UNCTAD/DITE/3(Vol. VII)

United Nations Conference on Trade and Development
Division on Investment, Technology and Enterprise Development

International Investment Instruments: A Compendium

Volume VII

United Nations
New York and Geneva, 2002

Note

UNCTAD serves as the focal point within the United Nations Secretariat for all matters related to foreign direct investment and transnational corporations. In the past, the Programme on Transnational Corporations was carried out by the United Nations Centre on Transnational Corporations (1975-1992) and the Transnational Corporations and Management Division of the United Nations Department of Economic and Social Development (1992-1993). In 1993, the Programme was transferred to the United Nations Conference on Trade and Development. UNCTAD seeks to further the understanding of the nature of transnational corporations and their contribution to development and to create an enabling environment for international investment and enterprise development. UNCTAD's work is carried out through intergovernmental deliberations, technical assistance activities, seminars, workshops and conferences.

The term "country", as used in the boxes added by the UNCTAD secretariat at the beginning of the instruments reproduced in this volume, also refers, as appropriate, to territories or areas; the designations employed and the presentation of the material do not imply the expression of any opinion whatsoever on the part of the Secretariat of the United Nations concerning the legal status of any country, territory, city or area or of its authorities, or concerning the delimitation of its frontiers or boundaries. Moreover, the country or geographical terminology used in the boxes may occasionally depart from standard United Nations practice when this is made necessary by the nomenclature used at the time of negotiation, signature, ratification or accession of a given international instrument.

To preserve the integrity of the texts of the instruments reproduced in this volume, references to the sources of the instruments that are not contained in their original text are identified as "note added by the editor".

The texts of the instruments included in this volume are reproduced as they were written in one of their original languages or as an official translation thereof. When an obvious linguistic mistake has been found, the word "sic" has been added in brackets.

The materials contained in this volume have been reprinted with special permission of the relevant institutions. For those materials under copyright protection, all rights are reserved by the copyright holders.

It should be further noted that this collection of instruments has been prepared for documentation purposes only, and its contents do not engage the responsibility of UNCTAD.

UNCTAD/DITE/3 Vol. VII

UNITED NATIONS PUBLICATION

Sales No. E.02.II.D.14

ISBN 92-1-112563-4

PREFACE

International Investment Instruments: A Compendium contains a collection of international instruments relating to foreign direct investment (FDI) and transnational corporations (TNCs). The collection is presented in nine volumes. The first three volumes were published in 1996. *Volumes IV* and *V* were published in 2000 followed by *Volume VI* in 2001. *Volumes VII, VIII and IX* bring the collection up to date. Most of the instruments reproduced in these volumes were adopted in the 1990s, the rest were adopted between 2000 and 2002.

The collection has been prepared to make the texts of international investment instruments conveniently available to interested policy-makers, scholars and business executives. The need for such a collection has increased in recent years as bilateral, regional, interregional and multilateral instruments dealing with various aspects of FDI have proliferated, and as new investment instruments are being negotiated or discussed at all levels.

While by necessity selective, the present collection seeks to provide a faithful record of the evolution and present status of intergovernmental cooperation concerning FDI and TNCs. Although the emphasis of the collection is on relatively recent documents (the majority of the instruments reproduced date from after 1990), it was deemed useful to include important older instruments as well, with a view towards providing some indications of the historical development of international concerns over FDI in the decades since the end of the Second World War.

The core of this collection consists of legally binding international instruments, mainly multilateral conventions, regional agreements, and bilateral treaties that have entered into force. In addition, a number of "soft law" documents, such as guidelines, declarations and resolutions adopted by intergovernmental bodies, have been included since these instruments also play a role in the elaboration of an international framework for FDI. In an effort to enhance the understanding of the efforts behind the elaboration of this framework, certain draft instruments that never entered into force, or texts of instruments on which the negotiations were not concluded, are also included; prototypes of bilateral investment treaties are reproduced as well. Included also are a number of influential documents prepared by business, consumer and labour organizations, as well as by other non-governmental organizations. It is clear from the foregoing that no implications concerning the legal status or the legal effect of an instrument can be drawn from its inclusion in this collection.

In view of the great diversity of the instruments in this *Compendium* -- in terms of subject matter, approach, legal form and extent of participation of States -- the simplest possible method of presentation was deemed the most appropriate. Thus, the relevant instruments are distributed among the *nine volumes of the Compendium* as follows:

- *Volume I* is devoted to multilateral instruments, that is to say, multilateral conventions as well as resolutions and other documents issued by multilateral organizations.

- *Volume II* covers interregional and regional instruments, including agreements, resolutions and other texts from regional organizations with an inclusive geographical context.

- *Volume III* is divided into three annexes covering three types of instruments that differ in their context or their origin from those included in the first two volumes:

  - Annex A reproduces investment-related provisions in free trade and regional integration agreements. The specific function and, therefore, the effect of such provisions is largely determined by the economic integration process which they are intended to promote and in the context of which they operate.

  - Annex B (the only section that departs from the chronological pattern) offers the texts of prototype bilateral treaties for the promotion and protection of foreign investments (BITs) of several developed and developing countries, as well as a list of these treaties concluded up to July 1995. The bilateral character of these treaties differentiates them from the bulk of the instruments included in this *Compendium*. Over 900 such treaties had been adopted by July 1995.

  - Annex C supplies the texts of documents prepared by non-governmental organizations; these give an indication of the broader environment in which the instruments collected here are prepared.

- *Volume IV*, divided into two parts, covers additional multilateral (Part One) and regional instruments (Part Two) not covered in *Volumes I* and *II*, including, but not limited to, those adopted between 1996 and the end of 1999.

- *Volume V* is divided into four parts, as follows:

  - Part One reproduces investment-related provisions in a number of additional free trade and economic integration agreements not covered in *Volume III*.

  - Part Two includes for the first time investment-related provisions in association agreements as well as bilateral and interregional cooperation agreements. These are divided into three annexes. Annex A is devoted to agreements signed between the countries members of the European Free Trade Association (EFTA) and third countries. Annex B covers investment-related provisions in agreements signed between the countries members of the European Community (EC) and third countries as well as other regional groups. Annex C includes types of bilateral agreements related to investment that differ from those covered in other parts.

  - Part Three contains the texts of a number of additional prototype BITs of several developed and developing countries, as well as a list of these treaties concluded between July 1995 and the end of 1998, when the total number of BITs concluded since 1959 reached over 1,730.

- Part Four reproduces additional texts of recent documents prepared by non-governmental organizations.

- *Volume VI* is divided into the following six parts:

  - Part One contains an additional multilateral instrument.

  - Part Two covers additional interregional and regional instruments, including agreements, resolutions and other texts from regional organizations with an inclusive geographical context.

  - Part Three reproduces investment-related provisions in a number of additional free trade and economic integration agreements not covered in previous volumes.

  - Part Four includes investment-related provisions in association agreements as well as bilateral and interregional cooperation agreements not covered in previous volumes.

  - Part Five contains the texts of a number of additional prototype BITs of several developed and developing countries not covered in previous volumes.

  - Part Six includes for the first time prototype double taxation treaties (DTTs).

- *Volume VII* is divided into the following three parts:

  - Part One contains an additional multilateral instrument.

  - Part Two reproduces investment-related provisions in a number of additional free trade and cooperation agreements signed between countries members of the European Free Trade Association (EFTA) and countries members of the European Community (EC) with third countries not covered in previous volumes.

  - Part Three contains the texts of a number of additional prototype BITs not covered in previous volumes.

- *Volume VIII* is divided into the following three parts:

  - Part One covers additional interregional and regional instruments, including agreements and other texts from regional organizations with an inclusive geographical context.

- Part Two reproduces investment-related provisions in a number of additional free trade, economic integration and cooperation agreements not covered in previous volumes.

- Part Three contains the texts of a number of additional prototype BITs not covered in previous volumes.

- *Volume IX* is divided into the following three parts:

  - Part One covers additional interregional and regional instruments, including agreements and other texts from regional organizations with an inclusive geographical context.

  - Part Two reproduces investment-related provisions in a number of additional free trade, economic integration and cooperation agreements not covered in previous volumes.

  - Part Three contains the texts of a number of additional prototype BITs not covered in previous volumes.

Within each of these subdivisions, instruments are reproduced in chronological order, except for the sections dedicated to prototype instruments.

The multilateral and regional instruments covered are widely differing in scope and coverage. Some are designed to provide an overall, general framework for FDI and cover many, although rarely all, aspects of investment operations. Most instruments deal with particular aspects and issues concerning FDI. A significant number address core FDI issues, such as the promotion and protection of investment, investment liberalization, dispute settlement and insurance and guarantees. Others cover specific issues, of direct but not exclusive relevance to FDI and TNCs, such as transfer of technology, intellectual property, avoidance of double taxation, competition and the protection of consumers and the environment. A relatively small number of instruments of this last category has been reproduced, since each of these specific issues often constitutes an entire system of legal regulation of its own, whose proper coverage would require an extended exposition of many kinds of instruments and arrangements.[a]

The *Compendium* is meant to be a collection of instruments, not an anthology of relevant provisions. Indeed, to understand a particular instrument, it is normally necessary to take its entire text into consideration. An effort has been made, therefore, to reproduce complete instruments, even though, in a number of cases, reasons of space and relevance have dictated the inclusion of excerpts.

The UNCTAD secretariat has deliberately refrained from adding its own commentary to the texts reproduced in the *Compendium*. The only exception to this rule is the boxes added to

---

[a] For a collection of instruments (or excerpts therefrom) dealing with transfer of technology, see UNCTAD, *Compendium of International Arrangements on Transfer of Technology: Selected Instruments* (Geneva: United Nations), United Nations publication, Sales No. E.01.II.D.28.

each instrument. They provide some basic facts, such as its date of adoption and date of entry into force and, where appropriate, signatory countries. Also, a list of agreements containing investment-related provisions signed by the EFTA countries and by the EC countries with third countries or regional groups are reproduced in the *Compendium*. Moreover, to facilitate the identification of each instrument in the table of contents, additional information has been added, in brackets, next to each title, on the year of its signature and the name of the relevant institution involved.

Rubens Ricupero
Secretary-General of UNCTAD

Geneva, June 2002

ACKNOWLEDGEMENTS

Volume VII of the *Compendium* was prepared by Abraham Negash under the overall direction of Karl P. Sauvant. Comments were received from Victoria Aranda, Americo Beviglia Zampetti and Joerg Weber. The volume was proof-read by Stijn Mentrop. Secretarial assistance was provided by Florence Hudry. The cooperation of the relevant countries and organizations from which the relevant instruments originate is acknowledged with gratitude.

CONTENTS

VOLUME VII

PART ONE

MULTILATERAL INSTRUMENTS

PART TWO

BILATERAL INSTRUMENTS

PART THREE

PROTOTYPE INSTRUMENTS

CONTENTS OF OTHER VOLUMES

VOLUME I
MULTILATERAL INSTRUMENTS

VOLUME II
REGIONAL INSTRUMENTS

REGIONAL INSTRUMENTS

VOLUME III

REGIONAL INTEGRATION, BILATERAL AND NON-GOVERNMENTAL INSTRUMENTS

ANNEX C. NON-GOVERNMENTAL INSTRUMENTS

VOLUME IV

MULTILATERAL AND REGIONAL INSTRUMENTS

PART ONE

MULTILATERAL INSTRUMENTS

PART TWO

REGIONAL INSTRUMENTS

VOLUME V

REGIONAL INTEGRATION, BILATERAL AND NON-GOVERNMENTAL INSTRUMENTS

PART ONE

INVESTMENT-RELATED PROVISIONS IN FREE TRADE AND ECONOMIC INTEGRATION AGREEMENTS

PART TWO

INVESTMENT-RELATED PROVISIONS IN ASSOCIATION AGREEMENTS, BILATERAL AND INTERREGIONAL COOPERATION AGREEMENTS

ANNEX A. **INVESTMENT-RELATED PROVISIONS IN FREE TRADE AGREEMENTS SIGNED BETWEEN THE COUNTRIES MEMBERS OF THE EUROPEAN FREE TRADE ASSOCIATION AND THIRD COUNTRIES AND LIST OF AGREEMENTS SIGNED (END-1999)**

ANNEX B. **INVESTMENT-RELATED PROVISIONS IN ASSOCIATION, PARTNERSHIP AND COOPERATION AGREEMENTS SIGNED BETWEEN THE COUNTRIES MEMBERS OF THE EUROPEAN COMMUNITY AND THIRD COUNTRIESAND LIST OF AGREEMENTS SIGNED (END-1999)**

ANNEX C.   OTHER BILATERAL INVESTMENT-RELATED AGREEMENTS

PART THREE

PROTOTYPE BILATERAL INVESTMENT TREATIES AND LIST OF BILATERAL INVESTMENT TREATIES (MID-1995 — END-1998)

PART FOUR

NON-GOVERNMENTAL INSTRUMENTS

VOLUME VI

PART THREE

INVESTMENT-RELATED PROVISIONS IN FREE TRADE AND ECONOMIC INTEGRATION AGREEMENTS

PART FOUR

INVESTMENT-RELATED PROVISIONS IN ASSOCIATION AGREEMENTS, BILATERAL AND INTERREGIONAL COOPERATION AGREEMENTS

PART FIVE

PROTOTYPE BILATERAL INVESTMENT TREATIES

PART SIX

PROTOTYPE BILATERAL DOUBLE TAXATION TREATIES

PART THREE
PROTOTYPE INSTRUMENTS

CONTENTS
VOLUME IX

PART ONE
INTERREGIONAL AND REGIONAL INSTRUMENTS

PART TWO

BILATERAL INSTRUMENTS

PART THREE

PROTOTYPE INSTRUMENTS

PART ONE

MULTILATERAL INSTRUMENTS

DOHA MINISTERIAL DECLARATION *
[excerpts]

(WORLD TRADE ORGANIZATION)

The Doha Ministerial Declaration was adopted on 14 November 2001 by the Fourth WTO Ministerial Conference held in Doha, Qatar between 9 and 14 November 2001.

WORK PROGRAMME

...

Services

15.   The negotiations on trade in services shall be conducted with a view to promoting the economic growth of all trading partners and the development of developing and least-developed countries. We recognize the work already undertaken in the negotiations, initiated in January 2000 under Article XIX of the General Agreement on Trade in Services, and the large number of proposals submitted by members on a wide range of sectors and several horizontal issues, as well as on movement of natural persons. We reaffirm the Guidelines and Procedures for the Negotiations adopted by the Council for Trade in Services on 28 March 2001 as the basis for continuing the negotiations, with a view to achieving the objectives of the General Agreement on Trade in Services, as stipulated in the Preamble, Article IV and Article XIX of that Agreement. Participants shall submit initial requests for specific commitments by 30 June 2002 and initial offers by 31 March 2003.

Trade-related aspects of intellectual property rights

17.   We stress the importance we attach to implementation and interpretation of the Agreement on Trade-Related Aspects of Intellectual Property Rights (TRIPS Agreement) in a manner supportive of public health, by promoting both access to existing medicines and research and development into new medicines and, in this connection, are adopting a separate declaration.

18.   With a view to completing the work started in the Council for Trade-Related Aspects of Intellectual Property Rights (Council for TRIPS) on the implementation of Article 23.4, we agree to negotiate the establishment of a multilateral system of notification and registration of geographical indications for wines and spirits by the Fifth Session of the Ministerial Conference. We note that issues related to the extension of the protection of geographical indications provided for in Article 23 to products other than wines and spirits will be addressed in the Council for TRIPS pursuant to paragraph 12 of this declaration.

---

*   *Source*: World Trade Organization (2001). "Doha Ministerial declaration", World Trade Organization, Ministerial Conference, Fourth Session, Doha, 9-14 November 2001, WT/MIN(01)/DEC/1, available on the Internet (http://www.wto.org). [Note added by the editor.]

19.   We instruct the Council for TRIPS, in pursuing its work programme including under the review of Article 27.3(b), the review of the implementation of the TRIPS Agreement under Article 71.1 and the work foreseen pursuant to paragraph 12 of this declaration, to examine, inter alia, the relationship between the TRIPS Agreement and the Convention on Biological Diversity, the protection of traditional knowledge and folklore, and other relevant new developments raised by members pursuant to Article 71.1. In undertaking this work, the TRIPS Council shall be guided by the objectives and principles set out in Articles 7 and 8 of the TRIPS Agreement and shall take fully into account the development dimension.

Relationship between trade and investment

20.   Recognizing the case for a multilateral framework to secure transparent, stable and predictable conditions for long-term cross-border investment, particularly foreign direct investment, that will contribute to the expansion of trade, and the need for enhanced technical assistance and capacity-building in this area as referred to in paragraph 21, we agree that negotiations will take place after the Fifth Session of the Ministerial Conference on the basis of a decision to be taken, by explicit consensus, at that session on modalities of negotiations.

21.   We recognize the needs of developing and least-developed countries for enhanced support for technical assistance and capacity building in this area, including policy analysis and development so that they may better evaluate the implications of closer multilateral cooperation for their development policies and objectives, and human and institutional development. To this end, we shall work in cooperation with other relevant intergovernmental organisations, including UNCTAD, and through appropriate regional and bilateral channels, to provide strengthened and adequately resourced assistance to respond to these needs.

22.   In the period until the Fifth Session, further work in the Working Group on the Relationship Between Trade and Investment will focus on the clarification of: scope and definition; transparency; non-discrimination; modalities for pre-establishment commitments based on a GATS-type, positive list approach; development provisions; exceptions and balance-of-payments safeguards; consultation and the settlement of disputes between members. Any framework should reflect in a balanced manner the interests of home and host countries, and take due account of the development policies and objectives of host governments as well as their right to regulate in the public interest. The special development, trade and financial needs of developing and least-developed countries should be taken into account as an integral part of any framework, which should enable members to undertake obligations and commitments commensurate with their individual needs and circumstances. Due regard should be paid to other relevant WTO provisions. Account should be taken, as appropriate, of existing bilateral and regional arrangements on investment.

Interaction between trade and competition policy

23.   Recognizing the case for a multilateral framework to enhance the contribution of competition policy to international trade and development, and the need for enhanced technical assistance and capacity-building in this area as referred to in paragraph 24, we agree that negotiations will take place after the Fifth Session of the Ministerial Conference on the basis of a decision to be taken, by explicit consensus, at that session on modalities of negotiations.

24.   We recognize the needs of developing and least-developed countries for enhanced support for technical assistance and capacity building in this area, including policy analysis and

development so that they may better evaluate the implications of closer multilateral cooperation for their development policies and objectives, and human and institutional development. To this end, we shall work in cooperation with other relevant intergovernmental organisations, including UNCTAD, and through appropriate regional and bilateral channels, to provide strengthened and adequately resourced assistance to respond to these needs.

25.   In the period until the Fifth Session, further work in the Working Group on the Interaction between Trade and Competition Policy will focus on the clarification of: core principles, including transparency, non-discrimination and procedural fairness, and provisions on hardcore cartels; modalities for voluntary cooperation; and support for progressive reinforcement of competition institutions in developing countries through capacity building. Full account shall be taken of the needs of developing and least-developed country participants and appropriate flexibility provided to address them.

Transparency in government procurement

26.   Recognizing the case for a multilateral agreement on transparency in government procurement and the need for enhanced technical assistance and capacity building in this area, we agree that negotiations will take place after the Fifth Session of the Ministerial Conference on the basis of a decision to be taken, by explicit consensus, at that session on modalities of negotiations. These negotiations will build on the progress made in the Working Group on Transparency in Government Procurement by that time and take into account participants' development priorities, especially those of least-developed country participants. Negotiations shall be limited to the transparency aspects and therefore will not restrict the scope for countries to give preferences to domestic supplies and suppliers. We commit ourselves to ensuring adequate technical assistance and support for capacity building both during the negotiations and after their conclusion.

Trade and transfer of technology

37.   We agree to an examination, in a Working Group under the auspices of the General Council, of the relationship between trade and transfer of technology, and of any possible recommendations on steps that might be taken within the mandate of the WTO to increase flows of technology to developing countries. The General Council shall report to the Fifth Session of the Ministerial Conference on progress in the examination.

Technical cooperation and capacity building

38.   We confirm that technical cooperation and capacity building are core elements of the development dimension of the multilateral trading system, and we welcome and endorse the New Strategy for WTO Technical Cooperation for Capacity Building, Growth and Integration. We instruct the Secretariat, in coordination with other relevant agencies, to support domestic efforts for mainstreaming trade into national plans for economic development and strategies for poverty reduction. The delivery of WTO technical assistance shall be designed to assist developing and least-developed countries and low-income countries in transition to adjust to WTO rules and disciplines, implement obligations and exercise the rights of membership, including drawing on the benefits of an open, rules-based multilateral trading system. Priority shall also be accorded to small, vulnerable, and transition economies, as well as to members and observers without representation in Geneva. We reaffirm our support for the valuable work of the International Trade Centre, which should be enhanced.

39.   We underscore the urgent necessity for the effective coordinated delivery of technical assistance with bilateral donors, in the OECD Development Assistance Committee and relevant international and regional intergovernmental institutions, within a coherent policy framework and timetable. In the coordinated delivery of technical assistance, we instruct the Director-General to consult with the relevant agencies, bilateral donors and beneficiaries, to identify ways of enhancing and rationalizing the Integrated Framework for Trade-Related Technical Assistance to Least-Developed Countries and the Joint Integrated Technical Assistance Programme (JITAP).

40.   We agree that there is a need for technical assistance to benefit from secure and predictable funding. We therefore instruct the Committee on Budget, Finance and Administration to develop a plan for adoption by the General Council in December 2001 that will ensure long-term funding for WTO technical assistance at an overall level no lower than that of the current year and commensurate with the activities outlined above.

41.   We have established firm commitments on technical cooperation and capacity building in various paragraphs in this Ministerial Declaration. We reaffirm these specific commitments contained in paragraphs 16, 21, 24, 26, 27, 33, 38-40, 42 and 43, and also reaffirm the understanding in paragraph 2 on the important role of sustainably financed technical assistance and capacity-building programmes. We instruct the Director-General to report to the Fifth Session of the Ministerial Conference, with an interim report to the General Council in December 2002 on the implementation and adequacy of these commitments in the identified paragraphs.

Least-developed countries

42.   We acknowledge the seriousness of the concerns expressed by the least-developed countries (LDCs) in the Zanzibar Declaration adopted by their ministers in July 2001. We recognize that the integration of the LDCs into the multilateral trading system requires meaningful market access, support for the diversification of their production and export base, and trade-related technical assistance and capacity building. We agree that the meaningful integration of LDCs into the trading system and the global economy will involve efforts by all WTO members. We commit ourselves to the objective of duty-free, quota-free market access for products originating from LDCs. In this regard, we welcome the significant market access improvements by WTO members in advance of the Third UN Conference on LDCs (LDC-III), in Brussels, May 2001. We further commit ourselves to consider additional measures for progressive improvements in market access for LDCs. Accession of LDCs remains a priority for the Membership. We agree to work to facilitate and accelerate negotiations with acceding LDCs. We instruct the Secretariat to reflect the priority we attach to LDCs' accessions in the annual plans for technical assistance. We reaffirm the commitments we undertook at LDC-III, and agree that the WTO should take into account, in designing its work programme for LDCs, the trade-related elements of the Brussels Declaration and Programme of Action, consistent with the WTO's mandate, adopted at LDC-III. We instruct the Sub-Committee for Least-Developed Countries to design such a work programme and to report on the agreed work programme to the General Council at its first meeting in 2002.

43.   We endorse the Integrated Framework for Trade-Related Technical Assistance to Least-Developed Countries (IF) as a viable model for LDCs' trade development. We urge development partners to significantly increase contributions to the IF Trust Fund and WTO extra-budgetary trust funds in favour of LDCs. We urge the core agencies, in coordination with development

partners, to explore the enhancement of the IF with a view to addressing the supply-side constraints of LDCs and the extension of the model to all LDCs, following the review of the IF and the appraisal of the ongoing Pilot Scheme in selected LDCs. We request the Director-General, following coordination with heads of the other agencies, to provide an interim report to the General Council in December 2002 and a full report to the Fifth Session of the Ministerial Conference on all issues affecting LDCs.

Special and differential treatment

44.   We reaffirm that provisions for special and differential treatment are an integral part of the WTO Agreements. We note the concerns expressed regarding their operation in addressing specific constraints faced by developing countries, particularly least-developed countries. In that connection, we also note that some members have proposed a Framework Agreement on Special and Differential Treatment (WT/GC/W/442). We therefore agree that all special and differential treatment provisions shall be reviewed with a view to strengthening them and making them more precise, effective and operational. In this connection, we endorse the work programme on special and differential treatment set out in the Decision on Implementation-Related Issues and Concerns.

*

Part Two

BILATERAL INSTRUMENTS

EUROPE AGREEMENT ESTABLISHING AN ASSOCIATION BETWEEN THE EUROPEAN COMMUNITIES AND THEIR MEMBER STATES, OF THE ONE PART, AND THE REPUBLIC OF POLAND, OF THE OTHER PART[*]
[excerpts]

The Europe Agreement Establishing an Association between the European Communities and Their Member States, of the One Part, and the Republic of Poland, of the Other Part was signed on 16 December 1991. It entered into force on 1 February 1994. The member States of the European Communities are: Austria, Belgium, Denmark, Finland, France, Germany, Greece, Ireland, Italy, Luxembourg, the Netherlands, Portugal, Spain, Sweden and the United Kingdom.

TITLE IV
MOVEMENT OF WORKERS, ESTABLISHMENT, SUPPLY OF SERVICES CHAPTER

CHAPTER II
Establishment

Article 44

1.   Poland shall, during the transitional periods referred to in Article 6, facilitate the setting up of operations on its territory by Community companies and nationals. To that end, it shall:

(i)   grant for the establishment of Community companies and nationals as defined in Article 48 a treatment no less favourable than that accorded to its own nationals and companies in accordance with the following timetable:

- from entry into force of the Agreement for the sectors included in Annex XIIa, and for all sectors not referred to in Annexes XIIa, XIIb, XIIc, XIId and XIIe,

- gradually, and at the latest by the end of the transitional period referred to in Article 6 for the sectors included in Annex XIIb;

- gradually, and at the latest by the end of the transitional period referred to in Article 6 for the sectors included in Annexes XIIc and XIId; and

(ii)   grant, from entry into force of this Agreement, in the operation of Community companies and nationals established in Poland a treatment no less favourable than that accorded to its own companies and nationals.

---

[*]   *Source*: European Communities (1993). "Europe Agreement Establishing an Association between the European Communities and Their Member States, of the One Part, and the Republic of Poland, of the Other Part", *Official Journal of the European Communities*, L 348, 31 December 1993, pp. 2 - 180; available also on the Internet (http://www.europa.eu.int). [Note added by the editor.]

Should the existing laws and regulations not grant such treatment of Community companies and nationals for certain economic activities in Poland upon entry into force of this Agreement, Poland shall amend such laws and regulations as to ensure such treatment at the latest at the end of the first stage referred to in Article 6.

2.   Poland shall, during the transitional periods referred to in paragraph 1, not adopt any new regulations or measures which introduce discrimination as regards the establishment and operations of Community companies and nationals in its territory in comparison to its own companies and nationals.

3.   Each Member State shall grant, from entry into force of this Agreement, a treatment no less favourable than that accorded to its own companies and nationals for the establishment of Polish companies and nationals as defined in Article 48 and shall grant in the operation of Polish companies and nationals established in its territory a treatment no less favourable than that accorded to its own companies and nationals.

4.   For the purposes of this Agreement:

    (a)   'establishment` shall mean

        (i)   as regards nationals, the right to take up and pursue economic activities as self-employed persons and to set up and manage undertakings, in particular companies, which they effectively control. Self-employment and business undertakings by nationals shall not extend to seeking or taking employment in the labour market or confer a right of access to the labour market of another Party. The provisions of this chapter do not apply to those who are not exclusively self-employed;

        (ii)   as regards companies, the right to take up and pursue economic activities by means of the setting up and management of subsidiaries, branches and agencies;

    (b)   'subsidiary` of a company shall mean a company which is effectively controlled by the first company;

    (c)   'economic activities` shall in particular include activities of an industrial character, activities of a commercial character, activities of craftsmen and activities of the professions.

5.   The Association Council shall during the transitional periods referred to in paragraph 1 (i) examine regularly the possibility of accelerating the granting of national treatment in the sectors referred to in Annexes XIIb, XIIc and XIId and the inclusion of areas or matters listed in Annex XIIe within the scope of application of the provisions of paragraphs 1, 2 and 3. Amendments may be made to these Annexes by decision of the Association Council.

Following the expiration of the transitional periods referred to in paragraph 1 (i), the Association Council may exceptionally, upon request of Poland, and if the necessity arises, decide to prolong the duration of exclusion of certain areas or matters listed in Annexes XIIb, XIIc and XIId for a limited period of time.

6.   The provisions concerning establishment and operation of Community and Polish companies and nationals contained in paragraphs 1, 2 and 3 shall not apply to the areas or matters listed in Annex XIIe.

7.   Notwithstanding the provisions of this Article, Community companies established in the territory of Poland shall have, from entry into force of this Agreement, the right to acquire, use, rent and sell real property, and as regards natural resources, agricultural land and forestry, the right to lease, where these are directly necessary for the conduct of the economic activities for which they are established.

Poland shall grant these rights to branches and agencies established in Poland of Community companies at the latest by the end of the first stage referred to in Article 6.

Poland shall grant these rights to Community nationals established as self-employed persons in Poland at the latest by the end of the transitional period referred to in Article 6.

Article 45

1.   Subject to the provisions of Article 44, with the exception of financial services described in Annex XIIc, each Party may regulate the establishment and operation of companies and nationals on its territory, in so far as these regulations do not discriminate against companies and nationals of the other Party in comparison to its own companies and nationals.

2.   In respect of financial services, described in Annex XIIc, this Agreement does not prejudice the right of the Parties to adopt measures necessary for the conduct of the Party's monetary policy, or for prudential grounds in order to ensure the protection of investors, depositors, policy holders, or persons to whom a fiduciary duty is owed, or to ensure the integrity and stability of the financial system. These measures shall not discriminate against companies and nationals of the other Party in comparison to its own companies and nationals.

Article 46

In order to make it easier for Community nationals and Polish nationals to take up and pursue regulated professional activities in Poland and the Community respectively, the Association Council shall examine which steps are necessary to be taken to provide for the mutual recognition of qualifications. It may take all necessary measures to that end.

Article 47

The provisions of Article 45 do not preclude the application by a Contracting Party of particular rules concerning the establishment and operation in its territory of branches and agencies of companies of another Party not incorporated in the territory of the first Party, which are justified by legal or technical differences between such branches and agencies as compared to branches and agencies of companies incorporated in its territory, or, as regards financial services, for prudential reasons. The difference in treatment shall not go beyond what is strictly necessary as a result of such legal or technical differences, or, as regards financial services, described in Annex XIIc, for prudential reasons.

Article 48

1.   A 'Community company` and a 'Polish company` respectively shall for the purpose of this Agreement mean a company or a firm set up in accordance with the laws of a Member State or of Poland respectively and having its registered office, central administration, or principal place of business in the territory of the Community or Poland respectively. However, should the company or firm, set up in accordance with the laws of a Member State or of Poland respectively, have only its registered office in the territory of the Community or Poland respectively, its operations must possess a real and continuous link with the economy of one of the Member States or Poland respectively.

2.   With regard to international maritime transport, shall also be beneficiaries of the provisions of this chapter and chapter III of this Title, a national or a shipping company of the Member States or of Poland respectively established outside the Community or Poland respectively and controlled by nationals of a Member State, or Polish nationals respectively, if their vessels are registered in that Member State or in Poland respectively in accordance with their respective legislations.

3.   A Community and a Polish national respectively shall, for the purpose of this Agreement, mean a natural person who is a national of one of the Member States or of Poland respectively.

4.   The provisions of this Agreement shall not prejudice the application by each Party of any measure necessary to prevent the circumvention of its measures concerning third country access to its market through the provisions of this Agreement.

Article 49

For the purpose of this Agreement 'financial services` shall mean those activities described in Annex XIIc. The Association Council may extend or modify the scope of Annex XIIc.

Article 50

During the first stage referred to in Article 6 for the sectors included in Annexes XIIa and XIIb, or for the sectors included in Annexes XIIc and XIId during the transitional period referred to in Article 6, Poland may introduce measures which derogate from the provisions of this chapter as regards the establishment of Community companies and nationals if certain industries:

- are undergoing restructuring, or

- are facing serious difficulties, particularly where these entail serious social problems in Poland, or

- face the elimination or a drastic reduction of the total market share held by Polish companies or nationals in a given sector or industry in Poland, or

- are newly emerging industries in Poland.

Such measures:

- shall cease to apply at the latest two years after the expiration of the first stage referred to in Article 6 for the sectors included in Annexes XIIa and XIIb, or for the sectors included in Annexes XIIc and XIId upon the expiration of the transitional period referred to in Article 6, and

- shall be reasonable and necessary in order to remedy the situation, and

- shall only relate to establishments in Poland to be created after the entry into force of such measures and shall not introduce discrimination concerning the operations of Community companies or nationals already established in Poland at the time of introduction of a given measure compared to Polish companies or nationals.

While devising and applying such measures, Poland shall grant whenever possible to Community companies and nationals a preferential treatment, and in no case a treatment less favourable than that accorded to companies or nationals from any third country.

Prior to the introduction of these measures, Poland shall consult the Association Council and shall not put them into effect before a one-month period following the notification to the Association Council of the concrete measures to be introduced by Poland, except where the threat of irreparable damage requires the taking of urgent measures in which case Poland shall consult the Association Council immediately after their introduction.

Upon the expiration of the first stage referred to in Article 6 for the sectors included in Annex XIIb, or for the sectors included in Annexes XIIc and XIId upon expiration of the transitional period referred to in Article 6, Poland may introduce such measures only with the authorization of the Association Council and under conditions determined by the latter.

Article 51

1.   The provisions of this chapter shall not apply to air transport services, inland-waterways transport services and maritime cabotage transport services.

2.   The Association Council may make recommendations for improving establishment and operations in the areas covered by paragraph 1.

Article 52

1.   Notwithstanding the provisions of Chapter I of this Title, the beneficiaries of the rights of establishment granted by Poland and the Community respectively shall be entitled to employ, or have employed by one of their subsidiaries, in accordance with the legislation in force in the host country of establishment, in the territory of Poland and the Community respectively, employees who are nationals of Community Member States and Poland respectively, provided that such employees are key personnel as defined in paragraph 2 and that they are employed exclusively by such beneficiaries or their subsidiaries. The residence and work permits of such employees shall only cover the period of such employment.

2.   Key personnel of the beneficiaries of the rights of establishment herein referred to as 'organization` are:

(a)   senior employees of an organization who primarily direct the management of the organization, receiving general supervision or direction principally from the board of directors or shareholders of the business, including:

- directing the organization or a department or sub-division of the organization,

- supervising and controlling the work of other supervisory, professional or managerial employees,

- having the authority personally to engage and dismiss or recommend engaging, dismissing or other personnel actions;

(b)   persons employed by an organization who possess high or uncommon:

- qualifications referring to a type of work or trade requiring specific technical knowledge,

- knowledge essential to the organization's service, research equipment, techniques or management.

These may include, but are not limited to, members of accredited professions.

Each such employee must have been employed by the organization concerned for at least one year preceding the detachment by the organization.

Article 53

1.   The provisions of this chapter shall be applied subject to limitations justified on grounds of public policy, public security or public health.

2.   The provisions of this chapter shall not apply to activities which in the territory of each Party are connected, even occasionally, with the exercise of official authority.

Article 54

Companies which are controlled and exclusively owned jointly by Polish companies or nationals and Community companies or nationals shall also be beneficiaries of the provisions of this chapter and Chapter III of this Title.

CHAPTER III
Supply of services between the Community and Poland

Article 55

1.   The Parties undertake in accordance with the provisions of this chapter to take the necessary steps to allow progressively the supply of services by Community or Polish companies or nationals who are established in a Party other than that of the person for whom the services are intended taking into account the development of the services sector in the Parties.

2.   In step with the liberalization process mentioned in paragraph 1, and subject to the provisions of Article 58 (1), the Parties shall permit the temporary movement of natural persons providing the service or who are employed by the service provider as key personnel as defined in Article 52 (2), including natural persons who are representatives of a Community or Polish company or national and are seeking temporary entry for the purpose of negotiating for the sale of services or entering into agreements to sell services for that service provider, where those representatives will not be engaged in making direct sales to the general public or in supplying services themselves.

3.   The Association Council shall take the measures necessary to implement progressively the provisions of paragraph 1.

Article 56

With regard to supply of transport services between the Community and Poland, the following replaces the provisions of Article 55:

1.   With regard to international maritime transport the Parties undertake to apply effectively the principle of unrestricted access to the market and traffic on a commercial basis.

    (a)   the above provision does not prejudice the rights and obligations under the United Nations Code of Conduct for Liner Conferences, as applied by one or the other Contracting Party to this Agreement. Non-conference liners will be free to operate in competition with a conference as long as they adhere to the principle of fair competition on a commercial basis;

    (b)   the parties affirm their commitment to a freely competitive environment as being an essential feature of the dry and liquid bulk trade.

2.   In applying the principles of paragraph 1, the Parties shall:

    (a)   not introduce cargo sharing clauses in future bilateral agreements with third countries, other than in those exceptional circumstances where liner shipping companies from one or other Party to this Agreement would not otherwise have an effective opportunity to ply for trade to and from the third country concerned;

    (b)   prohibit cargo sharing arrangements in future bilateral agreements concerning dry and liquid bulk trade;

    (c)   abolish, upon entry into force of this Agreement, all unilateral measures, administrative, technical and other obstacles which could have restrictive or discriminatory effects on the free supply of services in international maritime transport.

3.   With a view to assuring a coordinated development and progressive liberalization of transport between the Parties adapted to their reciprocal commercial needs, the conditions of mutual market access in air transport and in inland transport shall be dealt with by special transport agreements to be negotiated between the Parties after the entry into force of this Agreement.

4.   Prior to the conclusion of the agreements referred to in paragraph 3, the Parties shall not take any measures or actions which are more restrictive or discriminatory as compared to the situation existing on the day preceding the day of entry into force of this Agreement.

5.   During the transitional period, Poland shall progressively adapt its legislation including administrative, technical and other rules to that of the Community legislation existing at any time in the field of air and inland transport in so far as it serves liberalization purposes and mutual access to markets of the Parties and facilitates the movement of passengers and of goods.

6.   In step with the common progress in the achievement of the objectives of this chapter, the Association Council shall examine ways of creating the conditions necessary for improving freedom to provide air and inland transport services.

Article 57

The provisions of Article 53 shall apply to the matters covered by this chapter.

CHAPTER IV
General provisions

Article 58

1.   For the purpose of Title IV of this Agreement, nothing in the Agreement shall prevent the Parties from applying their laws and regulations regarding entry and stay, work, labour conditions and establishment of natural persons, and supply of services, provided that, in so doing, they do not apply them in a manner as to nullify or impair the benefits accruing to any Party under the terms of a specific provision of this Agreement. This provision does not prejudice the application of Article 53.

2.   The provisions of Chapters II, III and IV of Title IV shall be adjusted by decision of the Association Council in the light of the result of the negotiations on services taking place in the Uruguay Round and in particular to ensure that under any provision of the present Agreement a Party grants to the other Party a treatment no less favourable than that accorded under the provisions of a future GATS Agreement.

3.   The exclusion of Community companies and nationals established in Poland in accordance with the provisions of Chapter II of Title IV from public aid granted by Poland in the areas of public education services, health related and social services and cultural services shall, for the duration of the transitional period referred to in paragraph 6, be deemed compatible with the provisions of Title IV and with the competition rules referred to in Title V.

TITLE V
PAYMENTS, CAPITAL, COMPETITION AND OTHER ECONOMIC PROVISIONS, APPROXIMATION OF LAWS

CHAPTER I
Current payments and movement of capital

Article 59

The Contracting Parties undertake to authorize, in freely convertible currency, any payments on the current account of balance of payments to the extent that the transaction underlying the payments concern movements of goods, services or persons between the Parties which have been liberalized pursuant to this Agreement.

Article 60

1.   With regard to transactions on the capital account of balance of payments, from the entry into force of this Agreement, the Member States and Poland respectively shall ensure the free movement of capital relating to direct investments made in companies formed in accordance with the laws of the host country and investments made in accordance with the provisions of Chapter II of Title IV, and the liquidation or repatriation of these investments and of any profit stemming therefrom. Notwithstanding the above provision, such free movement, liquidation and repatriation shall be ensured by the end of the first stage referred to in Article 6 for all investments linked to establishment of nationals establishing in Poland as self-employed persons pursuant to Chapter II of Title IV.

2.   Without prejudice to paragraph 1, the Member States, as from the entry into force of this Agreement, and Poland as from the start of the second stage referred to in Article 6, shall not introduce any new foreign exchange restrictions on the movement of capital and current payments connected therewith between residents of the Community and Poland and shall not make the existing arrangements more restrictive.

3.   The Parties shall consult each other with a view to facilitating the movement of capital between the Community and Poland in order to promote the objectives of this Agreement.

Article 61

1.   During the first stage referred to in Article 6 the Contracting Parties shall take measures permitting the creation of the necessary conditions for the further gradual application of Community rules on the free movement of capital.

2.   During the second stage referred to in Article 6 the Association Council shall examine ways of enabling Community rules on the movement of capital to be applied in full.

Article 62

With reference to the provisions of this chapter, and notwithstanding the provisions of Article 64, until a full convertibility of the Polish currency in the meaning of Article VIII of the International Monetary Fund is introduced, Poland may in exceptional circumstances apply exchange restrictions connected with the granting or taking up of short- and medium-term credits to the extent that such restrictions are imposed on Poland for the granting of such credits and are permitted according to Poland's status under the IMF.

Poland shall apply these restrictions in a non-discriminatory manner. They shall be applied in such a manner as to cause the least possible disruption to this Agreement. Poland shall inform the Association Council promptly of the introduction of such measures and of any changes therein.

CHAPTER II
Competition and other economic provisions

Article 63

1.   The following are incompatible with the proper functioning of the Agreement, in so far as they may affect trade between the Community and Poland:

(i)   all agreements between undertakings, decisions by associations of undertakings and concerted practices between undertakings which have as their object or effect the prevention, restriction or distortion of competition;

(ii)   abuse by one or more undertakings of a dominant position in the territories of the Community or of Poland as a whole or in a substantial part thereof;

(iii)   any public aid which distorts or threatens to distort competition by favouring certain undertakings or the production of certain goods.

2.   Any practices contrary to this Article shall be assessed on the basis of criteria arising from the application of the rules of Articles 85, 86 and 92 of the Treaty establishing the European Community.

3.   The Association Council shall, within three years of the entry into force of this Agreement, adopt by decision the necessary rules for the implementation of paragraphs 1 and 2. Until these rules are adopted, the provisions of the Agreement on interpretation and application of Articles VI, XVI and XXIII of the General Agreement on Tariffs and Trade shall be applied as the rules for the implementation of paragraphs 1 (iii) and related parts of paragraph 2.

4.   (a)   For the purposes of applying the provisions of paragraph 1 (iii), the Parties recognize that during the first five years after the entry into force of this Agreement, any public aid granted by Poland shall be assessed taking into account the fact that Poland shall be regarded as an area identical to those areas of the Community described in Article 92 (3) (a) of the Treaty establishing the European Community. The Association Council shall, taking into account the economic situation of Poland, decide whether that period should be extended by further periods of five years.

(b)   Each Party shall ensure transparency in the area of public aid, inter alia by reporting annually to the other Party on the total amount and the distribution of the aid given and by providing, upon request, information on aid schemes. Upon request by one Party, the other Party shall provide information on particular individual cases of public aid.

5.   With regard to products referred to in Chapters II and III of Title III:

- the provisions of paragraph 1 (iii) do not apply,

- any practices contrary to paragraph 1 (i) should be assessed according to the criteria established by the Community on the basis of Articles 42 and 43 of the Treaty establishing the European Economic Community, and in particular of those established in Council Regulation No 26/62.

6.   If the Community or Poland considers that a particular practice is incompatible with the terms of paragraph 1, and:

- is not adequately dealt with under the implementing rules referred to in paragraph 3, or

- in the absence of such rules, and if such practice causes or threatens to cause serious prejudice to the interest of the other Party or material injury to its domestic industry, including its services industry, it may take appropriate measures after consultation within the Association Council or after 30 working days following referral for such consultation.

In the case of practices incompatible with paragraph 1 (iii) of this Article, such appropriate measures may, where the General Agreement on Tariffs and Trade applies thereto, only be adopted in accordance with the procedures and under the conditions laid down by the General Agreement on Tariffs and Trade and any other relevant instrument negotiated under its auspices which are applicable between the Parties.

7.   Notwithstanding any provisions to the contrary adopted in accordance with paragraph 3, the Parties shall exchange information taking into account the limitations imposed by the requirements of professional and business secrecy.

8.   This Article shall not apply to the products covered by the Treaty establishing the European Coal and Steel Community which are the subject of Protocol 2.

Article 64

1.   The Parties shall endeavour to avoid the imposition of restrictive measures including measures relating to imports for balance of payments purposes. In the event of their introduction, the Party having introduced the same shall present to the other Party as soon as possible, a time schedule for their removal.

2.   Where one or more Member States of the Community or Poland is in serious balance of payments difficulties, or under imminent threat thereof, the Community or Poland, as the case may be, may, in accordance with the conditions established under the General Agreement on Tariffs and Trade, adopt restrictive measures, including measures relating to imports, which shall be of limited duration and may not go beyond what is necessary to remedy the balance of payments situation. The Community or Poland, as the case may be, shall inform the other Party forthwith.

3.   Any restrictive measures shall not apply to transfers related to investment and in particular to the repatriation of amounts invested or reinvested and of any kind of revenues stemming therefrom.

Article 65

With regard to public undertakings, and undertakings to which special or exclusive rights have been granted, the Association Council shall ensure that as from the third year following the date of entry into force of this Agreement, the principles of the Treaty establishing the European Economic Community, in particular Article 90, and the principles of the concluding document of the April 1990 Bonn meeting of the Conference on Security and Cooperation in Europe, in particular entrepreneurs' freedom of decision, are upheld.

Article 66

1.   Poland shall continue to improve the protection of intellectual, industrial and commercial property rights in order to provide, by the end of the fifth year from the entry into force of this Agreement, a level of protection similar to that existing in the Community, including comparable means of enforcing such rights.

2.   By the end of the fifth year from the entry into force of this Agreement, Poland shall apply to accede to the Munich Convention on the Grant of European Patents of 5 October 1973 and shall accede to the other multilateral conventions on intellectual, industrial and commercial property rights referred to in Annex XIII paragraph 1 to which Member States are Parties, or which are de facto applied by Member States.

Article 67

1.   The Contracting Parties consider the opening up of the award of public contracts on the basis of non-discrimination and reciprocity, in particular in the GATT context, to be a desirable objective.

2.   Polish companies as defined in Article 48, shall be granted access to contract award procedures in the Community pursuant to Community procurement rules under a treatment no less favourable than that accorded to Community companies as of the entry into force of this Agreement.

Community companies as defined in Article 48 shall be granted access to contract award procedures in Poland under a treatment no less favourable than that accorded to Polish companies at the latest at the end of the transitional period referred to in Article 6.

Community companies established in Poland under the provisions of Chapter II of Title IV shall have, upon entry into force of the Agreement, access to contract award procedures under a treatment no less favourable than that accorded to Polish companies.

The Association Council shall periodically examine the possibility for Poland to introduce access to award procedures in Poland for all Community companies prior to the end of the transitional period.

3.   As regards establishment, operations, supply of services between the Community and Poland, as well as employment and movement of labour linked to the fulfilment of public contracts, the provisions of Articles 37 to 58 are applicable.

CHAPTER III
Approximation of laws

Article 68

The Contracting Parties recognize that the major precondition for Poland's economic integration into the Community is the approximation of that country's existing and future legislation to that of the Community. Poland shall use its best endeavours to ensure that future legislation is compatible with Community legislation.

Article 69

The approximation of laws shall extend to the following areas in particular: customs law, company law, banking law, company accounts and taxes, intellectual property, protection of workers at the workplace, financial services, rules on competition, protection of health and life of humans, animals and plants, consumer protection, indirect taxation, technical rules and standards, transport and the environment.

Article 70

The Community shall provide Poland with technical assistance for the implementation of these measures which may include inter alia:

- the exchange of experts,

- the provision of information,

- organization of seminars,

- training activities,

- aid for the translation of Community legislation in the relevant sectors.

TITLE VI
ECONOMIC COOPERATION

Article 71

1.   The Community and Poland shall establish cooperation aimed at contributing to Poland's development. Such cooperation shall back up Poland's achievements and shall strengthen existing economic links on the widest possible foundation, to the benefit of both Parties.

2.   Policies designed to bring about the economic and social development of Poland, in particular policies relating to industry including the mining sector, investment, agriculture,

energy, transport, regional development and tourism should be guided by the principle of sustainable development. This entails ensuring that environmental considerations are fully incorporated into such policies from the outset.

These policies shall also take into account the requirements of sustainable social development.

3.   Special attention must be devoted to measures capable of fostering cooperation between the countries of central and Eastern Europe with a view to integrated development of the region.

Article 72
Industrial cooperation

1.   Cooperation shall seek to promote the following in particular:

- industrial cooperation between economic operators in the Community and in Poland, with the particular aim of strengthening the private sector,

- Community participation in Poland's efforts in both public and private sectors to modernize and restructure its industry, which will effect the transition from a centrally planned system to a market economy under conditions which ensure that the environment is protected,

- the restructuring of individual sectors,

- the establishment of new undertakings in areas offering potential for growth.

2.   Industrial cooperation initiatives take into account priorities determined by Poland. The initiatives should seek in particular to establish a suitable framework for undertakings, to improve management know-how and to promote transparency as regards markets and conditions for undertakings.

Article 73
Investment promotion and protection

1.   Cooperation shall aim to establish a favourable climate for private investment, both domestic and foreign, which is so essential to economic and industrial reconstruction in Poland.

2.   The particular aims of cooperation shall be:

- for Poland to establish a legal framework which favours investment; this could be achieved where appropriate by the Member States and Poland extending agreements for the promotion and protection of investment,

- to implement suitable arrangements for the transfer of capital,

- to bring about better investment protection,

- to carry through deregulation and improve economic infrastructure,

- to exchange information on investment opportunities in the form of trade fairs, exhibitions, trade weeks and other events.

Article 75
Cooperation in science and technology

1.   The Parties shall undertake to promote cooperation in research and technological development. They shall devote special attention to the following:

- the exchange of scientific and technological information, including information on each other's science and technology policies and activities,

- the organization of joint scientific meetings (seminars and workshops),

- joint R& D activities aimed at encouraging scientific progress and the transfer of technology and know-how,

- training activities and mobility programmes for researchers and specialists from both sides,

- the development of an environment conducive to research and the application of new technologies and adequate protection of the intellectual property of the results of research,

- participation in the Community programmes in accordance with paragraph 3.

Technical assistance shall be provided where appropriate.

2.   The Association Council shall determine the appropriate procedures for developing cooperation.

3.   Cooperation under the Community's framework programme in the field of research and technological development shall be implemented according to specific arrangements to be negotiated and concluded in accordance with the procedures adopted by each Party.

ANNEX XIIc Concerning articles 44, 45, 49 and 50

FINANCIAL SERVICES

Financial services: definitions

A financial service is any service of a financial nature offered by a financial service provider of a party. Financial services include the following activities:

A.   All insurance and insurance-related services.

      1.   Direct insurance (including co-insurance):

            i)   life;

      ii)   non-life.

2.   Reinsurance and retrocession.

3.   Insurance intermediation, such as brokerage and agency.

4.   Services auxiliary to insurance, such as consultancy, actuarial, risk assessment and claim settlement services.

B.   Banking and other financial services (excluding insurance).

1.   Acceptance of deposits and other repayable funds from the public.

2.   Lending of all types, including, inter-alia, consumer credit, mortgage credit, factoring and financing of commercial transaction.

3.   Financial leasing.

4.   All payment and money transmission services, including credit charge and debit cards, travellers cheques and bankers draft.

5.   Guarantees and commitments.

6.   Trading for own account of customers, whether on an exchange, in an over the counter market or otherwise, the following:

     (a)   money market instruments (cheques, bills, certificates of deposits, etc.);

     (b)   foreign exchange;

     (c)   derivative products including, but not limited to, futures and options;

     (d)   exchange rates and interest rate instruments, including products such as swaps, forward rate agreements, etc;

     (e)   transferable securities;

     (f)   other negotiable instruments and financial assets, including bullion.

7.   Participation in issues of all kinds of securities, including underwriting and placement as agent (whether publicly or privately) and provision of services related to such issues.

8.   Money broking.

9.   Asset management, such as cash or portfolio management, all forms of collective investment management, pension-fund management, custodial depository and trust services.

10. Settlement and clearing services for financial assets, including securities, derivative products, and other negotiable instruments.

11. Advisory intermediation and other auxiliary financial services on all the activities listed in Points 1 to 10 above, including credit reference and analysis, investment and portfolio research and advice, advice on acquisitions and on corporate restructuring and strategy.

12. Provision and transfer of financial information, and financial data processing and related software by providers of other financial services.

Are excluded from the definition of financial services the following activities:

(a) activities carried out by central banks or by any other public institution in pursuit of monetary and exchange rate policies;

(b) activities conducted by central banks, government agencies or departments, or public institutions, for the account or with the guarantee of the government, except when those activities may be carried out by financial service providers in competition with such public entities.

(c) activities forming part of a statutory system of social security or public retirement plans, except when those activities may be carried out by financial service providers in competition with public entities or private institutions.

ANNEX XIII

1. Paragraph 2 of Article 66 refers to the following multilateral conventions:

- Berne Convention for the Protection of Literary and Artistic Works in the Act of Paris of 24 July 1971,

- International Convention for the Protection of Performers, Producers of Phonograms and Broadcasting Organizations signed at Rome on 26 October 1961,

- Budapest Treaty on the International Recognition of the Deposit of Micro-organisms for the Purpose of Patent Procedure, signed at Budapest in 1977 and amended in 1980,

- the Madrid Protocol concerning the international recognition of trade marks (Madrid 1989).

2. The Association Council may decide that paragraph 2 of Article 66 applies to other multilateral conventions.

3. The Contracting Parties express their attachment to observing the obligations flowing from the following multilateral conventions:

- Paris Convention for the Protection of Industrial Property in the 1967 Act of Stockholm (Paris Union),

- Madrid Arrangement on the International Registration of Marks in the 1967 Act of Stockholm (Madrid Union),

- Patent Cooperation Treaty signed at Washington in 1970 (PCT Union).

4.   Before the end of the first stage, Poland shall comply in its internal legislation with the stubstantial provisions of the Nice Agreement concerning the international classification of goods and services for the purposes of registration of marks (Geneva 1977, amended 1979).

5.   For the purposes of paragraph 3 of this Annex and of the provisions of Article 75 (1) referring to intellectual property, the Contracting Parties shall be Poland, the European Economic Community and the Member States, each in as far as they are respectively competent for matters concerning industrial, intellectual and commercial property covered by these conventions or by Article 75 (1).

6.   The provisions of this Annex and those of Article 75 (1) referring to intellectual property are without prejudice to the competences of the European Economic Community and its Member States in matters of industrial, intellectual and commercial property.

*

EUROPE AGREEMENT ESTABLISHING AN ASSOCIATION BETWEEN THE EUROPEAN COMMUNITIES AND THEIR MEMBER STATES, OF THE ONE PART, AND THE REPUBLIC OF HUNGARY, OF THE OTHER PART[*]
[excerpts]

> The Europe Agreement Establishing an Association between the European Communities and Their Member States, of the One Part, and the Republic of Hungary, of the Other Part was signed on 16 December 1991. It entered into force on 1 February 1994. The member States of the European Communities are: Austria, Belgium, Denmark, Finland, France, Germany, Greece, Ireland, Italy, Luxembourg, the Netherlands, Portugal, Spain, Sweden and the United Kingdom.

TITLE IV
MOVEMENT OF WORKERS, ESTABLISHMENT, SUPPLY OF SERVICES

CHAPTER II
Establishment

Article 44

1.   Hungary shall, during the transitional period referred to in Article 6, facilitate the setting up of operations on its territory by Community companies and nationals as defined in Article 48. To that end, it shall:

   (i)   gradually, and at the latest by the end of the first stage referred to in Article 6, grant for the establishment of Community companies and nationals a treatment no less favourable than that accorded to its own nationals and companies, save for the sectors referred to in Annexes XIIa and XIIb, where such treatment shall be granted at the latest by the end of the transitional period referred to in Article 6; and

   (ii)   grant, from entry into force of this agreement, in the operation of Community companies and nationals established in Hungary a treatment no less favourable than that accorded to its own companies and nationals. Should the existing laws and regulations not grant such treatment of Community companies and nationals for certain economic activities in Hungary upon entry into force of this Agreement, Hungary shall amend such laws and regulations as to ensure such treatment at the latest at the end of the first stage referred to in Article 6.

---

[*] *Source*: European Communities (1993). "Europe Agreement Establishing an Association between the European Communities and Their Member States, of the One Part, and the Republic of Hungary, of the Other Part" *Official Journal of the European Communities*, L 347, 31 December 1993 pp. 2 - 266; available also on the Internet (http://www.europa.eu.int/eur-lex/en/lif/dat/1993/en_293A1231_13.html). [Note added by the editor.]

2.   Hungary shall, during the transitional periods referred to in paragraph 1, not adopt any new regulations or measures which introduce discrimination as regards the establishment and operations of Community companies and nationals in its territory in comparison to its own companies and nationals.

3.   Each Member State shall grant, from entry into force of this Agreement, a treatment no less favourable than that accorded to its own companies and nationals for the establishment of Hungarian companies and nationals as defined in Article 48 and shall grant in the operation of Hungarian companies and nationals established in its territory a treatment no less favourable than that accorded to its own companies and nationals.

4.   Notwithstanding the provisions of paragraphs 1, 2 and 3, the national treatment as decribed in paragraphs 1 and 3 shall be applicable for branches, agencies and nationals establishing as self-employed persons only from the start of the second stage referred to in Article 6.

5.   For the purposes of this Agreement:

   (a)   'establishment` shall mean:

      (i)   as regards nationals, the right to take up and pursue economic activities as self-employed persons and to set up and manage undertakings, in particular companies, which they effectively control. Self-employment and business undertakings by nationals shall not extend to seeking or taking employment in the labour market or confer a right of access to the labour market of another Party. The provisions of this chapter do not apply to those who are not exclusively self-employed;

      (ii)   as regards companies, the right to take up and pursue economic activities by means of the setting up and management of subsidiaries, branches and agencies;

   (b)   'subsidiary` of a company shall mean a company which is effectively controlled by the first company;

   (c)   'economic activities` shall in particular include activities of an industrial character, activities of a commercial character, activities of craftsmen and activities of the professions.

6.   The Association Council shall during the transitional periods referred to in paragraph 1 (i) examine regularly the possibility of accelerating the granting of national treatment in the sectors referred to in Annexes XIIa and XIIb and the inclusion of areas or matters listed in Annex XIIc within the scope of application of the provisions of paragraphs 1, 2 and 3.

Amendments may be made to these Annexes by decision of the Association Council.
Following the expiration of the transitional periods referred to in paragraph 1 (i), the Association Council may exceptionally, upon request of Hungary, and if the necessity arises, decide to prolong the duration of exclusion of certain areas or matters listed in Annexes XIIa and XIIb for a limited period of time.

7.   The provisions concerning establishment and operation of Community and Hungarian companies and nationals contained in paragraphs 1, 2, 3 and 4 shall not apply to the areas or matters listed in Annex XIIc.

8.   Notwithstanding the provisions of this Article, Community companies established in the territory of Hungary shall have, from entry into force of this Agreement, the right to acquire, use, rent and sell real property, and as regards natural resources, agricultural land and forestry, the right to lease, where these are directly necessary for the conduct of the economic activities for which they are established. This right does not include establishment for the purpose of dealing and agency in the area of real estate and natural resources. Hungary shall grant these rights to branches and agencies of Community companies and Community nationals established as self-employed persons in Hungary at the latest by the end of the first stage referred to in Article 6. This right does not include establishment for the purpose of dealing and agency in the area of real estate and natural resources.

Article 45

1.   Subject to the provisions of Article 44, with the exception of financial services described in Annex XIIa, each Party may regulate the establishment and operation of companies and nationals on its territory, in so far as these regulations do not discriminate against companies and nationals of the other Party in comparison to its own companies and nationals.

2.   In respect of financial services, described in Annex XIIa, this Agreement does not prejudice the right of the Parties to adopt measures necessary for the conduct of the Party's monetary policy, or for prudential grounds in order to ensure the protection of investors, depositors, policy holders, or to whom a fiduciary duty is owed, or to ensure the integrity and stability of the financial system. These measures shall not discriminate against companies and nationals of the other Party in comparison to its own companies and nationals.

Article 46

In order to make it easier for Community nationals and Hungarian nationals to take up and pursue regulated professional activities in Hungary and the Community respectively, the Association Council shall examine which steps are necessary to be taken to provide for the mutual recognition of qualifications. It may take all necessary measures to that end.

Article 47

The provisions of Article 45 do not preclude the application by a Contracting Party of particular rules concerning the establishment and operation in its territory of branches and agencies of companies of another Party not incorporated in the territory of the first Party, which are justified by legal or technical differences between such branches and agencies as compared to branches and agencies of companies incorporated in its territory, or, as regards financial services, for prudential reasons. The difference in treatment shall not go beyond what is strictly necessary as a result of such legal or technical differences, or, as regards financial services, described in Annex XIIa, for prudential reasons.

Article 48

1.   A 'Community company` and an 'Hungarian company` respectively shall for the purpose of this Agreement mean a company or a firm set up in accordance with the laws of a Member State or of Hungary respectively and having its registered office, central administration, or principal place of business in the territory of the Community or Hungary respectively. However, should the company or firm, set up in accordance with the laws of a Member State or of Hungary respectively, have only its registered office in the territory of the Community or Hungary respectively, its operations must possess a real and continuous link with the economy of one of the Member States or Hungary respectively.

2.   With regard to international maritime transport, shall also be beneficiaries of the provisions of this Chapter and Chapter III of this Title, a national or a shipping company of the Member States or of Hungary respectively established outside the Community or Hungary respectively and controlled by nationals of a Member State, or Hungarian nationals respectively, if their vessels are registered on that Member State or in Hungary respectively in accordance with their respective legislations.

3.   A Community and a Hungarian national respectively shall, for the purpose of this Agreement, mean a natural person who is a national of one of the Member States or of Hungary respectively.

4.   The provisions of this Agreement shall not prejudice the application by each Party of any measure necessary to prevent the circumvention of its measures concerning third-country access to its market through the provisions of this Agreement.

Article 49

For the purpose of this Agreement 'financial services` shall mean those activities described in Annex XIIa. The Association Council may extend or modify the scope of Annex XIIa.

Article 50

During the first stage referred to in Article 6, or for the sectors included in Annexes XIIa and XIIb during the transitional period referred to in Article 6, Hungary may introduce measures which derogate from the provisions of this Chapter as regards the establishment of Community companies and nationals if certain industries:

- are undergoing restructuring, or

- are facing serious difficulties, particularly where these entail serious social problems in Hungary, or

- face the elimination or a drastic reduction of the total market share held by Hungarian companies or nationals in a given sector or industry in Hungary, or

- are newly emerging industries in Hungary.

Such measures:

- shall cease to apply at the latest two years after the expiration of the first stage referred to in Article 6, or for the sectors included in Annexes XIIa and XIIb upon the expiration of the transitional period referred to in Article 6, and

- shall be reasonable and necessary in order to remedy the situation, and

- shall only relate to establishments in Hungary to be created after the entry into force of such measures and shall not introduce discrimination concerning the operations of Community companies or nationals already established in Hungary at the time of introduction of a given measure compared to Hungarian companies or nationals.

While devising and applying such measures, Hungary shall grant whenever possible to Community companies and nationals a preferential treatment, and in no case a treatment less favourable than that accorded to companies or nationals from any third country.

Prior to the introduction of these measures, Hungary shall consult the Association Council and shall not put them into effect before a one-month period following the notification to the Association Council of the concrete measures to be introduced by Hungary, except where the threat of irreparable damage requires the taking of urgent measures in which case Hungary shall consult the Association Council immediately after their introduction.

Upon the expiration of the first stage referred to in Article 6, or for the sectors included in Annexes XIIa and XIIb upon expiration of the transitional period referred to in Article 6, Hungary may introduce such measures only with the authorization of the Association Council and under conditions determined by the latter.

Article 51

1. The provisions of this Chapter shall not apply to air transport services, inland-waterways transport services and maritime cabotage transport services.

2. The Association Council may make recommendations for improving establishment and operations in the areas covered by paragraph 1.

Article 52

1.   Notwithstanding the provisions of Chapter I of this Title, the beneficiaries of the rights of establishment granted by Hungary and the Community respectively shall be entitled to employ, or have employed by one of their subsidiaries, in accordance with the legislation in force in the host country of establishment, in the territory of Hungary and the Community respectively, employees who are nationals of Member States and Hungary respectively, provided that such employees are key personnel as defined in paragraph 2 and that they are employed exclusively by such beneficiaries or their subsidiaries. The residence and work permits of such employees shall only cover the period of such employment.

2.   Key personnel of the beneficiaries of the rights of establishment herein referred to as 'organization` are:

(a)   senior employees of an organization who primarily direct the management of the organization, receiving general supervision or direction principally from the board of directors or shareholders of the business, including:

- directing the organization or a department or sub-division of the organization,

- supervising and controlling the work of other supervisory, professional or managerial employees,

- having the authority personally to engage and dismiss or recommend engaging, dismissing or other personnel actions;

(b)   persons employed by an organization who possess high or uncommon:

- qualifications referring to a type of work or trade requiring specific technical knowledge,

- knowledge essential to the organization's service, research equipment, techniques or management.

These may include, but are not limited to, members of accredited professions.

Each such employee must have been employed by the organization concerned for at least one year preceding the detachment by the organization.

Article 53

1.   The provisions of this Chapter shall be applied subject to limitations justified on grounds of public policy, public security or public health.

2.   The provisions of this Chapter shall not apply to activities which in the territory of each Party are connected, even occasionally, with the exercise of official authority.

Article 54

Companies which are controlled and exclusively owned jointly by Hungarian companies or nationals and Community companies or nationals shall also be beneficiaries of the provisions of this Chapter and Chapter III of this Title.

CHAPTER III
Supply of services between the Community and Hungary

Article 55

1.   The Parties undertake in accordance with the provisions of this Chapter to take the necessary steps to allow progressively the supply of services by Community or Hungarian companies or nationals who are established in a Party other than that of the person for whom the services are intended taking into account the development of the services sector in the Parties.

2.   In step with the liberalization process mentioned in paragraph 1, and subject to the provisions of Article 58 (1), the Parties shall permit the temporary movement of natural persons providing the service or who are employed by the service provider as key personnel as defined in Article 52 (2), including natural persons who are representatives of a Community or Hungarian company or national and are seeking temporary entry for the purpose of negotiating for the sale of services or entering into agreements to sell services for that service provider, where those representatives will not be engaged in making direct sales to the general public or in supplying services themselves.

3.   The Association Council shall take the measures necessary to implement progressively the provisions of paragraph 1.

Article 56

With regard to supply of transport services between the Community and Hungary, the following replaces the provisions of Article 55:

1.   With regard to international maritime transport the Parties undertake to apply effectively the principle of unrestricted access to the market and traffic on a commercial basis:

   (a)   the above provision does not prejudice the rights and obligations under the United Nations Code of Conduct for Liner Conferences, as applied by one or the other Contracting Party to this Agreement. Non-conference liners will be free to operate in competition with a conference as long as they adhere to the principle of fair competition on a commercial basis;

   (b)   the Parties affirm their commitment to a freely competitive environment as being an essential feature of the dry and liquid bulk trade.

2.   In applying the principles of paragraph 1, the Parties shall:

   (a)   not introduce cargo sharing clauses in future bilateral agreements with third countries, other than in those exceptional circumstances where liner shipping companies from one or other Party to this Agreement would not otherwise have an effective opportunity to ply for trade to and from the third country concerned;

   (b)   prohibit cargo sharing arrangements in future bilateral agreements concerning dry and liquid bulk trade;

   (c)   abolish, upon entry into force of this Agreement, all unilateral measures, administrative, technical and other obstacles which could have restrictive or discriminatory effects on the free supply of services in international maritime transport.

3.   With a view to assuring a coordinated development and progressive liberalization of transport between the Parties adapted to their reciprocal commercial needs, the conditions of mutual market access in air transport and in inland transport shall be dealt with by special transport agreements to be negotiated between the Parties after the entry into force of this Agreement.

4.   Prior to the conclusion of the agreements referred to in paragraph 3, the Parties shall not take any measures or actions which are more restrictive or discriminatory as compared to the situation existing on the day preceding the day of entry into force of this Agreement.

5.   During the transitional period, Hungary shall progressively adapt its legislation including administrative, technical and other rules to that of the Community legislation existing at any time in the field of air and inland transport in so far as it serves liberalization purposes and mutual access to markets of the Parties and facilitates the movement of passengers and of goods.

6.   In step with the common progress in the achievement of the objectives of this Chapter, the Association Council shall examine ways of creating the conditions necessary for improving freedom to provide air and inland transport services.

Article 57

The provisions of Article 53 shall apply to the matters covered by this Chapter.

CHAPTER IV
General provisions

Article 58

1.   For the purpose of Title IV of this Agreement, nothing in the Agreement shall prevent the Parties from applying their laws and regulations regarding entry and stay, work, labour conditions and establishment of natural persons, and supply of services, provided that, in so doing, they do not apply them in a manner as to nullify or impair the benefits accruing to any Party under the terms of a specific provision of this Agreement. This provision does not prejudice the application of Article 53.

2.   The provisions of Chapters II, III and IV of Title IV shall be adjusted by decision of the Association Council in the light of the result of the negotiations on services taking place in the Uruguay Round and in particular to ensure that under any provision of this Agreement a Party grants to the other Party a treatment no less favourable than that accorded under the provisions of a future GATT Agreement.

TITLE V
PAYMENTS, CAPITAL, COMPETITION AND OTHER
ECONOMIC PROVISIONS, APPROXIMATION OF LAWS

CHAPTER I
Current payments and movement of capital

Article 59

The Contracting Parties undertake to authorize, in freely convertible currency, any payments on the current account of balance of payments to the extent that the transaction underlying the payments concern movements of goods, services or persons between the Parties which have been liberalized pursuant to this Agreement.

Article 60

1.   With regard to transactions on the capital account of balance of payments, from the entry into force of this Agreement, the Member States and Hungary respectively shall ensure the free movement of capital relating to direct investments made in companies formed in accordance with the laws of the host country and investments made in accordance with the provisions of Chapter II of Title IV, and the liquidation or repatriation of these investments and of any profit stemming therefrom. Notwithstanding the above provision, such free movement, liquidation and repatriation shall be ensured by the end of the first stage referred to in Article 6 for all investments linked to establishment of branches and agencies of Community companies and of Community nationals establishing in Hungary as self-employed persons pursuant to Chapter II of Title IV.

2.   Without prejudice to paragraph 1, the Member States, as from the entry into force of this Agreement, and Hungary as from the start of the second stage referred to in Article 6, shall not introduce any new foreign exchange restrictions on the movement of capital and current payments connected therewith between residents of the Community and Hungary and shall not make the existing arrangements more restrictive.

3.   The provisions of paragraph 1 and 2 shall not prevent Hungary from applying restrictions on outward investments by Hungarian nationals and companies.

4.   The Parties shall consult each other with a view to facilitating the movement of capital between the Community and Hungary in order to promote the objectives of this Agreement.

Article 61

1.   During the first stage referred to in Article 6 the Contracting Parties shall take measures permitting the creation of the necessary conditions for the further gradual application of Community rules on the free movement of capital.

2.   During the second stage referred to in Article 6 the Association Council shall examine ways of enabling Community rules on the movement of capital to be applied in full.

CHAPTER II
Competition and other economic provisions

Article 62

1.   The following are incompatible with the proper functioning of the Agreement, in so far as they may affect trade between the Community and Hungary:

(i)   all agreements between undertakings, decisions by associations of undertakings and concerted practices between undertakings which have as their object or effect the prevention, restriction or distortion of competition;

(ii)   abuse by one or more undertakings of a dominant position in the territories of the Community or of Hungary as a whole or in a substantial part thereof;

(iii)   any public aid which distorts or threatens to distort competition by favouring certain undertakings or the production of certain goods.

2.   Any practices contrary to this Article shall be assessed on the basis of criteria arising from the application of the rules of Articles 85, 86 and 92 of the Treaty establishing the European Economic Community.

3.   The Association Council shall, within three years of the entry into force of this Agreement, adopt by decision the necessary rules for the implementation of paragraphs 1 and 2.

4.   (a)   For the purposes of applying the provisions of paragraph 1 (iii), the Parties recognize that during the frist five years after the entry into force of this Agreement, any public aid granted by Hungary shall be assessed taking into account the fact that Hungary shall be regarded as an area identical to those areas of the Community described in Article 92 (3) (a) of the Treaty establishing the European Economic Community. The Association Council shall, taking into account the economic situation of Hungary, decide whether that period should be extended by further periods of five years.

(b)   Each Party shall ensure transparency in the area of public aid, inter alia by reporting annually to the other Party on the total amount and the distribution of the aid given and by providing, upon request, information on aid schemes. Upon request by one Party, the other Party shall provide information on particular individual cases of public aid.

5.   With regard to products referred to in Chapters II and III of Title III:

- the provisions of paragraph 1 (iii) do not apply,

- any practices contrary to paragraph 1 (i) should be assessed according to the criteria established by the Community on the basis of Articles 42 and 43 of the Treaty establishing the European Economic Community and in particular of those established in Council Regulation No 26/1962.

6.   If the Community or Hungary considers that a particular practice is incompatible with the terms of paragrah 1, and:

- is not adequately dealt with under the implementing rules referred to in paragraph 3, or

- in the absence of such rules, and if such practice causes or threatens to cause serious prejudice to the interest of the other Party or material injury to its domestic industry, including its services industry, it may take appropriate measures after consultation within the Association Council or after 30 working days following referral for such consultation.

In the case of practices incompatible with paragraph 1 (iii), such appropriate measures may, where the General Agreement on Tariffs and Trade applies thereto, only be adopted in accordance with the procedures and under the conditions laid down by the General Agreement on Tariffs and Trade and any other relevant instrument negotiated under its auspices which are applicable between the Parties.

7.   Notwithstanding any provisions to the contrary adopted in accordance with paragraph 3, the Parties shall exchange information taking into account the limitations imposed by the requirements of professional and business secrecy.

8.   This Article shall not apply to the products covered by the Treaty establishing the European Coal and Steel Community which are the subject of Protocol 2.

Article 63

1.   The Parties shall endeavour to avoid the imposition of restrictive measures including measures relating to imports for balance of payments purposes. In the event of their introduction, the Party having introduced the same shall present to the other Party as soon as possible, a time schedule for their removal.

2.   Where one or more Member States of the Community or Hungary is in serious balance of payments difficulties, or under imminent threat thereof, the Community or Hungary as the case may be, may, in accordance with the conditions established under the General Agreement on Tariffs and Trade, adopt restrictive measures, including measures relating to imports, which shall be of limited duration and may not go beyond what is necessary to remedy the balance of payments situation. The Community or Hungary, as the case may be, shall inform the other Party forthwith.

3.   Any restrictive measures shall not apply to transfers related to investment and in particular to the repatriation of amounts invested or reinvested and of any kind of revenues stemming therefrom.

Article 64

With regard to public undertakings, and undertakings to which special or exclusive rights have been granted, the Association Council shall ensure that as from the third year following the date of entry into force of this Agreement, the principles of the Treaty establishing the European Economic Community, in particular Article 90, and the principles of the concluding document of the April 1990 Bonn meeting of the Conference on Security and Cooperation in Europe, in particular entrepreneurs' freedom of decision, are upheld.

Article 65

1.   Hungary shall continue to improve the protection of intellectual, industrial and commercial property rights in order to provide, by the end of the fifth year from the entry into force of this Agreement, a level of protection similar to that existing in the Community, including comparable means of enforcing such rights.

2.   By the end of the fifth year from the entry into force of this Agreement, Hungary shall apply to accede to the Munich Convention on the Grant of European Patents of 5 October 1973 and shall accede to the other multilateral conventions on intellectual, industrial and commercial property rights referred to in Annex XIII point 1 to which Member States are Parties, or which are de facto applied by Member States.

Article 66

1.   The Contracting Parties consider the opening up of the award of public contracts on the basis of non-discrimination and reciprocity, in particular in the GATT context, to be a desirable objective.

2.   Hungarian companies as defined in Article 48, shall be granted access to contract award procedures in the Community pursuant to Community procurement rules under a treatment no less favourable than that accorded to Community companies as of the entry into force of this Agreement.

Community companies as defined in Article 48 shall be granted access to contract award procedures in Hungary under a treatment no less favourable than that accorded to Hungarian companies at the latest at the end of the transitional period referred to in Article 6.

Community companies established in Hungary under the provisions of Chapter II of Title IV shall have from the entry into force of this Agreement access to contract award procedures under a treatment no less favourable than that accorded to Hungarian companies.

The Association Council shall periodically examine the possibility for Hungary to introduce access to award procedures in Hungary for all Community companies prior to the end of the transitional period.

3.   As regards establishment, operations, supply of services between the Community and Hungary as well as employment and movement of labour linked to the fulfilment of public contracts, the provisions of Articles 37 to 57 are applicable.

CHAPTER III
Approximation of laws

Article 67

The Contracting Parties recognize that the major precondition for Hungary's economic integration into the Community is the approximation of that country's existing and future legislation to that of the Community. Hungary shall act to ensure that future legislation is compatible with Community legislation as far as possible.

Article 68

The approximation of laws shall extend to the following areas in particular; customs law, company law, banking law, company accounts and taxes, intellectual property, protection of workers at the workplace, financial services, rules on competition, protection of health and life of humans, animals and plants, food legislation, consumer protection including product liability, indirect taxation, technical rules and standards, transport and the environment.

Article 69

The Community shall provide Hungary with technical assistance for the implementation of these measures which may include inter alia:

- the exchange of experts,

- the provision of information,

- organization of seminars,

- training activities,

- aid for the translation of Community legislation in the relevant sectors.

TITLE VI
ECONOMIC COOPERATION

Article 70

1.   The Community and Hungary shall establish cooperation aimed at strengthening economic links on the widest possible foundation to the benefit of both Parties and at contributing to Hungary's development.

2.   Policies designed to bring about the economic and social development of Hungary, in particular policies relating to industry including the mining sector, construction industry, investment, agriculture, energy, transport, telecommunications, regional development and tourism should be guided by the principle of sustainable development. This entails ensuring that environmental considerations are fully incorporated into such policies from the outset.

These policies shall also take into account the requirements of sustainable and harmonious social development.

3.   Particular attention should also be devoted to measures capable of fostering regional cooperation.

Article 71
Industrial cooperation

1.   Cooperation shall seek to promote the following in particular:

- industrial cooperation between economic operators in the Community and in Hungary, with the particular aim of strengthening the private sector,

- Community participation in Hungary's efforts in both public and private sectors to modernize and restructure its industry under conditions which ensure that the environment is protected,

- the restructuring of individual sectors,

- the establishment of new undertakings in areas offering potential for growth,

- transfer of the technology and know-how.

2.   Industrial cooperation initiatives take into account priorities determined by Hungary. The initiatives should seek in particular to establish a suitable and transparent framework for undertakings and to improve management know-how.

Article 72
Investment promotion and protection

1.   The cooperation shall aim at maintaining and, if necessary, improving a favourable climate and legal framework for private investment, both domestic and foreign, which is essential to economic and industrial reconstruction in Hungary. The cooperation shall also aim to encourage and promote foreign investment and privatization in Hungary.

2.   The cooperation shall take the following forms:

- the conclusion, where appropriate of agreements between Member States and Hungary on investment promotion and protection, including the transfer of benefits and the repatriation of capital,

- further deregulation in Hungary and improving economic infrastructure,

- exchange of information on laws, regulations and administrative practices in the field of investments,

- exchange of information on investment opportunities in the form of trade fairs, exhibitions, trade weeks and other events,

- organization of investment missions both in Hungary and in the Community.

Article 74
Cooperation in science and technology

1.   The Parties shall promote cooperation in research and technological development. They shall devote special attention to the following:

- the exchange of information on each other's science and technology policies,

- the organization of joint scientific and technological development meetings (seminars and workshops),

- joint research and development (R& D) activities aimed at encouraging scientific progress and the transfer of technology and know-how,

- training activities and mobility programmes for researchers and specialists from both sides,

- the development of an environment conducive to research and the application of new technologies and adequate protection of the intellectual property results of research,

- participation in the Community programmes in accordance with paragraph 3,

- support by the Community for Hungary's participation in relevant European research and development (R& D) programmes.

Technical assistance shall be provided where appropriate.

2.   The Association Council shall determine the appropriate procedures for developing cooperation.

3.   Cooperation under the Community's framework programme in the field of research and technological development shall be implemented according to specific arrangements to be negotiated and concluded in accordance with the procedures adopted by each Party.

Article 90
Small and medium-sized enterprises

1.   The Parties shall aim to develop and strengthen small and medium-sized enterprises and cooperation between SMEs in the Community and Hungary.

2.   They shall encourage the exchange of information and know-how in the following areas:

- improving, where appropriate, the legal, administrative, technical, tax and financial conditions necessary for the development and expansion of SMEs and for cross-border cooperation,

- the provision of the specialized services required by SMEs (management training, accounting, marketing, quality control, etc.) and the strengthening of agencies providing such services,

- the establishment of appropriate links with Community operators with the aim of improving the flow of information to SMEs and promoting cross-border cooperation (e.g. the Business Cooperation Network (BC-NET), Euro-Info Centres, conferences, etc.).

ANNEX XII a Related to Articles 44 and 49

FINANCIAL SERVICES

Financial services: definitions

A financial service is any service of a financial nature offered by a financial service provider of a party. Financial services include the following activities.
A.   All insurance and insurance-related services:

1.   direct insurance (including co-insurance):

(i)   life;

(ii)   non-life;

2.   reinsurance and retrocession;

3.   insurance intermediation, such as brokerage and agency;

4.   services auxiliary to insurance, such as consultancy, actuarial, risk assessment and claim-settlement services.

B.   Banking and other financial services (excluding insurance):

1.   acceptance of deposits and oher repayable funds from the public;

2.   lending of all types, including, inter alia, consumer credit, mortgage credit, factoring and financing of commercial transaction;

3.   financial leasing;

4.   all payment and money transmission services, including credit charge and debit cards, travellers cheques and bankers drafts;

5.   guarantees and commitments;

6.   trading for own account of customers, whether on an exchange, in an over-the-counter-market or otherwise, the following;

    (a)   money market instruments (cheques, bills, certificates of deposits, etc);

    (b)   foreign exchange;

    (c)   derivate products including, but not limited to, futures and options;

    (d)   exchange rates and interest rate instruments, including products such as swaps, forward rate agreements, etc;

    (e)   transferable securities;

    (f)   other negotiable instruments and financial assets, including bullion;

7.   participation in issues of all kinds of securities, including under-writing and placement as agent (whether publicly or privately) and provision of services related to such issues;

8.   money broking;

9.   asset management, such as cash or portfolio management, all forms of collective investment management, pension fund management, custodial depository and trust services.

10.   settlement and clearing services for financial assets, including securities, derivative products, and other negotiable instruments.

11.   advisory intermediation and other auxiliary financial services on all the activities listed in points 1 to 10 above, including credit reference and analysis, investment

and portfolio research and advice, advice on acquisitions and on corporate restructuring and strategy.

12.   provision and transfer of financial information, and financial data processing and related software by providers of other financial services.

Are excluded from the definition of financial services the following activities:

(a)   Activities carried out by central banks or by any other public institution in pursuit of monetary and exchange rate policies.

(b)   Activities conducted by central banks, government agencies or departments, or public institutions, for the account or with the guarantee of the government, except when those activities may be carried out by financial service providers in competition with such public entities.

(c)   Activities forming part of a statutory system of social security or public retirement plans, except when those activities may be carried out by financial service providers in competition with public entities or private institutions.

ANNEX XIII

1.   Paragraph 2 of Article 65 concerns the following multilateral conventions:

- Protocol relating to the Madrid Agreement concerning the international registration of marks (Madrid 1989),

- International Convention for the Protection of Performers, Producers and Phonograms and Broadcasting Organizations (Rome, 1961).

2.   The Association Council may decide that paragraph 2 of Article 65 shall apply to other multilateral conventions.

3.   The Contracting Parties confirm the importance they attach to the obligations arising from the following multilateral conventions:

- Berne Convention for the Protection of Literary and Artistic Works (Paris Act, 1971),

- Paris Convention for the Protection of Industrial Property (Stockholm Act, 1967 and amended in 1979),
- Madrid Agreement concerning the international registration of marks (Stockholm Act, 1967 and amended in 1979),

- Nice Agreement concerning the international classification of goods and services for the purposes of the registration of marks (Geneva 1977, amended 1979),

- Budapest Treaty on the international recognition of the deposit of micro-organisms for the purposes of patent procedures (1977, modified in 1980);

- Patent Cooperation Treaty (Washington 1979, amended 1979 and modified in 1984).

4.   For the purposes of paragraph 3 of this Annex and the provisions of Article 74 (1) referring to intellectual property, Contracting Parties shall be Hungary, the European Economic Community and the Member States, each in as far as they are respectively competent for matters concerning industrial, intellectual and commercial property covered by these conventions or by Article 74 (1).

5.   The provisions of this Annex and the provisions of Article 74 (1) referring to intellectual property are without prejudice to the competence of the European Economic Community and its Member States in matters of industrial, intellectual and commercial property.

*

FREE TRADE AGREEMENT BETWEEN THE EFTA STATES AND THE CZECH REPUBLIC*
[excerpts]

The Free Trade Agreement between the EFTA States and the Czech Republic was signed on 20 March 1992. It entered into force on 1 July 1992.

Article 16
Public procurement

1. The States Parties to this Agreement consider the effective liberalization of their respective public procurement markets as a desirable and important objective of this Agreement.

2. As of the entry into force of this Agreement, the EFTA States shall grant companies from the Czech Republic access to contract award procedures on their respective public procurement markets according to the Agreement on Government procurement of 12 April 1979, as amended by a Protocol of Amendments of 2 February 1987 negotiated under the auspices of the General Agreement on Tariffs and Trade. The Czech Republic shall, taking into account the restructuring and development process of its economy, gradually ensure that companies from the EFTA States have access on the same principles to contract award procedures on its public procurement market.

3. As soon as possible after the entry into force of the Agreement the States Parties to this Agreement shall progressively develop and adjust the rules, conditions and practices governing the participation in public procurement contracts awarded by public authorities and public undertakings, and by private undertakings which have been granted special or exclusive rights, so as to ensure free access and transparency, and that there is no discrimination between potential suppliers from the States Parties to this Agreement. A full balance of rights and obligations between the States Parties to this Agreement shall be established not later than at the end of the transitional period.

4. The Joint Committee shall recommend or agree, as appropriate, the practical modalities for this development including, inter alia, scope, timetable and rules to be applied.

5. The States Parties to this Agreement concerned shall endeavour to accede to the relevant Agreements negotiated under the auspices of the General Agreement on Tariffs and Trade.

---

* *Source*: European Free Trade Association Secretariat (1992). "Free Trade Agreement between the EFTA States and the Czech Republic", available on the Internet (http://secretariat.efta.int). [Note added by the editor.]

ARTICLE 17[1]
Protection of intellectual property

1.   The States Parties to this Agreement shall grant and ensure adequate, effective and non-discriminatory protection of intellectual property rights, including measures for the enforcement of such rights against infringement thereof, counterfeiting and piracy, in accordance with the provisions of this Article, Annex XI to this Agreement and the international agreements referred to therein.

2.   The States Parties to this Agreement shall accord to each other's nationals treatment no less favourable than that they accord to their own nationals. Exemptions from this obligation must be in accordance with the substantive provisions of Article 3 of the TRIPS Agreement.

3.   The States Parties to this Agreement shall grant to each others' nationals treatment no less favourable than that accorded to nationals of any other State. Exemptions from this obligation must be in accordance with the substantive provisions of the TRIPS Agreement, in particular Articles 4 and 5 thereof.

4.   The States Parties to this Agreement agree, upon request of any State Party, to review the provisions on the protection of intellectual property rights contained in the present Article and in Annex XI, with a view to further improve levels of protection and to avoid or remedy trade distortions caused by actual levels of protection of intellectual property rights.

Article 18
Rules of competition concerning undertakings

1.   The following are incompatible with the proper functioning of this Agreement in so far as they may affect trade between an EFTA State and the Czech Republic:

  (a)   all agreements between undertakings, decisions by associations of undertakings and concerted practices between undertakings which have as their object or effect the prevention, restriction or distortion of competition;

  (b)   abuse by one or more undertakings of a dominant position in the territories of the States Parties to this Agreement as a whole or in a substantial part thereof.

2.   As from the third year from the entry into force of this Agreement, the provisions of paragraph 1 shall also apply to the activities of public undertakings, and undertakings for which the Parties grant special or exclusive rights, in so far as the application of these provisions does not obstruct the performance, in law or in fact, of the particular public tasks assigned to them.

3.   If a State Party to this Agreement considers that a given practice is incompatible with the provisions of paragraphs 1 and 2 and if such practice causes or threatens to cause serious prejudice to the interest of that State Party or material injury to its domestic industry, it may take appropriate measures after consultations within the Joint Committee or after thirty days following referral for such consultation.

---

[1]   Article 17 and Annex X1 were amended by Joint Committee Decision No. 1 of 1997 (14 January 1997).

ARTICLE 30
Services and investment

1.   The States Parties to this Agreement recognize the growing importance of certain areas, such as services and investments. In their efforts to gradually develop and broaden their co-operation, in particular in the context of European integration, they will co-operate with the aim of achieving a gradual liberalization and mutual opening of markets for investments and trade in services, taking into account relevant GATT work.

2.   The EFTA States and the Czech Republic will discuss in the Joint Committee this co-operation with the aim to develop and deepen their relations under the Agreement.

ANNEX XI[1]

ON INTELLECTUAL PROPERTY
Referred to in Article 17

Article 1
Definition and scope of protection

"Intellectual property protection" comprises in particular protection of copyright and neighbouring rights, including computer programmes and databases, trademarks for goods and services, geographical indications, including appellations of origin, industrial designs, patents, plant varieties, topographies of integrated circuits, as well as undisclosed information.

Article 2
International conventions

(1)   The States Parties to this Agreement reaffirm their commitment to comply with the obligations set out in the following multilateral agreements:

- WTO Agreement of 15 April 1994 on Trade-Related Aspects of Intellectual Property Rights (TRIPS Agreement);

- Paris Convention of 20 March 1883 for the Protection of Industrial Property (Stockholm Act, 1967);

- Bern Convention of 9 September 1886 for the Protection of Literary and Artistic Works (Paris Act, 1971).

(2)   The States Parties to this Agreement which are not States Parties to the agreement listed below shall undertake to obtain their adherence to this multilateral agreement within two years from the date of entry into force of this Annex.

- International Convention for the Protection of Performers Producers of Phonograms and Broadcasting Organisations (Rome Convention 1961).

---

[1]   As amended by Joint Committee Decision No. 1 of 1997 (14 January 1997).

(3)   The States Parties to this Agreement agree to promptly hold expert consultations, upon request of any State Party, on activities relating to the identified or to future international conventions on harmonization, administration and enforcement of intellectual property rights and on activities in international organizations, such as the WTO and the World Intellectual Property Organization (WIPO), as well as relations of the States Parties with third countries on matters concerning intellectual property.

Article 3
Additional substantive standards

The States Parties to this Agreement shall ensure in their national laws at least the following:

- adequate and effective means to protect geographical indications, including appellations of origin, with regard to all products and services;

- adequate and effective protection of industrial designs by providing in particular a period of protection of five years from the date of application with a possibility of renewal for two consecutive periods of five years each;

- adequate and effective patent protection for inventions in all fields of technology on a level similar to that prevailing in the European Patent Convention of 5 October 1973;

- compulsory licensing of patents shall only be granted under the conditions of Article 31 of the TRIPS Agreement. Licences granted on the grounds of nonworking shall be used only to the extent necessary to satisfy the domestic market on reasonable commercial terms.

Article 4
Acquisition and maintenance of intellectual property rights

Where the acquisition of an intellectual property right is subject to the right being granted or registered, the States Parties to this Agreement shall ensure that the procedures for grant or registration are of the same level as that provided in the TRIPS Agreement, in particular Article 62.

Article 5
Enforcement of intellectual property rights

The States Parties to this Agreement shall provide for enforcement provisions under their national laws of the same level as that provided in the TRIPS Agreement, in particular Articles 41 to 61.

Article 6
Technical co-operation

The States Parties to this Agreement shall agree upon appropriate modalities for technical assistance and co-operation of the respective authorities of the States Parties. To this end, they shall co-ordinate efforts with relevant international.

*

FREE TRADE AGREEMENT BETWEEN THE EFTA STATES AND ISRAEL[*]
[excerpts]

The Free Trade Agreement between the EFTA States and Israel was signed on 17 September 1992. It entered into force on1 January 1993.

ARTICLE 14
Public procurement

1.   The Parties consider the effective liberalisation of their respective public procurement markets an integral objective of this Agreement.

2.   As of the entry into force of this Agreement, the Parties shall grant each other's companies access to contract award procedures on their respective public procurement markets on a reciprocal basis according to the Agreement on Government Procurement of 12 April 1979, as amended by a Protocol of Amendments of 2 February 1987, negotiated under the auspices of the General Agreement on Tariffs and Trade.

3.   Taking into account the rules and disciplines agreed upon within the General Agreement on Tariffs and Trade and with third countries in this field, the Parties foresee to extend the scope of paragraph 2 of this Article after the entry into force of this Agreement in accordance with the following provisions:

   (a)   The Parties agree to further ensure effective transparency and free access and that there is no discrimination between the potential suppliers from the Parties.

   To this end the Parties shall progressively adjust the relevant rules, conditions, procedures and practices governing the participation in contracts awarded by public authorities and public undertakings, and by private undertakings which have been granted special or exclusive rights.

   (b)   The Parties agree to entrust the Joint Committee to decide, as soon as possible, on all practical modalities, including the scope, timetable and rules for this adjustment, taking into account the need to maintain a full balance of the rights and obligations between the Parties.

4.   As soon as conceivable after the entry into force of this Agreement, the Joint Committee shall discuss with a view to reaching an agreement on a progressive extension of the list of the procuring entities to be covered as regards their procurements in the supplies and utilities sectors, above the respective thresholds.

---

[*]   *Source*: European Free Trade Association Secretariat (1992). "Free Trade Agreement between the EFTA States and Israel", available on the Internet (http://secretariat.efta.int). [Note added by the editor.]

ARTICLE 15
Protection of intellectual property

1.   The Parties shall grant and ensure adequate, effective and non-discriminatory protection of intellectual property rights, as defined in Article 1 of Annex V. They shall adopt and take adequate, effective and non-discriminatory measures for the enforcement of such rights against infringement thereof, and in particular against counterfeiting and piracy.

Particular obligations of the Parties shall be listed in Annex V.

2.   The Parties agree to comply with the substantive provisions of the multilateral conventions which are specified in Article 2 of Annex V and make their best endeavours to adhere to them as well as to multilateral agreements facilitating co-operation in the field of protection of intellectual property rights.

3.   In the field of intellectual property, the Parties shall not grant treatment to each other's nationals less favourable than that accorded to nationals of any other State. Any advantage, favour, privilege or immunity in the field of intellectual property deriving from:

(a)   bilateral agreements in force for a Party at the entry into force of this Agreement as notified to the other Party at the latest before the entry into force,

(b)   existing and future multilateral agreements, including regional agreements on economic integration to which not all of the Parties are parties, may be exempted from this obligation, provided that it does not constitute an arbitrary or unjustifiable discrimination of nationals of the other Party.

4.   Two or more Parties may conclude further agreements exceeding the terms of this Agreement and of Annex V, provided that such agreements shall be open to all other Parties on terms equivalent to those under the agreements and that they shall be ready to enter into good faith negotiations to this end.

5.   The Parties agree to keep under mutual review the implementation of the provisions on intellectual property with a view to further improve levels of protection and to avoid or remedy trade distortions caused by actual levels of protection of intellectual property rights.

6.   If any Party considers that any other Party has failed to fulfil its obligations under this Article and the Annex thereto, it may take appropriate measures under the conditions and in accordance with the procedures laid down in Article 23.

7.   The Parties shall agree upon appropriate modalities for technical assistance and cooperation of respective authorities of the Parties. To this end, they shall co-ordinate efforts with relevant international organizations.

ARTICLE 17
Rules of competition applying to undertakings

1.   The following are incompatible with the proper functioning of this Agreement in so far as they may affect trade between an EFTA State and Israel:

(a)   all agreements between undertakings, decisions by associations of undertakings and concerted practices between undertakings which have as their object or effect the prevention, restriction or distortion of competition;

(b)   abuse by one or more undertakings of a dominant position in the territories of the Parties as a whole or in a substantial part thereof.

2.   These provisions shall also apply to the activities of public undertakings, and undertakings for which the Parties grant special or exclusive rights, in so far as the application of these provisions does not obstruct the performance, in law or in fact, of their particular public tasks.

3.   If a Party considers that a given practice is incompatible with this Article, it may take appropriate measures under the conditions and in accordance with the procedures laid down in Article 23.

ARTICLE 29
Services and investments

1.   The Parties recognize the growing importance of certain areas, such as services and investments. In their efforts to gradually deepen and broaden their co-operation, they will cooperate with the aim of achieving a progressive liberalization and mutual opening of markets for investments and trade in services, taking into account relevant GATT work. They will endeavour to accord treatment no less favourable than that accorded to domestic and foreign operators in their territories on condition that a balance of rights and obligations exists between the Parties.

2.   The modalities for this co-operation will be negotiated in the Joint Committee. Arrangements resulting therefrom will, where necessary, be subject to ratification or approval by the Parties in accordance with their own procedures and be applied within the framework of this Agreement.

ANNEX V

REFERRED TO IN ARTICLE 15
PROTECTION OF INTELLECTUAL PROPERTY

Article 1
Definition and scope of protection

"Intellectual property protection" includes in particular protection of copyright and neighbouring rights, trademarks, geographical indications, industrial designs, patents, topographies of integrated circuits, as well as undisclosed information on know-how.

Article 2
International conventions

(1)   In accordance with paragraph 2 of Article 15, the Parties agree to comply with the substantive standards of, and to adhere to, the following multilateral agreements:

- Paris Convention of 20 March 1883, for the Protection of Industrial Property (Stockholm Act, 1967),

- Berne Convention of 9 September 1886, for the Protection of Literary and Artistic Works (Paris Act 1971).

(2)   The Parties agree to promptly hold expert consultations, upon request of any Party, on activities relating to the identified or to future international conventions on harmonization, administration and enforcement of intellectual property and on activities in international organizations, such as the General Agreement on Tariffs and Trade, the World Intellectual Property Organization (WIPO), as well as arrangements between any Parties and third countries on matters concerning intellectual property.

Article 3
Additional substantive standards

(1)   The Parties shall ensure in their national laws at least the following:

- adequate and effective legal protection of copyright, including computer programmes and data bases, as well as of neighbouring rights;

- adequate and effective legal protection of trademarks for goods and services, in particular of internationally well known trademarks;

- adequate and effective legal means to protect geographical indications, including appellations of origin, with regard to all products, at least to the extent that their use is misleading the public;

- adequate and effective legal protection of industrial designs by providing in particular a period of protection of five years from the date of application with a possibility of renewal for two consecutive periods of five years each;

- adequate and effective legal protection of patents on a basis similar to that prevailing in the European Free Trade Area;

- compulsory licensing of patents shall be non-exclusive, non-discriminatory, subject to compensation commensurate with the market value for the licence of the patent and to judicial review.

The scope and duration of such licence shall be limited to the purpose for which it was granted;

- adequate and effective legal protection of topographies of integrated circuits;

- adequate and effective legal protection of undisclosed information on knowhow.

Article 4
Acquisition and maintenance of intellectual property rights

Where the acquisition of an intellectual property right is subject to the right being granted or registered, the Parties shall ensure that the procedures for grant or registration be non-discriminatory, fair and equitable. They shall not be unnecessarily complicated and costly, or entail unreasonable time limits or unwarranted delays.

Article 5
Enforcement of intellectual property rights

(1)   The Parties shall ensure that the enforcement procedures be non-discriminatory, fair and equitable. They shall not be unnecessarily complicated and costly, or entail unreasonable time limits or unwarranted delays.

 (2)   The Parties shall provide for enforcement provisions that are adequate, effective and non-discriminatory so as to guarantee full protection of intellectual property rights against infringement. Such provisions shall include in particular injunctions, damages adequate to compensate for the injury suffered by the right holder, as well as provisional measures, including inaudita altera parte ones.

*

FREE TRADE AGREEMENT BETWEEN THE EFTA STATES AND THE SLOVAK REPUBLIC[*]
[excerpts]

The Free Trade Agreement between the EFTA States and the Slovak Republic was signed on 20 March 1992. It entered into force on 1 July 1992.

ARTICLE 16
Public procurement

1.   The States Parties to this Agreement consider the effective liberalization of their respective public procurement markets as a desirable and important objective of this Agreement.

2.   As of the entry into force of this Agreement, the EFTA States shall grant companies from the Slovak Republic access to contract award procedures on their respective public procurement markets according to the Agreement on Government procurement of 12 April 1979, as amended by a Protocol of Amendments of 2 February 1987 negotiated under the auspices of the General Agreement on Tariffs and Trade. The Slovak Republic shall, taking into account the restructuring and development process of its economy, gradually ensure that companies from the EFTA States have access on the same principles to contract award procedures on its public procurement market.

3.   As soon as possible after the entry into force of the Agreement the States Parties to this Agreement shall progressively develop and adjust the rules, conditions and practices governing the participation in public procurement contracts awarded by public authorities and public undertakings, and by private undertakings which have been granted special or exclusive rights, so as to ensure free access and transparency, and that there is no discrimination between potential suppliers from the States Parties to this Agreement. A full balance of rights and obligations between the States Parties to this Agreement shall be established not later than at the end of the transitional period.

4.   The Joint Committee shall recommend or agree, as appropriate, the practical modalities for this development including, inter alia, scope, timetable and rules to be applied.

5.   The States Parties to this Agreement concerned shall endeavour to accede to the relevant Agreements negotiated under the auspices of the General Agreement on Tariffs and Trade.

---

[*]   *Source*: European Free Trade Association Secretariat (1992). "Free Trade Agreement between the EFTA States and the Slovak Republic", available on the Internet (http://secretariat.efta.int). [Note added by the editor.]

ARTICLE 17[1]
Protection of intellectual property

1.   The States Parties to this Agreement shall grant and ensure adequate, effective and non-discriminatory protection of intellectual property rights, including measures for the enforcement of such rights against infringement thereof, counterfeiting and piracy, in accordance with the provisions of this Article, Annex XI to this Agreement and the international agreements referred to therein.

2.   The States Parties to this Agreement shall accord to each other's nationals treatment no less favourable than that they accord to their own nationals. Exemptions from this obligation must be in accordance with the substantive provisions of Article 3 of the TRIPS Agreement.

3.   The States Parties to this Agreement shall grant to each others' nationals treatment no less favourable than that accorded to nationals of any other State. Exemptions from this obligation must be in accordance with the substantive provisions of the TRIPS Agreement, in particular Articles 4 and 5 thereof.

4.   The States Parties to this Agreement agree, upon request of any State Party, to review the provisions on the protection of intellectual property rights contained in the present Article and in Annex XI, with a view to further improve levels of protection and to avoid or remedy trade distortions caused by actual levels of protection of intellectual property rights.

ARTICLE 18
Rules of competition concerning undertakings

1.   The following are incompatible with the proper functioning of this Agreement in so far as they may affect trade between an EFTA State and the Slovak Republic:

(a)   all agreements between undertakings, decisions by associations of undertakings and concerted practices between undertakings which have as their object or effect the prevention, restriction or distortion of competition;

(b)   abuse by one or more undertakings of a dominant position in the territories of the States Parties to this Agreement as a whole or in a substantial part thereof.

2.   As from the third year from the entry into force of this Agreement, the provisions of paragraph 1 shall also apply to the activities of public undertakings, and undertakings for which the Parties grant special or exclusive rights, in so far as the application of these provisions does not obstruct the performance, in law or in fact, of the particular public tasks assigned to them.

3.   If a State Party to this Agreement considers that a given practice is incompatible with the provisions of paragraphs 1 and 2 and if such practice causes or threatens to cause serious prejudice to the interest of that State Party or material injury to its domestic industry, it may take appropriate measures after consultations within the Joint Committee or after thirty days following referral for such consultation.

---

[1]   As amended by Joint Committee Decision No. 9 of 1996 (16 and 17 October 1996).

ARTICLE 30
Services and investment

1.   The States Parties to this Agreement recognize the growing importance of certain areas, such as services and investments. In their efforts to gradually develop and broaden their co-operation, in particular in the context of European integration, they will co-operate with the aim of achieving a gradual liberalization and mutual opening of markets for investments and trade in services, taking into account relevant GATT work.

2.   The EFTA States and the Slovak Republic will discuss in the Joint Committee this cooperation with the aim to develop and deepen their relations under the Agreement.

ANNEX XI[1]
ON INTELLECTUAL PROPERTY
Referred to in Article 17

Article 1
Definition and scope of protection

"Intellectual property protection" comprises in particular protection of copyright and neighbouring rights, including computer programmes and databases, trademarks for goods and services, geographical indications, including appellations of origin, industrial designs, patents, plant varieties, topographies of integrated circuits, as well as undisclosed information.

Article 2
International conventions

(1)   The States Parties to this Agreement reaffirm their commitment to comply with the obligations set out in the following multilateral agreements:

- WTO Agreement of 15 April 1994 on Trade-Related Aspects of Intellectual Property Rights (TRIPS Agreement);

- Paris Convention of 20 March 1883 for the Protection of Industrial Property (Stockholm Act, 1967);

- Bern Convention of 9 September 1886 for the Protection of Literary and Artistic Works (Paris Act, 1971).

(2)   The State Parties to this Agreement which are not States Parties to the agreement listed below shall undertake to obtain their adherence to the following multilateral agreement before the end of 1997:

- Protocol of 27 June 1989 Relating to the Madrid Agreement Concerning the International Registration of Marks.

---

[1]   As amended by Joint Committee Decision No. 9 of 1996 (16 and 17 October 1996).

(3)   The States Parties to this Agreement agree to promptly hold expert consultations, upon request of any State Party, on activities relating to the identified or to future international conventions on harmonization, administration and enforcement of intellectual property rights and on activities in international organizations, such as the WTO and the World Intellectual Property Organization (WIPO), as well as relations of the States Parties with third countries on matters concerning intellectual property.

Article 3
Additional substantive standards

The States Parties to this Agreement shall ensure in their national laws at least the following:

- adequate and effective means to protect geographical indications, including appellations of origin, with regard to all products and services;

- adequate and effective protection of industrial designs by providing in particular a period of protection of five years from the date of application with a possibility of renewal for two consecutive periods of five years each;

- adequate and effective patent protection for inventions in all fields of technology on a level similar to that prevailing in the European Patent Convention of 5 October 1973;

- compulsory licensing of patents shall only be granted under the conditions of Article 31 of the TRIPS Agreement. Licences granted on the grounds of nonworking shall be used only to the extent necessary to satisfy the domestic market on reasonable commercial terms.

Article 4
Acquisition and maintenance of intellectual property rights

Where the acquisition of an intellectual property right is subject to the right being granted or registered, the States Parties to this Agreement shall ensure that the procedures for grant or registration are of the same level as that provided in the TRIPS Agreement, in particular Article 62.

Article 5
Enforcement of intellectual property rights

The States Parties to this Agreement shall provide for enforcement provisions under their national laws of the same level as that provided in the TRIPS Agreement, in particular Articles 41 to 61.

Article 6
Technical co-operation

The States Parties to this Agreement shall agree upon appropriate modalities for technical assistance and co-operation of the respective authorities of the States Parties. To this end, they shall co-ordinate efforts with relevant international organizations.

*

FREE TRADE AGREEMENT BETWEEN THE EFTA STATES AND POLAND*
[excerpts]

> The Free Trade Agreement between the EFTA States and Poland was signed on 10 December 1992. It entered into force on 1 September 1993.

ARTICLE 16
Public procurement

1.   The States Parties to this Agreement consider the effective liberalization of their respective public procurement markets as a desirable and important objective of this Agreement.

2.   As of the entry into force of this Agreement, the EFTA States shall grant Polish companies access to contract award procedures on their respective public procurement markets according to the Agreement on Government Procurement of 12 April 1979, as amended by a Protocol of Amendments of 2 February 1987, negotiated under the auspices of the General Agreement on Tariffs and Trade. Poland shall, taking into account the restructuring and development process of its economy, gradually ensure that companies from the EFTA States have access on the same principles to contract award procedures on its public procurement market.

3.   As soon as possible after the entry into force of the Agreement, the States Parties to this Agreement shall progressively develop and adjust the rules, conditions and practices governing the participation in public procurement contracts, so as to ensure free access and transparency, and that there is no discrimination between potential suppliers from the States Parties to this Agreement. After a period of decreasing asymmetry in favour of Poland in their relations, a full balance of rights and obligations between the States Parties to this Agreement shall be established not later than at the end of the transitional period.

4.   The Joint Committee shall recommend or agree, as appropriate, the practical modalities for this development including, inter alia, scope, timetable and rules to be applied, and designation of entities awarding public procurement contracts, that is public authorities, public undertakings and private undertakings which have been granted special or exclusive rights.

5.   The States Parties concerned shall endeavour to accede to the relevant Agreements negotiated under the auspices of the General Agreement on Tariffs and Trade.

ARTICLE 17
Protection of intellectual property

1.   The States Parties to this Agreement shall grant and ensure non-discriminatory protection of intellectual property rights, including measures for the grant and enforcement of such rights.

---

* *Source*: European Free Trade Association Secretariat (1992). "Free Trade Agreement between the EFTA States and Poland", available on the Internet (http://secretariat.efta.int). [Note added by the editor.]

The protection shall be gradually improved and, before 31 December 1996, shall be of a level similar to that prevailing in the area of the States Parties to this Agreement.

2.   The States Parties to this Agreement agree to comply before 31 December 1996 with the substantive standards of the multilateral agreements which are specified in Annex XII; they shall make best endeavours to adhere to them as well as to other multilateral agreements facilitating co-operation in the field of intellectual property rights, reserving the sovereign right of the States Parties to this Agreement to decide on it.

3.   For the purpose of this Agreement, "intellectual property protection" includes in particular protection of copyright, comprising computer programmes and databases, and neighbouring rights, trademarks, geographical indications, industrial designs, patents, topographies of integrated circuits, as well as undisclosed information on know-how.

4.   (a)   The States Parties to this Agreement shall not grant treatment less favourable to nationals of each other in the field of intellectual property than that accorded to nationals of any other country. Any advantage, favour, privilege or immunity deriving from:

           (i)   bilateral agreements in force for a State Party to this Agreement at the entry into force of this Agreement as notified to the other States Parties by 1 January 1994,

           (ii)   existing and future multilateral agreements, including regional agreements on economic integration to which not all of the States Parties to this Agreement are Parties, may be exempted from this obligation, provided that it does not constitute an arbitrary or unjustifiable discrimination of nationals of the other States Parties.

       (b)   Two or more States Parties to this Agreement may conclude further agreements exceeding the requirements of this Agreement, provided that such agreements shall be open to all other States Parties to this Agreement on terms equivalent to those under the agreements and that they shall be ready to enter into good faith negotiations to this end.

5.   The States Parties to this Agreement shall ensure in their national laws that compulsory licensing of patents shall be non-exclusive, non-discriminatory, subject to compensation commensurate with the market value for the licence of the patent and to judicial review. The scope and duration of such licence shall be limited to the purpose for which it was granted.

Licences granted on the ground of non-working shall be used only to the extent necessary to satisfy the local market on reasonable commercial terms.

6.   The States Parties to this Agreement shall ensure that the procedures for grant or registration or maintenance of intellectual property rights and the enforcement procedures be fair and equitable. They shall not be unnecessarily complicated and costly, or entail unreasonable time-limits or unwarranted delays. Enforcement provisions shall include in particular injunctions, damages adequate to compensate for the injury suffered by the right holder, as well as provisional measures, including *inaudita altera parte* ones.

7.   (a)   The States Parties to this Agreement shall establish appropriate modalities for technical assistance and co-operation of their respective authorities. To this end, they shall co-ordinate efforts with relevant international organizations, such as the World Intellectual Property Organization (WIPO) and the European Patent Organisation (EPO).

      (b)   The States Parties to this Agreement agree to promptly hold expert consultations, at the request of any State Party to this Agreement, on activities relating to the existing or to future international conventions on harmonization, administration and enforcement of intellectual property and on activities in international organizations, such as the General Agreement on Tariffs and Trade and the World Intellectual Property Organization, as well as relations of States Parties with third countries on matters concerning intellectual property.

ARTICLE 18
Rules of competition concerning undertakings

1.   The following are incompatible with the proper functioning of this Agreement in so far as they may affect trade between an EFTA State and Poland:

      (a)   all agreements between undertakings, decisions by associations of undertakings and concerted practices between undertakings which have as their object or effect the prevention, restriction or distortion of competition;

      (b)   abuse by one or more undertakings of a dominant position in the territories of the States Parties to this Agreement as a whole or in a substantial part thereof.

2.   These provisions shall also apply to the activities of public undertakings and undertakings for which the States Parties to this Agreement grant special or exclusive rights, in so far as the application of these provisions does not obstruct the performance, in law or fact, of their particular public tasks.

3.   If a State Party to this Agreement considers that a given practice is incompatible with this Article, it may take appropriate measures it considers necessary to deal with the serious difficulties resulting from the practices in question under the conditions and in accordance with the procedures laid down in Article 25.

ARTICLE 30
Services and investment

1.   The States Parties to this Agreement recognize the growing importance of certain areas, such as services and investments. In their efforts to gradually develop and broaden their co-operation, in particular in the context of European integration, they will co-operate with the aim of achieving a progressive liberalization and mutual opening of markets for investments and trade in services, taking into account relevant GATT work.

2.   The EFTA States and Poland will discuss in the Joint Committee the possibilities to extend their trade relations to the fields of foreign direct investment and trade in services.

ANNEX XII

ON INTELLECTUAL PROPERTY

The multilateral Agreements mentioned in paragraph 2 of Article 17 are the following:

- Paris Convention of 20 March 1883 for the Protection of Industrial Property (Stockholm Act, 1967);

- Berne Convention of 9 September 1886 for the Protection of Literary and Artistic Works (Paris Act, 1971);

- International Convention of 26 October 1961 for the Protection of Performers, Producers of Phonograms and Broadcasting Organisations (Rome Convention);

- European Patent Convention of 5 October 1973.

*

FREE TRADE AGREEMENT BETWEEN THE EFTA STATES AND ROMANIA[*]
[excerpts]

The Free Trade Agreement between the EFTA States and Romania was signed on 10 December 1992. It entered into force on 1 May 1992.

ARTICLE 16
Public procurement

1.   The States Parties to this Agreement consider the effective liberalization of their respective public procurement markets as a desirable and important objective of this Agreement.

2.   As of the entry into force of this Agreement, the EFTA States shall grant companies from Romania access to contract award procedures on their respective public procurement markets according to the Agreement on Government Procurement of 12 April 1979, as amended by a Protocol of Amendments of 2 February 1987, negotiated under the auspices of the General Agreement on Tariffs and Trade. Romania shall, taking into account the restructuring and development process of its economy, gradually ensure that companies from the EFTA States have access on the same principles to contract award procedures on its public procurement market.

3.   As soon as possible after the entry into force of this Agreement, the States Parties to this Agreement shall progressively develop and adjust the rules, conditions and practices governing the participation in public procurement contracts awarded by public authorities and public undertakings, and by private undertakings which have been granted special or exclusive rights, so as to ensure free access and transparency, and that there is no discrimination between potential suppliers from the States Parties to this Agreement. A full balance of rights and obligations between the States Parties to this Agreement shall be established not later than at the end of the transitional period.

4.   The Joint Committee shall recommend or agree, as appropriate, the practical modalities for this development including, inter alia, scope, timetable and rules to be applied.

5.   The States Parties concerned shall endeavour to accede to the relevant Agreements negotiated under the auspices of the General Agreement on Tariffs and Trade.

---

[*]   *Source*: European Free Trade Association Secretariat (1992). "Free Trade Agreement between the EFTA States and Romania", available on the Internet (http://secretariat.efta.int). [Note added by the editor.]

ARTICLE 17[1]
Protection of intellectual property

1.   The States Parties to this Agreement shall grant and ensure adequate, effective and non-discriminatory protection of intellectual property rights. They shall adopt and take adequate, effective and non-discriminatory measures for the enforcement of such rights against infringement thereof, and in particular against counterfeiting and piracy. Particular obligations of the States Parties are contained in Annex XI.

2.   The States Parties to this Agreement shall take all necessary measures as soon as possible after the entry into force of the Agreement to comply with the substantive provisions of the multilateral conventions which are specified in Article 2 of Annex XI and shall make best endeavours to adhere to them as well as to multilateral agreements facilitating co-operation in the field of the protection of intellectual property rights.

3.   In the field of intellectual property, the States Parties to this Agreement shall not grant treatment less favourable to each others' nationals than that accorded to nationals of any other State. Any advantage, favour, privilege or immunity deriving from:

   (a)   bilateral agreements in force for a State Party to this Agreement at the entry into force of this Agreement as notified to the other States Parties by 1 January 1994,

   (b)   existing and future multilateral agreements, including regional agreements on economic integration, to which not all of the States Parties to this Agreement are Parties, may be exempted from this obligation, provided that it does not constitute an arbitrary or unjustifiable discrimination of nationals of the other States Parties.

4.   Two or more States Parties to this Agreement may conclude further agreements exceeding the requirements of this Agreement, provided that such agreements shall be open to all other States Parties to this Agreement on terms equivalent to those under the agreements and that they shall be ready to enter into good faith negotiations to this end.

5.   The States Parties to this Agreement shall agree upon appropriate modalities for technical assistance and co-operation of respective authorities of the States Parties to this Agreement. To this end, they shall co-ordinate efforts with relevant international organizations.

ARTICLE 18
Rules of competition concerning undertakings

1.   The following are incompatible with the proper functioning of this Agreement in so far as they may affect trade between an EFTA State and Romania:

   (a)   all agreements between undertakings, decisions by associations of undertakings and concerted practices between undertakings which have as their object or effect the prevention, restriction or distortion of competition;

---

[1]   Article 17 has been amended by Joint Committee Decision No. 8 of 1997 (18 December 1997). The Decision will enter into force when the instruments of acceptance have been deposited by all Parties with the Depositary. The current Article will then be replaced.

(b)   abuse by one or more undertakings of a dominant position in the territories of the States Parties to this Agreement as a whole or in a substantial part thereof.

2.   As from the third year from the entry into force of this Agreement, the provisions of paragraph 1 shall also apply to the activities of public undertakings, and undertakings for which the Parties grant special or exclusive rights, in so far as the application of these provisions does not obstruct the performance, in law or in fact, of the particular public tasks assigned to them.

3.   If a State Party to this Agreement considers that a given practice is incompatible with the provisions of paragraphs 1 and 2 and if such practice causes or threatens to cause serious prejudice to the interest of that State Party or material injury to its domestic industry, it may take appropriate measures after consultations within the Joint Committee or after thirty days following referral for such consultation.

ARTICLE 30
Services and investment

1.   The States Parties to this Agreement recognize the growing importance of certain areas, such as services and investments. In their efforts to gradually develop and broaden their co-operation, in particular in the context of European integration, they will co-operate with the aim of achieving a gradual liberalization and mutual opening of markets for investments and trade in services, taking into account relevant GATT work.

2.   The EFTA States and Romania will discuss in the Joint Committee this co-operation with the aim to develop and deepen their relations under the Agreement.

ANNEX XI[1]

ON INTELLECTUAL PROPERTY

Article 1 - Definition and scope of protection

"Intellectual property protection" includes in particular protection of copyright and neighbouring rights, trademarks, geographical indications, industrial designs, patents, topographies of integrated circuits, as well as undisclosed information on know-how.

Article 2 - Substantive standards according to international conventions

1.   In accordance with paragraph 2 of Article 17, the States Parties to this Agreement agree to comply with the substantive standards of the following multilateral agreements:

- Paris Convention of 20 March 1883 for the Protection of Industrial Property (Stockholm Act, 1967);

---

[1]Annex XI was amended by Joint Committee Decision No. 8 of 1997 (18 December 1997). The Decision will enter into force when the instruments of acceptance have been deposited by all Parties with the Depositary. The current Annex will then be replaced.

- Berne Convention of 9 September 1886 for the Protection of Literary and Artistic Works (Paris Act, 1971);

- International Convention of 26 October 1961 for the Protection of Performers, Producers of Phonograms and Broadcasting Organisations (Rome Convention);

2.   The States Parties to this Agreement agree to promptly hold expert consultations, upon request of any Party, on activities relating to the identified or to future international conventions on harmonization, administration and enforcement of intellectual property and on activities in international organizations, such as the General Agreement on Tariffs and Trade, the World Intellectual Property Organization (WIPO), as well as relations of the States Parties to third countries on matters concerning intellectual property.

Article 3 - Additional substantive standards

The States Parties to this Agreement shall ensure in their national laws at least the following:

- adequate and effective protection of copyright, including computer programmes and data bases, as well as neighbouring rights;

- adequate and effective protection of trademarks for goods and services, in particular of internationally well known trademarks;

- adequate and effective means to protect geographical indications, including appellations of origin, with regard to all products, at least to the extent that their use is misleading the public;

- adequate and effective protection of industrial designs by providing in particular a period of protection of five years from the date of application with a possibility of renewal for two consecutive periods of five years each;

- adequate and effective protection of patents on a level similar to that prevailing in the European Free Trade Area;

- compulsory licensing of patents shall be non-exclusive, nondiscriminatory, subject to compensation commensurate with the market value for the licence of the patent and to judicial review. The scope and duration of such licence shall be limited to the purpose for which it was granted. Licences granted on the grounds of non-working shall be used only to the extent necessary to satisfy the local market on reasonable commercial terms;

- adequate and effective protection of topographies of integrated circuits;

- adequate and effective protection of undisclosed information on knowhow.

Article 4 - Acquisition and maintenance of intellectual property rights

Where the acquisition of an intellectual property right is subject to the right being granted or registered, the States Parties to this Agreement shall ensure that the procedures for grant or registration be non-discriminatory, fair and equitable. They shall not be unnecessarily complicated and costly, or entail unreasonable time- limits or unwarranted delays.

Article 5 - Enforcement of intellectual property rights

1.   The States Parties to this Agreement shall ensure that the enforcement procedures be non-discriminatory, fair and equitable. They shall not be unnecessarily complicated and costly, or entail unreasonable time- limits or unwarranted delays.

2.   The States Parties to this Agreement shall provide for enforcement provisions that are adequate, effective and non-discriminatory so as to guarantee full protection of intellectual property rights against infringement. Such provisions shall include in particular injunctions, damages adequate to compensate for the injury suffered by the right holder, as well as provisional measures, including inaudita altera parte ones.

*

EUROPE AGREEMENT ESTABLISHING AN ASSOCIATION BETWEEN THE EUROPEAN COMMUNITIES AND THEIR MEMBER STATES, OF THE ONE PART, AND THE CZECH REPUBLIC, OF THE OTHER PART[*]
[excerpts]

> The Europe Agreement Establishing an Association between the European Communities and Their Member States, of the One Part, and the Czech Republic, of the Other Part was signed on 4 October 1993. It entered into force on 1 February 1995. The member States of the European Communities are: Austria, Belgium, Denmark, Finland, France, Germany, Greece, Ireland, Italy, Luxembourg, the Netherlands, Portugal, Spain, Sweden and the United Kingdom.

TITLE IV
MOVEMENT OF WORKERS, ESTABLISHMENT, SUPPLY OF SERVICES

CHAPTER II
Establishment

Article 45

1.   The Czech Republic shall, during the transitional periods referred to in Article 7, facilitate the setting up of operations on its territory by Community companies and nationals. To that end, it shall:

   (i)   grant, from entry into force of this Agreement for the establishment of Community companies and nationals a treatment no less favourable than that accorded to its own nationals and companies, save for the sectors and matters referred to in Annexes XVIa and XVIb, where such treatment shall be granted at the latest by the end of the transitional period referred to in Article 7; and

   (ii)   grant, from entry into force of this Agreement, in the operation of Community companies and nationals established in the Czech Republic a treatment no less favourable than that accorded to its own companies and nationals;

   (iii)   notwithstanding the provisions of indents (i) and (ii), the national treatment as described in indents (i) and (ii) shall be applicable for Community nationals establishing in the Czech Republic as self-employed persons only from the start of the sixth year following the entry into force of this Agreement.

2.   The Czech Republic shall, during the transitional periods referred to in paragraph 1, not adopt any new regulations or measures which introduce discrimination as regards the

---

[*]   *Source*: European Communities (1994). "Europe Agreement Establishing an Association between the European Communities and Their Member States, of the One Part, and the Czech Republic, of the Other Part ", *Official Journal of the European Communities*, L 360, 31 December 1994 pp. 2 - 210; available also on the Internet (http://www.europa.eu.int/eur-lex/en/lif/dat/1994/en_294A1231_34.html). [Note added by the editor.]

establishment and operations of Community companies and nationals in its territory in comparison to its own companies and nationals.

3.   Each Member State shall grant, from entry into force of this Agreement, a treatment no less favourable than that accorded to its own companies and nationals for the establishment of Czech Republic companies and nationals and shall grant in the operation of Czech Republic companies and nationals established in its territory a treatment no less favourable than that accorded to its own companies and nationals.

4.   For the purposes of this Agreement:

   (a)   establishment shall mean:

      (i)   as regards nationals, the right to take up and pursue economic activities as self-employed persons and to set up and manage undertakings, in particular companies, which they effectively control. Self-employment and business undertakings by nationals shall not extend to seeking or taking employment in the labour market of another Party.

      The provisions of this chapter do not apply to those who are not exclusively self-employed;

      (ii)   as regards companies, the right to take up and pursue economic activities by means of the setting up and management of subsidiaries, branches and agencies;

   (b)   subsidiary of a company shall mean a company which is effectively controlled by the first company;

   (c)   economic activities shall in particular include activities of an industrial character, activities of a commercial character, activities of craftsmen and activities of the professions.

5.   The Association Council shall during the transitional periods referred to in paragraph 1 (i) and (iii) examine regularly the possibility of accelerating the granting of national treatment in the sectors referred to in Annexes XVIa and XVIb and the inclusion of areas or matters listed in Annex XVIc within the scope of application of the provisions of paragraphs 1, 2 and 3 of this Article. Amendments may be made to these Annexes by decision of the Association Council.
Following the expiration of the transitional periods referred to in paragraph 1 (i) and (iii), the Association Council may exceptionally, upon request of the Czech Republic, and if the necessity arises, decide to prolong the duration of exclusion of certain areas or matters listed in Annexes XVIa and XVIb for a limited period of time.

6.   The provisions concerning establishment and operation of Community and Czech Republic companies and nationals contained in paragraphs 1, 2 and 3 of this Article shall not apply to the areas or matters listed in Annex XVIc.

7.   Notwithstanding the provisions of this Article, Community companies established in the territory of the Czech Republic shall have, upon entry into force of this Agreement, where necessary for the conduct of the economic activities for which they are established, the right to

acquire, use, rent and sell real property, and as regards natural resources, agricultural land and forestry, the right to lease.

The Czech Republic shall grant these rights, where necessary for the conduct of the economic activities for which they are established, to branches and agencies established in the Czech Republic of Community companies at the latest by the end of the sixth year following the entry into force of this Agreement.

The Czech Republic shall grant these rights, where necessary for the conduct of the economic activities for which they are established, to Community nationals established in the Czech Republic as self-employed persons at the latest by the end of the transitional period referred to in Article 7.

Article 46

1.   Subject to the provisions of Article 45, with the exception of financial services described in Annex XVIa, each Party may regulate the establishment and operation of companies and nationals on its territory, in so far as these regulations do not discriminate against companies and nationals of the other Party, in comparison to its own companies and nationals.

2.   In respect of financial services, described in Annex XVIa, this Agreement does not prejudice the right of the Parties to adopt measures necessary for the conduct of the Party's monetary policy, or for prudential grounds in order to ensure the protection of investors, depositors, policy holders, or persons to whom a fiduciary duty is owed, or to ensure the integrity and stability of the financial system. These measures shall not discriminate on grounds of nationality against companies and nationals of the other Party in comparison to its own companies and nationals.

Article 47

In order to make it easier for Community nationals and Czech Republic nationals to take up and pursue regulated professional activities in the Czech Republic and the Community respectively, the Association Council shall examine which steps are necessary to be taken to provide for the mutual recognition of qualifications. It may take all necessary measures to that end.

Article 48

The provisions of Article 46 do not preclude the application by a Contracting Party of particular rules concerning the establishment and operation in its territory of branches and agencies of companies of another Party not incorporated in the territory of the first Party, which are justified by legal or technical differences between such branches and agencies as compared to branches and agencies of companies incorporated in its territory, or, as regards financial services, for prudential reasons. The difference in treatment shall not go beyond what is strictly necessary as a result of such legal or technical differences, or, as regards financial services, described in Annex XVIa, for prudential reasons.

Article 49

1.   A 'Community company` and a 'Czech Republic company` respectively shall, for the purpose of this Agreement, mean a company or a firm set up in accordance with the laws of a

Member State or of the Czech Republic respectively and having its registered office, central administration, or principal place of business in the territory of the Community or the Czech Republic respectively. However, should the company or firm, set up in accordance with the laws of a Member State or of the Czech Republic respectively, have only its registered office in the territory of the Community or the Czech Republic respectively, its operations must possess a real and continuous link with the economy of one of the Member States or the Czech Republic respectively.

2.   With regard to international maritime transport, shall also be beneficiaries of the provisions of this Chapter and Chapter III of this Title, a national or a shipping company of the Member States or of the Czech Republic respectively established outside the Community or the Czech Republic respectively and controlled by nationals of a Member State, or Czech Republic nationals respectively, if their vessels are registered in that Member State or in the Czech Republic respectively in accordance with their respective legislations.

3.   A Community and a Czech Republic national respectively shall, for the purpose of this Agreement, mean a natural person who is a national of one of the Member States or of the Czech Republic respectively.

4.   The provisions of this Agreement shall not prejudice the application by each Party of any measure necessary to prevent the circumvention of its measures concerning third country access to its market through the provisions of this Agreement.

Article 50

For the purpose of this Agreement 'financial services' shall mean those activities described in Annex XVIa. The Association Council may extend or modify the scope of Annex XVIa.

Article 51

During the first six years following the date of entry into force of this Agreement, or for the sectors referred to in Annexes XVIa and XVIb, during the transitional period referred to in Article 7, the Czech Republic may introduce measures which derogate from the provisions of this chapter as regards the establishment of Community companies and nationals if certain industries:

　　　- are undergoing restructuring, or

　　　- are facing serious difficulties, particularly where these entail serious social problems in the Czech Republic, or

　　　- face the elimination or a drastic reduction of the total market share held by Czech Republic companies or nationals in a given sector or industry in the Czech Republic, or

　　　- are newly emerging industries in the Czech Republic.

Such measures:

　　　(i)　　shall cease to apply at the latest two years after the expiration of the sixth year following the date of entry into force of this Agreement or for the sectors included in Annex XVIa and in Annex XVIb upon the expiration of the transitional period referred to in Article 7; and

(ii)   shall be reasonable and necessary in order to remedy the situation; and

(iii)   shall only relate to establishments in the Czech Republic to be created after the entry into force of such measures and shall not introduce discrimination concerning the operations of Community companies or nationals already established in the Czech Republic at the time of introduction of a given measure compared to Czech Republic companies or nationals.

The Association Council may exceptionally, upon request of the Czech Republic, and if the necessity arises, decide to prolong the periods referred to in point (i) above for a given sector for a limited period of time.

While devising and applying such measures, the Czech Republic shall grant whenever possible to Community companies and nationals a preferential treatment, and in no case a treatment less favourable than that accorded to companies or nationals from any third country.

Prior to the introduction of these measures, the Czech Republic shall consult the Association Council and shall not put them into effect before a one-month period following the notification to the Association Council of the concrete measures to be introduced by the Czech Republic, except where the threat of irreparable damage requires the taking of urgent measures in which case the Czech Republic shall consult the Association Council immediately after their introduction.

Upon the expiration of the sixth year following the entry into force of this Agreement, or for the sectors included in Annexes XVIa and XVIb upon expiration of the transitional period referred to in Article 7, the Czech Republic may introduce such measures only with the authorization of the Association Council and under conditions determined by the latter.

Article 52

1.   The provisions of this Chapter shall not apply to air transport services, inland-waterways transport services and maritime cabotage transport services.

2.   The Association Council may make recommendations for improving establishment and operations in the areas covered by paragraph 1.

Article 53

1.   Notwithstanding the provisions of Chapter I of this Title, the beneficiaries of the rights of establishment granted by the Czech Republic and the Community respectively shall be entitled to employ, or have employed by one of their subsidiaries, in accordance with the legislation in force in the host country of establishment, in the territory of the Czech Republic and the Community respectively, employees who are nationals of Community Member States and the Czech Republic respectively, provided that such employees are key personnel as defined in paragraph 2, and that they are employed exclusively by such beneficiaries or their subsidiaries. The residence and work permits of such employees shall only cover the period of such employment.

2.   Key personnel of the beneficiaries of the rights of establishment herein referred to as organization are:

(a)   senior employees of an organization who primarily direct the management of the organization, receiving general supervision or direction principally from the board of directors or shareholders of the business, including:

- directing the organization or a department or sub-division of the organization,

- supervising and controlling the work of other supervisory, professional or managerial employees,

- having the authority personally to engage and dismiss or recommend engaging, dismissing or other personnel actions;

(b)   persons employed by an organization who possess high or uncommon:

- qualifications referring to a type of work or trade requiring specific technical knowledge,

- knowledge essential to the organization's service, research equipment, techniques or management.

These may include, but are not limited to, members of accredited professions.

Each such employee must have been employed by the organization concerned for at least one year preceding the detachment by the organization.

Article 54

1.   The provisions of this Chapter shall be applied subject to limitations justified on grounds of public policy, public security or public health.

2.   They shall not apply to activities which in the territory of each Party are connected, even occasionally, with the exercise of official authority.

Article 55

Companies which are controlled and exclusively owned jointly by Czech Republic companies or nationals and Community companies or nationals shall also be beneficiaries of the provisions of this Chapter and Chapter III of this Title.

CHAPTER III
Supply of services between the Community and the Czech Republic

Article 56

1.   The Parties undertake in accordance with the provisions of this Chapter to take the necessary steps to allow progressively the supply of services by Community or Czech Republic

companies or nationals who are established in a Party other than that of the person for whom the services are intended taking into account the development of the services sector in the Parties.

2.   In step with the liberalization process mentioned in paragraph 1, and subject to the provisions of Article 59 (1), the Parties shall permit the temporary movement of natural persons providing the service or who are employed by the service provider as key personnel as defined in Article 53 (2), including natural persons who are representatives of a Community or Czech Republic company or national and are seeking temporary entry for the purpose of negotiating for the sale of services or entering into agreements to sell services for that service provider, where those representatives will not be engaged in making direct sales to the general public or in supplying services themselves.

3.   The Association Council shall take the measures necessary to implement progressively the provisions of paragraph 1.

Article 57

With regard to supply of transport services between the Community and the Czech Republic, the following replaces the provisions of Article 56:

1.   With regard to international maritime transport the Parties undertake to apply effectively the principle of unrestricted access to the market and traffic on a commercial basis.

   (a)   The above provision does not prejudice the rights and obligations under the United Nations Code of Conduct for Liner Conferences, as applied by one or the other Contracting Party to this Agreement. Non-conference liners will be free to operate in competition with a conference as long as they adhere to the principle of fair competition on a commercial basis.

   (b)   The Parties affirm their commitment to a freely competitive environment as being an essential feature of the dry and liquid bulk trade.

2.   In applying the principles of paragraph 1, the Parties shall:

   (a)   not introduce cargo sharing clauses in future bilateral agreements with third countries, other than in those exceptional circumstances where liner shipping companies from one or other Party to this Agreement would not otherwise have an effective opportunity to ply for trade to and from the third country concerned;

   (b)   prohibit cargo sharing arrangements in future bilateral agreements concerning dry and liquid bulk trade;

   (c)   abolish, upon entry into force of this Agreement, all unilateral measures, administrative, technical and other obstacles which could have restrictive or discriminatory effects on the free supply of services in international maritime transport.

3.   With a view to assuring a coordinated development and progressive liberalization of transport between the Parties adapted to their reciprocal commercial needs, the conditions of mutual market access in air transport and in inland transport shall be dealt with by special

transport agreements to be negotiated between the Parties after the entry into force of this Agreement.

4.   Prior to the conclusion of the agreements referred to in paragraph 3, the Parties shall not take any measures or actions which are more restrictive or discriminatory as compared to the situation existing on the day preceding the day of entry into force of this Agreement.

5.   During the transitional period, the Czech Republic shall progressively adapt its legislation including administrative, technical and other rules to that of the Community legislation existing at any time in the field of air and inland transport in so far as it serves liberalization purposes and mutual access to markets of the Parties and facilitates the movement of passengers and of goods.

6.   In step with the common progress in the achievement of the objectives of this Chapter, the Association Council shall examine ways of creating the conditions necessary for improving freedom to provide air and inland transport services.

Article 58

The provisions of Article 54 shall apply to the matters covered by this Chapter.

CHAPTER IV
General provisions

Article 59

1.   For the purpose of Title IV of this Agreement, nothing in the Agreement shall prevent the Parties from applying their laws and regulations regarding entry and stay, work, labour conditions and establishment of natural persons, and supply of services, provided that, in so doing, they do not apply them in a manner as to nullify or impair the benefits accruing to any Party under the terms of a specific provision of this Agreement. This provision does not prejudice the application of Article 54.

2.   The provisions of Chapters, II, III and IV of Title IV shall be adjusted by decision of the Association Council in the light of the result of the negotiations on services taking place in the Uruguay Round and in particular to ensure that under any provision of this Agreement a Party grants to the other Party a treatment no less favourable than that accorded under the provisions of a future General Agreement on Trade and Services (GATS).

3.   The exclusion of Community companies and nationals established in the Czech Republic in accordance with the provisions of Chapter II of Title IV from public aid granted by the Czech Republic in the areas of public education services, health related and social services and cultural services shall, for the duration of the transitional period referred to in Article 7, be deemed compatible with the provisions of Title IV and with the competition rules referred to in Title V.

TITLE V
PAYMENTS, CAPITAL, COMPETITION AND OTHER
ECONOMIC PROVISIONS, APPROXIMATION OF LAWS

CHAPTER I
Current payments and movement of capital

Article 60

The Contracting Parties undertake to authorize, in freely convertible currency, any payments on the current account of balance of payments to the extent that the transaction underlying the payments concern movements of goods, services or persons between the Parties which have been liberalized pursuant to this Agreement.

Article 61

1.   With regard to transactions on the capital account of balance of payments, from the entry into force of this Agreement, the Member States and the Czech Republic respectively shall ensure the free movement of capital relating to direct investments made in companies formed in accordance with the laws of the host country and investments made in accordance with the provisions of Chapter II of Title IV, and the liquidation or repatriation of these investments and of any profit stemming therefrom. Notwithstanding the above provision, such free movement, liquidation and repatriation shall be ensured by the end of the fifth year following the entry into force of this Agreement for all investments linked to establishment of nationals establishing in the Czech Republic as self-employed persons pursuant to Chapter II of Title IV.

2.   Without prejudice to paragraph 1, the Member States, as from the entry into force of this Agreement, and the Czech Republic as from the end of the fifth year following the entry into force of this Agreement, shall not introduce any new foreign exchange restrictions on the movement of capital and current payments connected therewith between residents of the Community and the Czech Republic and shall not make the existing arrangements more restrictive.

3.   The Parties shall consult each other with a view to facilitating the movement of capital between the Community and the Czech Republic in order to promote the objectives of this Agreement.

Article 62

1.   During the five years following the date of entry into force of this Agreement, the Contracting Parties shall take measures permitting the creation of the necessary conditions for the further gradual application of Community rules on the free movement of capital.

2.   By the end of the fifth year from the entry into force of this Agreement, the Association Council shall examine ways of enabling Community rules on the movement of capital to be applied in full.

Article 63

With reference to the provisions of this Chapter, and notwithstanding the provisions of Article 65, until a full convertibility of the Czech Republic currency within the meaning of Article VIII of the International Monetary Fund is introduced, the Czech Republic may in exceptional circumstances apply exchange restrictions connected with the granting or taking up of short- and medium-term credits to the extent that such restrictions are imposed on the Czech Republic for the granting of such credits and are permitted according to the Czech Republic's status under the IMF.

The Czech Republic shall apply these restrictions in a non-discriminatory manner. They shall be applied in such a manner as to cause the least possible disruption to this Agreement. The Czech Republic shall inform the Association Council promptly of the introduction of such measures and of any changes therein.

CHAPTER II
Competition and other economic provisions

Article 64

1.   The following are incompatible with the proper functioning of the Agreement, in so far as they may affect trade between the Community and the Czech Republic:

   (i)   all agreements between undertakings, decisions by associations of undertakings and concerted practices between undertakings which have as their object or effect the prevention, restriction or distortion of competition;

   (ii)   abuse by one or more undertakings of a dominant position in the territories of the Community or of the Czech Republic as a whole or in a substantial part thereof;

   (iii)   any public aid which distorts or threatens to distort competition by favouring certain undertakings or the production of certain goods.

2.   Any practices contrary to this Article shall be assessed on the basis of criteria arising from the application of the rules of Articles 85, 86 and 92 of the Treaty establishing the European Economic Community.

3.   The Association Council shall, within three years of the entry into force of this Agreement, adopt the necessary rules for the implementation of paragraphs 1 and 2. Until the implementing rules are adopted, practices incompatible with paragraph 1 shall be dealt with by the Contracting Parties on their respective territories according to their respective legislations. This is without prejudice to paragraph 6.

4.   (a)   For the purposes of applying the provisions of paragraph 1 (iii), the Parties recognize that during the first five years after the entry into force of this Agreement, any public aid granted by the Czech Republic shall be assessed taking into account the fact that the Czech Republic shall be regarded as an area identical to those areas of the Community described in Article 92 (3) (a) of the Treaty establishing the European Economic Community. The Association Council shall,

taking into account the economic situation of the Czech Republic, decide whether that period should be extended by further periods of five years.

(b)   Each Party shall ensure transparency in the area of public aid, inter alia by reporting annually to the other Party on the total amount and the distribution of the aid given and by providing, upon request, information on aid schemes. Upon request by one Party, the other Party shall provide information on particular individual cases of public aid.

5.   With regard to products referred to in Chapters II and III of Title III:

- the provision of paragraph 1 (iii) does not apply,

- any practices contrary to paragraph 1 (i) should be assessed according to the criteria established by the Community on the basis of Articles 42 and 43 of the Treaty establishing the European Economic Community and in particular of those established in Council Regulation No 26/62.

6.   If the Community or the Czech Republic considers that a particular practice is incompatible with the terms of paragraph 1, and:

- is not adequately dealt with under the implementing rules referred to in paragraph 3, or

- in the absence of such rules, and if such practice causes or threatens to cause serious prejudice to the interest of the other Party or material injury to its domestic industry, including its services industry, it may take appropriate measures after consultation within the Association Council or after 30 working days following referral for such consultation.

In the case of practices incompatible with paragraph 1 (iii), such appropriate measures may, where the General Agreement on Tariffs and Trade applies thereto, only be adopted in accordance with the procedures and under the conditions laid down by the General Agreement on Tariffs and Trade and any other relevant instrument negotiated under its auspices which are applicable between the Parties.

7.   Notwithstanding any provisions to the contrary adopted in accordance with paragraph 3, the Parties shall exchange information taking into account the limitations imposed by the requirements of professional and business secrecy.

8.   This Article shall not apply to the products covered by the Treaty establishing the European Coal and Steel Community which are the subject of Protocol 2.

Article 65

1.   Where one or more Member States of the Community or the Czech Republic is in serious balance of payments difficulties, or under imminent threat thereof, the Community or the Czech Republic, as the case may be, may, in accordance with the conditions established under the General Agreement on Tariffs and Trade, adopt restrictive measures, including measures relating to imports, which shall be of limited duration and may not go beyond what is necessary to remedy the balance of payments situation. The measures shall be progressively relaxed as balance of payments conditions improve and they shall be eliminated when conditions no longer justify

their maintenance. The Community or the Czech Republic, as the case may be, shall inform the other Party forthwith of their introduction and, whenever practicable, of a time schedule for their removal.

2.   The Parties shall nevertheless endeavour to avoid the imposition of restrictive measures for balance of payments purposes.

3.   Any restrictive measures shall not apply to transfers related to investment and in particular to the repatriation of amounts invested or reinvested and of any kind of revenues stemming therefrom.

Article 66

With regard to public undertakings, and undertakings to which special or exclusive rights have been granted, the Association Council shall ensure that as from the third year following the date of entry into force of this Agreement, the principles of the Treaty establishing the European Economic Community, in particular Article 90, and the principles of the concluding document of the April 1990 Bonn meeting of the Conference on Security and Cooperation in Europe, in particular entrepreneurs' freedom of decision, are upheld.

Article 67

1.   The Czech Republic shall continue to improve the protection of intellectual, industrial and commercial property rights in order to provide, by the end of the fifth year after the entry into force of this Agreement, a level of protection similar to that existing in the Community, including comparable means of enforcing such rights.

2.   Within the same time, the Czech Republic shall apply to accede to the Munich Convention on the granting of European patents of 5 October 1973. The Czech Republic shall also accede to the other multilateral conventions on intellectual, industrial and commercial property rights referred to in Annex XVII paragraph 1 to which Member States are Parties, or which are de facto applied by Member States.

Article 68

1.   The Contracting Parties consider the opening up of the award of public contracts on the basis of non-discrimination and reciprocity, in particular in the GATT context, to be a desirable objective.

2.   The Czech Republic companies as defined in Article 49, shall be granted access to contract award procedures in the Community pursuant to Community procurement rules under a treatment no less favourable than that accorded to Community companies as of the entry into force of this Agreement.

Community companies as defined in Article 49 shall be granted access to contract award procedures in the Czech Republic under a treatment no less favourable than that accorded to Czech Republic companies at the latest at the end of the transitional period referred to in Article 7.

Community companies established in the Czech Republic under the provisions of Chapter II of Title IV shall have upon entry into force of this Agreement access to contract award procedures under a treatment no less favourable than that accorded to Czech Republic companies.

The Association Council shall periodically examine the possibility for the Czech Republic in introduce access to award procedures in the Czech Republic for all Community companies prior to the end of the transitional period.

3.   As regards establishment, operations, supply of services between the Community and the Czech Republic, as well as employment and movement of labour linked to the fulfilment of public contracts, the provisions of Articles 38 to 59 are applicable.

CHAPTER III
Approximation of laws

Article 69

The Contracting parties recognize that the major precondition for the Czech Republic's economic integration into the Community is the approximation of the Czech Republic's existing and future legislation to that of the Community. The Czech Republic shall endeavour to ensure that its legislation will be gradually made compatible with that of the Community.

Article 70

The approximation of laws shall extend to the following areas in particular: customs law, company law, banking law, company accounts and taxes, intellectual property, protection of workers at the workplace, financial services, rules on competition, protection of health and life of humans, animals and plants, consumer protection, indirect taxation, technical rules and standards, nuclear law and regulation, transport and the environment.

Article 71

The Community shall provide the Czech Republic with technical assistance for the implementation of these measures, which may include inter alia:

- the exchange of experts,

- the provision of early information especially on relevant legislation,

- organization of seminars,

- training activities,

- aid for the translation of Community legislation in the relevant sectors.

TITLE VI
ECONOMIC COOPERATION

Article 72

1.   The Community and the Czech Republic shall establish economic cooperation aimed at contributing to the Czech Republic's development and growth potential. Such cooperation shall strengthen existing economic links on the widest possible foundation, to the benefit of both Parties.

2.   Policies and other measures will be designed to bring about economic and social development of the Czech Republic and will be guided by the principle of sustainable development. These policies should ensure that environmental considerations are also fully incorporated from the outset and that they are linked to the requirements of harmonious social development.

3.   To this end the cooperation should focus in particular on policies and measures related to industry including the mining sector, investment, agriculture, energy, transport, regional development and tourism.

4.   Special attention must be devoted to measures capable of fostering cooperation between the countries of central and Eastern Europe with a view to a harmonious development of the region.

Article 73
Industrial cooperation

1.   Cooperation shall aim at promoting the modernization and restructuring of Czech Republic industry in both public and private sectors as well as industrial cooperation between economic operators of both sides, with the particular objective of strengthening the private sector.

2.   Particular attention shall be paid to:

   - the restructuring of individual sectors; in this context, the Association Council will examine in particular the problems affecting the sectors of coal and steel and the conversion of the defence industry,

   - the establishment of new undertakings in areas offering potential for growth.

3.   Industrial cooperation initiatives take into account priorities determined by the Czech Republic. The initiatives should seek in particular to establish a suitable framework for undertakings, to improve management know-how and to promote transparency as regards markets and conditions for undertakings, and will include technical assistance where appropriate.

Article 74
Investment promotion and protection

1.   Cooperation shall aim to establish a favourable climate for private investment, both domestic and foreign, which is essential to economic and industrial reconstruction in the Czech Republic.

2.   The particular aims of cooperation shall be:

- to improve the institutional framework for investments in the Czech Republic,

- the extension by the Member States and the Czech Republic of agreements for the promotion and protection of investment,

- to implement suitable arrangements for the transfer of capital,

- to proceed with deregulation and to improve economic infrastructure,

- to exchange information on investment opportunities in the form of trade fairs, exhibitions, trade weeks and other events.

ANNEX XVIa (Title IV, Chapter II)

ESTABLISHMENT: FINANCIAL SERVICES

Definitions

A financial service is any service of a financial nature offered by a financial service provider of a party. Financial services include the following activities:

A.   All insurance and insurance-related services

    1.   Direct insurance (including co-insurance).

        (i)   life;

        (ii)   non-life.

    2.   Reinsurance and retrocession.

    3.   Insurance intermediation, such as brokerage and agency.

    4.   Services auxiliary to insurance, such as consultancy, actuarial, risk assessment and claim settlement services.

B.   Banking and other financial services (excluding insurance)

1.   Acceptance of deposits and other repayable funds from the public.

2.   Lending of all types, including, inter-alia, consumer credit, mortgage credit, factoring and financing of commercial transaction.

3.   Financial leasing.

4.   All payment and money transmission services, including credit charge and debit cards, travellers cheques and bankers drafts.

5.   Guarantees and commitments.

6.   Trading for own account of customers, whether on an exchange, in an over the counter market or otherwise, the following:

    (a)   money market instruments (cheques, bills, certificates of deposits, etc.);

    (b)   foreign exchange;

    (c)   derivative products including, but not limited to, futures and options;

    (d)   exchange rates and interest rate instruments, including products such as swaps, forward rate agreements, etc.;

    (e)   transferable securities;

    (f)   other negotiable instruments and financial assets, including bullion.

7.   Participation in issues of all kinds of securities, including underwriting and placement as agent (whether publicly or privately) and provision of services related to such issues.

8.   Money broking.

9.   Asset management, such as cash or portfolio management, all forms of collective investment management, pension fund management, custodial depository and trust services.

10.   Settlement and clearing services for financial assets, including securities, derivative products, and other negotiable instruments.

11.   Advisory intermediation and other auxiliary financial services on all the activities listed in points 1 to 10 above, including credit reference and analysis, investment and portfolio research and advice, advice on acquisitions and on corporate restructuring and strategy.

12.   Provision and transfer of financial information, and financial data processing and related software by providers of other financial services.

Excluded from the definition of financial services are the following activities:

(a)   activities carried out by central banks or by any other public institution in pursuit of monetary and exchange rate policies;

(b)   activities conducted by central banks, government agencies or departments, or public institutions, for the account or with the guarantee of the government, except when those activities may be carried out by financial service providers in competition with such public entities;

(c)   activities forming part of a statutory system of social security or public retirement plans, except when those activities may be carried out by financial service providers in competition with public entities or private institutions.

ANNEX XVII

1.   Paragraph 2 of Article 67 concerns the following multilateral convention: Protocol relating to the Madrid Agreement concerning the International Registration of Marks (Madrid 1989).

2.   The Association Council may decide that paragraph 2 of Article 67 shall apply to other multilateral conventions.

3.   The Contracting Parties confirm the importance they attach to the obligations arising from the following multilateral conventions:

- Berne Convention for the protection of literary and artistic works (Paris Act, 1971),

- International Convention for the protection of performers, producers of phonograms and broadcasting organizations (Rome, 1961),

- Paris Convention for the protection of industrial property (Stockholm Act, 1967 and amended in 1979),

- Madrid Agreement concerning the international registration of marks (Stockholm Act, 1967 and amended in 1979),

- Nice Agreement concerning the international classification of goods and services for the purposes of the registration of marks (Geneva 1977, amended 1979),

- Budapest Treaty on the international recognition of the deposit of micro-organisms for the purposes of patent procedures (1977, modified in 1980),

- Patent Cooperation Treaty (Washington 1970, amended 1979 and modified in 1984).

4.   For the purposes of paragraph 3 of this Annex and of the provisions of Article 76 (1) referring to intellectual property, Contracting Parties shall be the Czech Republic, the European Economic Community and the Member States, each in, as far as they are respectively competent

for matters concerning industrial, intellectual and commercial property covered by these conventions or by Article 76 (1).

5.   The provisions of this Annex and those of Article 76 (1) referring to intellectual property are without prejudice to the competences of the European Economic Community and its Member States in matters of industrial, intellectual and commercial property.

*

EUROPE AGREEMENT ESTABLISHING AN ASSOCIATION BETWEEN THE EUROPEAN ECONOMIC COMMUNITIES AND THEIR MEMBER STATES, OF THE ONE PART, AND OF THE OTHER PART*
[excerpts]

> The Europe Agreement Establishing an Association between the European Economic Communities and Their Member States, of the One Part, and Romania, of the Other Part was signed on 1 February 1993. It entered into force on 1 February 1995. The member States of the European Communities are: Austria, Belgium, Denmark, Finland, France, Germany, Greece, Ireland, Italy, Luxembourg, the Netherlands, Portugal, Spain, Sweden and the United Kingdom.

TITLE IV
MOVEMENT OF WORKERS, ESTABLISHMENT, SUPPLY OF SERVICES

CHAPTER II
Establishment

Article 45

1.   Each Member State shall grant, from entry into force of the Agreement, for the establishment of Romanian companies and nationals and for the operation of Romanian companies and nationals established in its territory, a treatment no less favourable than that accorded to its own companies and nationals, save for the areas described in Annex XVI.

2.   Without prejudice to paragraph 3, Romania shall grant, from entry into force of the Agreement, for the establishment of Community companies and nationals and for the operation of Community companies and nationals established in its territory, a treatment no less favourable than that accorded to its own companies and nationals save for the areas described in Annex XVII. Should the existing laws and regulations not grant such treatment of Community companies and nationals for certain economic activities in Romania upon entry into force of this Agreement, Romania shall amend such laws and regulations as to ensure such treatment at the latest at the end of the fifth year following the date of entry into force of this Agreement.

3.   For the areas and matters described in Annex XVIII, except for banking activities as referred to in Law No 33 of 1991, Romania shall grant gradually and at the latest by the end of the transitional period referred to in Article 7, a treatment no less favourable than that accorded to its own nationals and companies for the establishment of Community companies and nationals.

---

* *Source*: European Communities (1994). "Europe Agreement Establishing an Association between the European Economic Communities and Their Member States, of the One Part, and Romania, of the Other Part", *Official Journal of the European Communities*, L 357, 31 December 1994 pp. 2 - 189; available also on the Internet (http://www.europa.eu.int/eur-lex/en/lif/dat/1994/en_294A1231_20.html). [Note added by the editor.]

As regards the abovementioned banking activities, national treatment shall be granted at the latest by the end of the fifth year following the entry into force of this Agreement.

4.   Romania shall, during the transitional periods referred to in paragraphs 2 and 3 not adopt any new regulations or measures which introduce discrimination as regards to establisment and operations of Community companies and nationals in its territory in comparison to its own companies and nationals.

5.   For the purposes of this Agreement:

(a)   establishment shall mean

(i)   as regards nationals, the right to take up and pursue economic activities as self-employed persons and to set up and manage undertakings, in particular companies, which they effectively control. Self-employment and business undertakings by nationals shall not extend to seeking or taking employment in the labour market or confer a right of access to the labour market of another Party. The provisions of this Chapter do not apply to those who are not exclusively self-employed;

(ii)   as regards companies, the right to take up and pursue economic activities by means of the setting up and management of subsidiaries, branches and agencies;

(b)   subsidiary of a company shall mean a company which is effectively controlled by the first company;

(c)   economic activities shall in particular include activities of an industrial character, activities of a commercial character, activities of craftsmen and activities of the professions.

6.   The Association Council shall examine regularly the possibility of accelerating the granting of national treatment in the sectors referred to in Annex XVIII and the inclusion of areas and matters listed in Annexes XVI and XVII within the scope of application of the provisions of paragraphs 1, 2, 3 and 4 of this Article. Amendments may be made to these Annexes by decision of the Association Council.

Following the expiration of the transitional periods referred to in paragraphs 2 and 3, the Association Council may exceptionally, upon request by Romania, and if the necessity arises, decide to prolong the duration of those transitional periods for certain areas or matters for a limited period of time.

7.   Notwithstanding the provisions of this Article, Community companies established in the territory of Romania shall have, from entry into force of the Agreement, the right to acquire, use, rent and sell real property, and as regards public property, land and forestry, the right to lease, where these are directly necessary for the conduct of the economic activities for which they are established. This right does not include establishment for the purpose of dealing and agency in the area of real estate and natural resources.

Romania shall grant these rights to branches and agencies established in Romania of Community companies at the latest by the end of the first five years following the date of entry into force of the Agreement.

Romania shall grant these rights to Community nationals established as self-employed persons in Romania at the latest by the end of the transitional period referred to in Article 7.

Article 46

1.   Subject to the provisions of Article 45 with the exception of financial services described in Annex XVIII, each Party may regulate the establishment and operation of companies and nationals on its territory, in so far as these regulations do not discriminate against companies and nationals of the other Party in comparison to its own companies and nationals.

2.   In respect of financial services, described in Annex XVIII, this Agreement does not prejudice the right of the Parties to adopt measures necessary for the conduct of the Party's monetary policy, or for prudential grounds in order to ensure the protection of investors, depositors, policy holders, or persons to whom a fiduciary duty is owed, or to ensure the integrity and stability of the financial system. These measures shall not discriminate on grounds of nationality against companies and nationals of the other Party in comparison to its own companies and nationals.

Article 47

In order to make it easier for Community nationals and Romanian nationals to take up and pursue regulated professional activities in Romania and the Community respectively, the Association Council shall examine which steps are necessary to be taken to provide for the mutual recognition of qualifications. It may take all necessary measures to that end.

Article 48

The provisions of Article 46 do not preclude the application by a Party of particular rules concerning the establishment and operation in its territory of branches and agencies of companies of another Party not incorporated in the territory of the first Party, which are justified by legal or technical differences between such branches and agencies as compared to branches and agencies of companies incorporated in its territory, or, as regards financial services, for prudential reasons. The difference in treatment shall not go beyond what is strictly necessary as a result of such legal or technical differences, or, as regards financial services, described in Annex XVIII, for prudential reasons.

Article 49

1.   A 'Community company` and a 'Romanian company` respectively shall, for the purpose of this Agreement, mean a company or a firm set up in accordance with the laws of a Member State or of Romania respectively and having its registered office, central administration, or principal place of business in the territory of the Community or Romania respectively. However, should the company or firm, set up in accordance with the laws of a Member State or of Romania respectively, have only its registered office in the territory of the Community or Romania respectively, its operations must possess a real and continuous link with the economy of one of the Member States or Romania respectively.

2.   With regard to international maritime transport, shall also be beneficiaries of the provisions of this Chapter and Chapter III of this Title, a national or a shipping company of the Member States or of Romania, respectively established outside the Community or Romania respectively and controlled by nationals of a Member State, or Romanian nationals respectively, if their vessels are registered in that Member State or in Romania respectively in accordance with their respective legislations.

3.   A Community and a Romanian national respectively shall, for the purpose of this Agreement, mean a natural person who is a national of one of the Member States or of Romania respectively.

4.   The provisions of this Agreement shall not prejudice the application by each Party of any measure necessary to prevent the circumvention of its measures concerning third country access to its market, through the provisions of this Agreement.

Article 50

For the purpose of this Agreement 'financial services` shall mean those activities described in Annex XVIII. The Association Council may extend or modify the scope of Annex XVIII.

Article 51

During the first five years following the date of entry into force of the Agreement, Romania may introduce measures which derogate from the provisions of this Chapter as regards the establishment of Community companies and nationals if certain industries:

- are undergoing restructuring, or

- are facing serious difficulties, particularly where these entail serious social problems in Romania, or

- face the elimination or a drastic reduction of the total market share held by Romanian companies or nationals in a given sector or industry in Romania, or

- are newly emerging industries in Romania.

Such measures:

(i)   shall cease to apply at the latest two years after the expiration of the fifth year following the date of entry into force of this Agreement; and

(ii)   shall be reasonable and necessary in order to remedy the situation; and

(iii)   shall only relate to establishments in Romania to be created after the entry into force of such measures and shall not introduce discrimination concerning the operations of Community companies or nationals already established in Romania at the time of introduction of a given measure compared to Romanian companies or nationals.

The Association Council may exceptionally, upon request by Romania, and if the necessity arises, decide to prolong the period referred to in indent (i) above for a given sector for a limited period of time not exceeding the duration of the transition period referred to in Article 7.

While devising and applying such measures, Romania shall grant whenever possible to Community companies and nationals a preferential treatment, and in no case a treatment less favourable than that accorded to companies or nationals from any third country.

Prior to the introduction of these measures, Romania shall consult the Association Council and shall not put them into effect before a one month period following the notification to the Association Council of the concrete measures to be introduced by Romania, except where the threat of irreparable damage requires the taking of urgent measures in which case Romania shall consult the Association Council immediately after their introduction.

Upon the expiration of the fifth year following the entry into force of the Agreement, Romania may introduce such measures only with the authorization of the Association Council and under conditions determined by the latter.

Article 52

1.   The provisions of this Chapter shall not apply to air transport services, inland-waterways transport services and maritime cabotage transport services.

2.   The Association Council may make recommendations for improving establishment and operations in the areas covered by paragraph 1.

Article 53

1.   Notwithstanding the provisions of Chapter I of this Title, the beneficiaries of the rights of establishment granted by Romania and the Community respectively shall be entitled to employ, or have employed by one of their subsidiaries, in accordance with the legislation in force in the host country of establishment, in the territory of Romania and the Community respectively, employees who are nationals of Community Member States and Romania respectively, provided that such employees are key personnel as defined in paragraph 2, and that they are employed exclusively by such beneficiaries or their subsidiaries. The residence and work permits of such employees shall only cover the period of such employment.

2.   Key personnel of the beneficiaries of the rights of establishment herein referred to as 'organization' are:

    (a)   senior employees of an organization who primarily direct the management of the organization, receiving general supervision or direction principally from the board of directors or shareholders of the business, including:

        - directing the organization or a department or sub-division of the organization,

        - supervising and controlling the work of other supervisory, professional or managerial employees,

- having the authority personally to engage and dismiss or recommend engaging, dismissing or other personnel actions;

(b)   persons employed by an organization who possess high or uncommon:
- qualifications referring to a type of work or trade requiring specific technical knowledge,

- knowledge essential to the organization's service, research equipment, techniques or management.

These may include, but are not limited to, members of accredited professions.
Each such employee must have been employed by the organization concerned for at least one year preceding the detachment by the organization.

Article 54

1.   The provisions of this Chapter shall be applied subject to limitations justified on grounds of public policy, public security or public health.

2.   They shall not apply to activities which in the territory of each Party are connected, even occasionally, with the exercise of official authority.

Article 55

Companies which are controlled and exclusively owned jointly by Romanian companies or nationals and Community companies or nationals shall also be beneficiaries of the provisions of this Chapter and Chapter III if this Title.

CHAPTER III
Supply of services between the Community and Romania

Article 56

1.   The Parties undertake in accordance with the provisions of this Chapter to take the necessary steps to allow progressively the supply of services by Community or Romanian companies or nationals who are established in a Party other than that of the person for whom the services are intended taking into account the development of the services sectors in the Parties.

2.   In step with the liberalization process mentioned in paragraph 1, and subject to the provisions of Article 59 (1), the Parties shall permit the temporary movement of natural persons providing the service or who are employed by the service provider as key personnel as defined in Article 53 (2), including natural persons who are representatives of a Community or Romanian company or national and are seeking temporary entry for the purpose of negotiating for the sale of services or entering into Agreements to sell services for that service provider, where those representatives will not be engaged in making direct sales to the general public or in supplying services themselves.

3.   The Association Council shall take the measures necessary to progressively implement the provisions of paragraph 1 of this Article.

Article 57

With regard to supply of transport services between the Community and Romania, the following replaces the provisions of Article 56:

1.   with regard to international maritime transport, the Parties undertake to apply effectively the principle of unrestricted access to the market and traffic on a commercial basis.

   (a)   The above provision does not prejudice the rights and obligations under the United Nations Code of Conduct for Liner Conferences, as applied by one or the other Contracting Party to this Agreement. Non-conference liners will be free to operate in competition with a conference as long as they adhere to the principle of fair competition on a commercial basis.

   (b)   The Parties affirm their commitment to a freely competitive environment as being an essential feature of the dry and liquid bulk trade;

2.   in applying the principles of point 1, the Parties shall:

   (a)   not introduce cargo sharing clauses in future bilateral Agreements with third countries, other than in those exceptional circumstances where liner shipping companies from one or other Party to this Agreement would not otherwise have an effective opportunity to ply for trade to and from the third country concerned;

   (b)   prohibit cargo sharing arrangements in future bilateral Agreements concerning dry and liquid bulk trade;

   (c)   abolish, upon entry into force of the Agreement, all unilateral measures, administrative, technical and other obstacles which could have restrictive or discriminatory effects on the free supply of services in international maritime transport.

3.   With a view to assuring a coordinated development and progressive liberalization of transport between the Parties adapted to their reciprocal commercial needs, the conditions of mutual market access in air transport and in inland transport shall be dealt with by special transport Agreements to be negotiated between the Parties after the entry into force of the Agreement.

4.   Prior to the conclusion of the Agreements referred to in paragraph 3, the Parties shall not take any measures or actions which are more restrictive or discriminatory as compared to the situation existing on the day preceding the day of entry into force of the Agreement.

5.   During the transitional period, Romania shall progressively adapt its legislation including administrative, technical and other rules to that of the Community legislation existing at any time in the field of air and inland transport insofar as it serves liberalization purposes and mutual access to markets of the Parties and facilitates the movement of passengers and of goods.

6.   In step with the common progress in the achievement of the objectives of this Chapter, the Association Council shall examine ways of creating the conditions necessary for improving freedom to provide air and inland transport services.

Article 58

The provisions of Article 54 shall apply to the matters covered by this Chapter.

CHAPTER IV
General Provisions

Article 59

1.   For the purpose of Title IV of this Agreement, nothing in the Agreement shall prevent the Parties from applying their laws and regulations regarding entry and stay, work, labour conditions and establishment of natural persons and supply of services, provided that, in so doing, they do not apply them in a manner as to nullify or impair the benefits accruing to any Party under the terms of a specific provision of the Agreement. The above provision does not prejudice the application of Article 54.

2.   The provisions of Chapter II, III and IV of Title IV shall be adjusted by decision of the Association Council in the light of the result of the negotiations on services taking place in the Uruguay Round and in particular to ensure that under any provision of this Agreement a Party grants to the other Party a treatment no less favourable than that accorded under the provisions of a future General Agreement on Trade and Services (GATS).

3.   The exclusion of Community companies and nationals established in Romania in accordance with the provisions of Chapter II of Title IV from public aid granted by Romania in the areas of public education services, health-related and social services and cultural services shall, for the duration of the transitional period referred to in Article 7, be deemed compatible with the provisions of Title IV and with the competition rules referred to in Title V.

TITLE V
PAYMENTS, CAPITAL, COMPETITION AND OTHER ECONOMIC PROVISIONS, APPROXIMATION OF LAWS

CHAPTER I
Current payments and movement of capital

Article 60

The Parties undertake to authorize in freely convertible currency, any payments on the current account of balance of payments to the extent that the transactions underlying the payments concern movements of goods, services, or persons between the Parties which have been liberalized pursuant to this Agreement.

Article 61

1.   With regard to transactions on the capital account of balance of payments, from entry into force of the Agreement, the Member States and Romania respectively shall ensure the free movement of capital relating to direct investments made in companies formed in accordance with the laws of the host country and investments made in accordance to the provisions of Chapter II

of Title IV, and the liquidation or repatriation of these investments and of any profit stemming therefrom.

2.   Notwithstanding the above provision, such free movement, liquidation and repatriation shall be ensured by the end of the first stage referred to in Article 7 for all investments linked to establishment of Community nationals establishing in Romania as self-employed persons pursuant to Chapter II of Title IV.

3.   Without prejudice to paragraph 1, the Member States, as from the entry into force of the Agreement, and Romania as from the end of the fifth year following the entry into force of the Agreement, shall not introduce any new foreign exchange restrictions on the movement of capital and current payments connected therewith between residents of the Community and Romania and shall not make the existing arrangements more restrictive.

4.   The Parties shall consult each other with a view to facilitating the movement of capital between the Community and Romania in order to promote the objectives of this Agreement.

Article 62

1.   During the five years following the date of entry into force of the Agreement, the Parties shall take measures permitting the creation of the necessary conditions for the further gradual application of Community rules on the free movement of capital.

2.   By the end of the fifth year from the entry into force of the Agreement, the Association Council shall examine ways of enabling Community rules on the movement of capital to be applied in full.

Article 63

With reference to the provisions of this Chapter, and notwithstanding the provisions of Article 65, until a full convertibility of Romanian currency in the meaning of Article VIII of the International Monetary Fund (IMF) is introduced, Romania may in exceptional circumstances apply exchange restrictions connected with the granting or taking up of short and medium-term credits to the extent that such restrictions are imposed on Romania for the granting of such credite and are permitted according to Romania's status under the IMF.

Romania shall apply these restrictions in a non-discriminatory manner. They shall be applied in such a manner as to cause the least possible disruption to this Agreement. Romania shall inform the Association Council promptly of the introduction of such measures and of any changes therein.

CHAPTER II
Competition and other economic provisions

Article 64

1.   The following are incompatible with the proper functioning of this Agreement, in so far as they may affect trade between the Community and Romania:

(i)   all Agreements between undertakings, decisions by associations of undertakings and concerted practices between undertakings which have as their object or effect the prevention, restriction or distortion of competition;

(ii)   abuse by one or more undertakings of a dominant position in the territories of the Community or of Romania as a whole or in a substantial part thereof;

(iii)   any public aid which distorts or threatens to distort competition by favouring certain undertakings or the production of certain goods.

2.   Any practices contrary to this Article shall be assessed on the basis of criteria arising from the application of the rules of Articles 85, 86, and 92 of the Treaty establishing the European Economic Community.

3.   The Association Council shall, within three years of the entry into force of the Agreement, adopt the necessary rules for the implementation of paragraphe 1 and 2.

4.   (a)   For the purposes of applying the provisions of paragraph 1, point (iii), the Parties recognize that during the first five years after the entry into force of the Agreement, any public aid granted by Romania shall be assessed taking into account the fact that Romania shall be regarded as an area indentical to those areas of the Community described in Article 92 (3) (a) of the Treaty establishing the European Economic Community. The Association Council shall, taking into account the economic situation of Romania, decide whether that period should be extended by further periods of five years.

        (b)   Each Party shall ensure transparency in the area of public aid, inter alia by reporting annually to the other Party on the total amount and the distribution of the aid given and by providing, upon request, information on aid schemes. Upon request by one Party, the other Party shall provide information on particular individual cases of public aid.

5.   With regard to products referred to in Chapters II and III of Title III:

- the provision of paragraph 1 (iii) does not apply,

- any practices contrary to paragraph 1 (i) should be assessed according to the criteria established by the Community on the basis of Articles 42 and 43 of the Treaty establishing the European Economic Community and in particular of those established in Council Regulation No 26/1962.

6.   If the Community or Romania considers that a particular practices is incompatible with the terms of paragraph 1 and:

- is not adequately dealt with under the implementing rules referred to in paragraph 3, or

- in the absence of such rules, and if such practice or threatens to cause serious prejudice to the interest of the other Party or material injury to its domestic industry, including its services industry, it may take appropriate measures after consultation within the Association Council or after 30 working days following referral for such consultation.

In the case of practices incompatible with paragraph 1 (iii) of this Article, such appropriate measures may, where the General Agreement on Tariffs and Trade applies thereto, only be adopted in conformity with the procedures and under the conditions laid down by the General Agreement on Tariffs and Trade and any other relevant instrument negotiated under its auspices which are applicable between the Parties.

7.   Notwithstanding any provisions to the contrary adopted in conformity with paragraph 3, the Parties shall exchange information taking into account the limitations imposed by the requirements of professional and business secrecy.

8.   This Article shall not apply to the products covered by the Treaty establishing the European Coal and Steel Community which are the subject of Protocol 2.

Article 65

1.   The Parties shall endeavour to avoid the imposition of restrictive measures including measures relating to imports for balance of payments purposes. In the event of their introduction, the Party having introduced the same shall present to the other Party a time schedule for their removal.

2.   Where one or more Member States or Romania is in serious balance of payments difficulties, or under imminent threat thereof, the Community or Romania, as the case may be, may, in accordance with the conditions established under the General Agreement on Tariffs and Trade, adopt restrictive measures, including measures relating to imports, which shall be of limited duration and may not go beyond what is necessary to remedy the balance of payments situation. The Community or Romania, as the case may be, shall inform the other Party forthwith.

3.   Any restrictive measures shall not apply to transfers related to investments and in particular to the repatriation of amounts invested or reinvested and of any kind of revenues stemming therefrom.

Article 66

With regard to public undertakings and undertakings to which special or exclusive rights have been granted, the Association Council shall ensure that, as from the third year from the date of entry into force of the Agreement, the principles of the Treaty establishing the European Economic Community, notably Article 90, and the principles of the concluding document of the April 1990 Bonn meeting of the Conference on Security and Cooperation in Europe (notably entrepreneurs' freedom of decision) are applied in the operation of this Agreement.

Article 67

1.   Romania shall continue to improve the protection of intellectual, industrial and commercial property rights in order to provide, by the end of the fifth year after the entry into force of the Agreement, for a level of protection similar to that existing in the Community, including comparable means of enforcing such rights.

2.   Within the same time, Romania shall apply to accede to the Munich Convention on the Grant of European Patents of 5 October 1973. Romania shall also accede to the other multilateral

conventions on intellectual, industrial and commercial property rights (referred to in paragraph 1 of Annex XIX) to which Member States are Parties, or which are de facto applied by Member States.

3.   Upon entry into force of the Agreement treatmet no less favourable than that granted to any third country under any bilateral agreement shall be granted by Romania.

Article 68

1.   The Parties consider the opening up of the award of public contracts on the basis of the principles of non-discrimination and reciprocity, in particular in the GATT context, to be a desirable objective.

2.   The Romanian companies as defined in Article 49 shall be granted access to contract award procedures in the Community pursuant to Community procurement rules under a treatment no less favourable than that accorded to Community companies as of the entry into force of the Agreement.

Community companies as defined in Article 49 shall be granted access to contract award procedures in Romania under a treatment no less favourable than that accorded to Romanian companies at the latest at the end of the transitional period referred to in Article 7.

Community companies established in Romania under the provisions of Chapter II of Title IV in the form of subsidiaries as described in Article 45 and in the forms described in Article 55 shall have upon entry into force of the Agreement access to contract award procedures under a treatment no less favourable than that accorded to Romanian companies. Community companies established in Romania in the form of branches and agencies as described in Article 45 shall be granted such treatment at the latest by the end of the transitional period referred to in Article 7.

The Association Council shall periodically examine the possibility for Romania to introduce access to award procedures in Romania for all Community companies prior to the end of the transitional period.

3.   As regards establishment, operations, supply of services between the Community and Romania, as well as employment and movement of labour linked to the fulfilment of public contracts, the provisions of Articles 38 to 59 are applicable.

CHAPTER III
Approximation of laws

Article 69

The Parties recognize that an important condition for Romania's economic integration into the Community is the approximation of Romania's existing and future legislation to that of the Community. Romania shall endeavour to ensure that its legislation will be gradually made compatible with that of the Community.

Article 70

The approximation of laws shall extend to the following areas in particular: customs law, company law, banking law, company accounts and taxes, intellectual property, protection of workers at the workplace, social security, financial services, rules on competition, protection of health and life of humans, animals and plants, consumer protection, indirect taxation, technical rules and standards, nuclear law and regulation, transport and the environment.

Article 71

The Community shall provide Romania with technical assistance for the implementation of these measures, which may include inter alia:

- the exchange of experts,

- the provision of early information especially on relevant legislation,

- organization of seminars,

- training activities,

- aid for the translation of Community legislation in the relevant sectors.

TITLE VI
ECONOMIC COOPERATION

Article 72

1.   The Community and Romania shall establish economic cooperation aimed at contributing to Romania's development and growth potential. Such cooperation shall strengthen existing economic links on the widest possible foundation, to the benefit of both Parties.

2.   Policies and other measures will be designed to bring about economic and social development of Romania and will be guided by the principle of sustainable development. These policies should ensure that environmental considerations are also fully incorporated from the outset and that they are linked to the requirements of harmonious social development.

3.   To this end the cooperation should focus in particular on policies and measures related to industry including the mining sector, investment, agriculture, energy, transport, regional development and tourism.

4.   Special attention shall be devoted to measures capable of fostering cooperation between the countries of central and eastern Europe with a view to a harmonious development of the region.

Article 73
Industrial cooperation

1.   Cooperation shall aim at promoting the following in particular:

- industrial cooperation between economic operators of both sides, with the particular objective of strengthening the private sector,

- Community participation in Romania's efforts in both public and private sectors to modernize and restructure its industry, which will effect the transition from a centrally planned system to a market economy under conditions which ensure that the environment is protected,

- the restructuring of individual sectors,

- the establishment of new undertakings in areas offering potential for growth,

- transfer of technology and know-how.

2.   Industrial cooperation initiatives shall take into account priorities determined by Romania. The initiatives should seek in particular to establish a suitable framework for undertakings, to improve management know-how and to promote transparency as regards markets and conditions for undertakings, and will include technical assistance where appropriate.

Article 74
Investment promotion and protection

1.   Cooperation shall aim to establish a favourable climate for private investment, both domestic and foreign, which is essential to economic and industrial reconstruction in Romania.

2.   The particular aims of cooperation shall be:

- for Romania to establish and improve a legal framework which favours and protects investment,

- the conclusion by the Member States and Romania of Agreements for the promotion and protection of investment,

- to implement suitable arrangements for the transfer of capital,

- to bring about better investment protection,

- to proceed with deregulation and to improve economic infrastructure,

- to exchange information on investment opportunities in the form of trade fairs, exhibitions, trade weeks and other events.

ANNEX XVIII

Establishment: Financial services (Articles 45, 46, 48 and 50)
Definitions

A financial service is any service of a financial nature offered by a financial service provider of a party. Financial services include the following activities:

A.   All insurance and insurance-related services

    1.   Direct insurance (including co-insurance)

        (i)   life;

        (ii)   non-life.

    2.   Reinsurance and retrocession.

    3.   Insurance intermediation, such as brokerage and agency.

    4.   Services auxiliary to insurance, such as consultancy, actuarial, risk asessment and claim settlement services.

B.   Banking and other financial services (excluding insurance)

    1.   Acceptance of deposits and other repayable funds from the public.

    2.   Lending of all types, including, inter alia, consumer credit, mortgage credit, factoring and financing of commercial transaction.

    3.   Financial leasing.

    4.   All payment and money transmission services, including credit charge and debit cards, travellers cheques and bankers drafts.

    5.   Guarantees and commitments.

    6.   Trading for own account of customers, whether on an exchange, in an over-the-counter market or otherwise, the following:

        (a)   money market instruments (cheques, bills, certificates of deposits, etc.);

        (b)   foreign exchange;

        (c)   derivative products including, but not limited to, futures and options;

        (d)   exchange rates and interest rate instruments, including products such as swaps, forward rate agreements, etc.;

        (e)   transferable securities;

        (f)   other negotiable instruments and financial assets, including bullion.

    7.   Participation in issues of all kinds of securities, including under-writing and placement as agent (whether publicly or privately) and provision of services related to such issues.

    8.   Money broking.

9.   Asset management, such as cash or portfolio management, all forms of collective investment management, pension fund management, custodial depository and trust services.

10.   Settlement and clearing services for financial assets, including securities, derivative products, and other negotiable instruments.

11.   Advisory intermediation and other auxiliary financial services on all the activities listed in Points 1 to 10 above, including credit reference and analysis, investment and portfolio research and advice, advice on acquisitions and on corporate restructuring and strategy.

12.   Provision and transfer of financial information, and financial data processing and related software by providers of other financial services.

Excluded from the definition of financial services are the following activities:

(a)   activities carried out by central banks or by any other public institution in pursuit of monetary and exchange rate policies;

(b)   activities conducted by central banks, government agencies or departments, or public institutions, for the account or with the guarantee of the government, except when those activities may be carried out by financial service providers in competition with such public entities;

(c)   activities forming part of a statutory system of social security or public retirement plans, except when those activities may be carried out by financial service providers in competition with public entities or private institutions.

ANNEX XIX

Intellectual property (Article 67)

1.   Paragraph 2 of Article 67 concerns the following multilateral conventions:

- Budapest Treaty on the international recognition of the deposit of micro-organisms for the purposes of patent procedures (1977, modified in 1980),

- Protocol relating to the Madrid Agreement concerning the international registration of marks (Madrid 1989),

- Berne Convention for the protection of literary and artistic works (Paris Act, 1971),

- International Convention for the protection of performers, producers of phonograms and broadcasting organizations (Rome, 1961).

2.   The Association Council may decide that paragraphe 2 of Article 67 shall aplly to other present or future mulitlateral conventions.

3.   The Contracting Parties confirm the importance they attach to the obligations arising from the following multilateral conventions:

- Paris Convention for the protection of industrial property (Stockholm Act, 1967 and amended in 1979),

- Madrid Agreement concerning the international registration of marks (Stockholm Act, 1967 and amended in 1979),

- Patent Cooperation Treaty (Washington 1970, amended 1979 and modified in 1984).

4.   Before the end of the first stage, Romania shall comply in its internal legislation with the substantial provisions of the Nice Agreement concerning the international classification of goods and services for the purposes of registration of marks (Geneva 1977, amended 1979).

5.   For the purposes of paragraph 3 of this Annex and the provisions of Article 76 (1) referring to intellectual property, Contracting Parties shall be Romania, the European Economic Community and the Member States, each in as far as they are respectively competent for matters concerning industrial, intellectual and commercial property covered by these conventions or by Article 76 (1).

6.   The provisions of this Annex and of the provisions of Article 76 (1), referring to intellectual property are without prejudice to the competence of the European Economic Community and its Member States in matters of industrial, intellectual and commercial property.

*

EUROPE AGREEMENT ESTABLISHING AN ASSOCIATION BETWEEN THE EUROPEAN COMMUNITIES AND THEIR MEMBER STATES, OF THE ONE PART, AND THE SLOVAK REPUBLIC, OF THE OTHER PART*
[excerpts]

The Europe Agreement Establishing an Association between the European Communities and Their Member States, of the One Part, and the Slovak Republic, of the Other Part was signed on 4 October 1993. It entered into force on 1 February 1995. The member States of the European Communities are: Austria, Belgium, Denmark, Finland, France, Germany, Greece, Ireland, Italy, Luxembourg, the Netherlands, Portugal, Spain, Sweden and the United Kingdom.

TITLE IV
MOVEMENT OF WORKERS, ESTABLISHMENT, SUPPLY OF SERVICES

CHAPTER II
Establishment

Article 45

1.   The Slovak Republic shall, during the transitional periods referred to in Article 7, facilitate the setting up of operations on its territory by Community companies and nationals. To that end, it shall:

   (i)   grant, from entry into force of this Agreement for the establishment of Community companies and nationals a treatment no less favourable than that accorded to its own nationals and companies, save for the sectors and matters referred to in Annexes XVIa and XVIb, where such treatment shall be granted at the latest by the end of the transitional period referred to in Article 7; and

   (ii)   grant, from entry into force of this Agreement, in the operation of Community companies and nationals established in the Slovak Republic a treatment no less favourable than that accorded to its own companies and nationals;

   (iii) notwithstanding the provisions of indents (i) and (ii), the national treatment as described in indents (i) and (ii) shall be applicable for Community nationals establishing in the Slovak Republic as self-employed persons only from the start of the sixth year following the entry into force of this Agreement.

---

* *Source*: European Communities (1994). "Europe Agreement Establishing an Association between the European Communities and Their Member States, of the One Part, and the Slovak Republic, of the Other Part", *Official Journal of the European Communities*, L 359, 31 December 1994 pp. 2 - 210; available also on the Internet: (http://www.europa.eu.int/eur-lex/en/lif/dat/1994/en_294A1231_30.html). [Note added by the editor.]

2.   The Slovak Republic shall, during the transitional periods referred to in paragraph 1, not adopt any new regulations or measures which introduce discrimination as regards the establishment and operations of Community companies and nationals in its territory in comparison to its own companies and nationals.

3.   Each Member State shall grant, from entry into force of this Agreement, a treatment no less favourable than that accorded to its own companies and nationals for the establishment of Slovak Republic companies and nationals and shall grant in the operation of Slovak Republic companies and nationals established in its territory a treatment no less favourable than that accorded to its own companies and nationals.

4.   For the purposes of this Agreement:

   (a)   establishment shall mean:

      (i)   as regards nationals, the right to take up and pursue economic activities as self-employed persons and to set up and manage undertakings, in particular companies, which they effectively control. Self-employment and business undertakings by nationals shall not extend to seeking or taking employment in the labour market of another Party.

         The provisions of this chapter do not apply to those who are not exclusively self-employed;

      (ii)   as regards companies, the right to take up and pursue economic activities by means of the setting up and management of subsidiaries, branches and agencies;

   (b)   subsidiary of a company shall mean a company which is effectively controlled by the first company;

   (c)   economic activities shall in particular include activities of an industrial character, activities of a commercial character, activities of craftsmen and activities of the professions.

5.   The Association Council shall during the transitional periods referred to in paragraph 1 (i) and (iii) examine regularly the possibility of accelerating the granting of national treatment in the sectors referred to in Annexes XVIa and XVIb and the inclusion of areas or matters listed in Annex XVIc within the scope of application of the provisions of paragraphs 1, 2 and 3 of this Article. Amendments may be made to these Annexes by decision of the Association Council.

Following the expiration of the transitional periods referred to in paragraph 1 (i) and (iii), the Association Council may exceptionally, upon request of the Slovak Republic, and if the necessity arises, decide to prolong the duration of exclusion of certain areas or matters listed in Annexes XVIa and XVIb for a limited period of time.

6.   The provisions concerning establishment and operation of Community and Slovak Republic companies and nationals contained in paragraphs 1, 2 and 3 of this Article shall not apply to the areas or matters listed in Annex XVIc.

7.   Notwithstanding the provisions of this Article, Community companies established in the territory of the Slovak Republic shall have, upon entry into force of this Agreement, where necessary for the conduct of the economic activities for which they are established, the right to acquire, use, rent and sell real property, and as regards natural resources, agricultural land and forestry, the right to lease.

The Slovak Republic shall grant these rights, where necessary for the conduct of the economic activities for which they are established, to branches and agencies established in the Slovak Republic of Community companies at the latest by the end of the sixth year following the entry into force of this Agreement.

The Slovak Republic shall grant these rights, where necessary for the conduct of the economic activities for which they are established, to Community nationals established in the Slovak Republic as self-employed persons at the latest by the end of the transitional period referred to in Article 7.

Article 46

1.   Subject to the provisions of Article 45, with the exception of financial services described in Annex XVIa, each Party may regulate the establishment and operation of companies and nationals on its territory, in so far as these regulations do not discriminate against companies and nationals of the other Party, in comparison to its own companies and nationals.

2.   In respect of financial services, described in Annex XVIa, this Agreement does not prejudice the right of the Parties to adopt measures necessary for the conduct of the Party's monetary policy, or for prudential grounds in order to ensure the protection of investors, depositors, policy holders, or persons to whom a fiduciary duty is owed, or to ensure the integrity and stability of the financial system. These measures shall not discriminate on grounds of nationality against companies and nationals of the other Party in comparison to its own companies and nationals.

Article 47

In order to make it easier for Community nationals and Slovak Republic nationals to take up and pursue regulated professional activities in the Slovak Republic and the Community respectively, the Association Council shall examine which steps are necessary to be taken to provide for the mutual recognition of qualifications. It may take all necessary measures to that end.

Article 48

The provisions of Article 46 do not preclude the application by a Contracting Party of particular rules concerning the establishment and operation in its territory of branches and agencies of companies of another Party not incorporated in the territory of the first Party, which are justified by legal or technical differences between such branches and agencies as compared to branches and agencies of companies incorporated in its territory, or, as regards financial services, for prudential reasons. The difference in treatment shall not go beyond what is strictly necessary as a result of such legal or technical differences, or, as regards financial services, described in Annex XVIa, for prudential reasons.

Article 49

1.   A 'Community company` and a 'Slovak Republic company` respectively shall, for the purpose of this Agreement, mean a company or a firm set up in accordance with the laws of a Member State or of the Slovak Republic respectively and having its registered office, central administration, or principal place of business in the territory of the Community or the Slovak Republic respectively. However, should the company or firm, set up in accordance with the laws of a Member State or of the Slovak Republic respectively, have only its registered office in the territory of the Community or the Slovak Republic respectively, its operations must possess a real and continuous link with the economy of one of the Member States or the Slovak Republic respectively.

2.   With regard to international maritime transport, shall also be beneficiaries of the provisions of this Chapter and Chapter III of this Title, a national or a shipping company of the Member States or of the Slovak Republic respectively established outside the Community or the Slovak Republic respectively and controlled by nationals of a Member State, or Slovak Republic nationals respectively, if their vessels are registered in that Member State or in the Slovak Republic respectively in accordance with their respective legislations.

3.   A Community and a Slovak Republic national respectively shall, for the purpose of this Agreement, mean a natural person who is a national of one of the Member States or of the Slovak Republic respectively.

4.   The provisions of this Agreement shall not prejudice the application by each Party of any measure necessary to prevent the circumvention of its measures concerning third country access to its market through the provisions of this Agreement.

Article 50

For the purpose of this Agreement 'financial services` shall mean those activities described in Annex XVIa. The Association Council may extend or modify the scope of Annex XVIa.

Article 51

During the first six years following the date of entry into force of this Agreement, or for the sectors referred to in Annexes XVIa and XVIb, during the transitional period referred to in Article 7, the Slovak Republic may introduce measures which derogate from the provisions of this chapter as regards the establishment of Community companies and nationals if certain industries:

   - are undergoing restructuring, or

   - are facing serious difficulties, particularly where these entail serious social problems in the Slovak Republic, or

   - face the elimination or a drastic reduction of the total market share held by Slovak Republic companies or nationals in a given sector or industry in the Slovak Republic, or

   - are newly emerging industries in the Slovak Republic.

Such measures:

(i) shall cease to apply at the latest two years after the expiration of the sixth year following the date of entry into force of this Agreement or for the sectors included in Annex XVIa and in Annex XVIb upon the expiration of the transitional period referred to in Article 7, and

(ii) shall be reasonable and necessary in order to remedy the situation and

(iii) shall only relate to establishments in the Slovak Republic to be created after the entry into force of such measures and shall not introduce discrimination concerning the operations of Community companies or nationals already established in the Slovak Republic at the time of introduction of a given measure compared to Slovak Republic companies or nationals.

The Association Council may exceptionally, upon request of the Slovak Republic, and if the necessity arises, decide to prolong the periods referred to in point (i) above for a given sector for a limited period of time.

While devising and applying such measures, the Slovak Republic shall grant whenever possible to Community companies and nationals a preferential treatment, and in no case a treatment less favourable than that accorded to companies or nationals from any third country.

Prior to the introduction of these measures, the Slovak Republic shall consult the Association Council and shall not put them into effect before a one-month period following the notification to the Association Council of the concrete measures to be introduced by the Slovak Republic, except where the threat of irreparable damage requires the taking of urgent measures in which case the Slovak Republic shall consult the Association Council immediately after their introduction.

Upon the expiration of the sixth year following the entry into force of this Agreement, or for the sectors included in Annexes XVIa and XVIb upon expiration of the transitional period referred to in Article 7, the Slovak Republic may introduce such measures only with the authorization of the Association Council and under conditions determined by the latter.

Article 52

1. The provisions of this Chapter shall not apply to air transport services, inland-waterways transport services and maritime cabotage transport services.

2. The Association Council may make recommendations for improving establishment and operations in the areas covered by paragraph 1.

Article 53

1. Notwithstanding the provisions of Chapter I of this Title, the beneficiaries of the rights of establishment granted by the Slovak Republic and the Community respectively shall be entitled to employ, or have employed by one of their subsidiaries, in accordance with the legislation in force in the host country of establishment, in the territory of the Slovak Republic and the Community respectively, employees who are nationals of Community Member States and the

Slovak Republic respectively, provided that such employees are key personnel as defined in paragraph 2, and that they are employed exclusively by such beneficiaries or their subsidiaries. The residence and work permits of such employees shall only cover the period of such employment.

2.   Key personnel of the beneficiaries of the rights of establishment herein referred to as organization are:

(a)   senior employees of an organization who primarily direct the management of the organization, receiving general supervision or direction principally from the board of directors or shareholders of the business, including:

- directing the organization or a department or sub-division of the organization,

- supervising and controlling the work of other supervisory, professional or managerial employees,

- having the authority personally to engage and dismiss or recommend engaging, dismissing or other personnel actions;

(b)   persons employed by an organization who possess high or uncommon:

- qualifications referring to a type of work or trade requiring specific technical knowledge,

- knowledge essential to the organization's service, research equipment, techniques or management.

These may include, but are not limited to, members of accredited professions.

Each such employee must have been employed by the organization concerned for at least one year preceding the detachment by the organization.

Article 54

1.   The provisions of this Chapter shall be applied subject to limitations justified on grounds of public policy, public security or public health.

2.   They shall not apply to activities which in the territory of each Party are connected, even occasionally, with the exercise of official authority.

Article 55

Companies which are controlled and exclusively owned jointly by Slovak Republic companies or nationals and Community companies or nationals shall also be beneficiaries of the provisions of this Chapter and Chapter III of this Title.

CHAPTER III
Supply of services between the Community and the Slovak Republic

Article 56

1.   The Parties undertake in accordance with the provisions of this Chapter to take the necessary steps to allow progressively the supply of services by Community or Slovak Republic companies or nationals who are established in a Party other than that of the person for whom the services are intended taking into account the development of the services sector in the Parties.

2.   In step with the liberalization process mentioned in paragraph 1, and subject to the provisions of Article 59 (1), the Parties shall permit the temporary movement of natural persons providing the service or who are employed by the service provider as key personnel as defined in Article 53 (2), including natural persons who are representatives of a Community or Slovak Republic company or national and are seeking temporary entry for the purpose of negotiating for the sale of services or entering into agreements to sell services for that service provider, where those representatives will not be engaged in making direct sales to the general public or in supplying services themselves.

3.   The Association Council shall take the measures necessary to implement progressively the provisions of paragraph 1.

Article 57

With regard to supply of transport services between the Community and the Slovak Republic, the following replaces the provisions of Article 56:

1.   With regard to international maritime transport the Parties undertake to apply effectively the principle of unrestricted access to the market and traffic on a commercial basis.

    (a)   The above provision does not prejudice the rights and obligations under the United Nations Code of Conduct for Liner Conferences, as applied by one or the other Contracting Party to this Agreement. Non-conference liners will be free to operate in competition with a conference as long as they adhere to the principle of fair competition on a commercial basis.

    (b)   The Parties affirm their commitment to a freely competitive environment as being an essential feature of the dry and liquid bulk trade.

2.   In applying the principles of paragraph 1, the Parties shall:

    (a)   not introduce cargo sharing clauses in future bilateral agreements with third countries, other than in those exceptional circumstances where liner shipping companies from one or other Party to this Agreement would not otherwise have an effective opportunity to ply for trade to and from the third country concerned;

    (b)   prohibit cargo sharing arrangements in future bilateral agreements concerning dry and liquid bulk trade;

(c)   abolish, upon entry into force of this Agreement, all unilateral measures, administrative, technical and other obstacles which could have restrictive or discriminatory effects on the free supply of services in international maritime transport.

3.   With a view to assuring a coordinated development and progressive liberalization of transport between the Parties adapted to their reciprocal commercial needs, the conditions of mutual market access in air transport and in inland transport shall be dealt with by special transport agreements to be negotiated between the Parties after the entry into force of this Agreement.

4.   Prior to the conclusion of the agreements referred to in paragraph 3, the Parties shall not take any measures or actions which are more restrictive or discriminatory as compared to the situation existing on the day preceding the day of entry into force of this Agreement.

5.   During the transitional period, the Slovak Republic shall progressively adapt its legislation including administrative, technical and other rules to that of the Community legislation existing at any time in the field of air and inland transport in so far as it serves liberalization purposes and mutual access to markets of the Parties and facilitates the movement of passengers and of goods.

6.   In step with the common progress in the achievement of the objectives of this Chapter, the Association Council shall examine ways of creating the conditions necessary for improving freedom to provide air and inland transport services.

Article 58

The provisions of Article 54 shall apply to the matters covered by this Chapter.

CHAPTER IV
General provisions

Article 59

1.   For the purpose of Title IV of this Agreement, nothing in the Agreement shall prevent the Parties from applying their laws and regulations regarding entry and stay, work, labour conditions and establishment of natural persons, and supply of services, provided that, in so doing, they do not apply them in a manner as to nullify or impair the benefits accruing to any Party under the terms of a specific provision of this Agreement. This provision does not prejudice the application of Article 54.

2.   The provisions of Chapters, II, III and IV of Title IV shall be adjusted by decision of the Association Council in the light of the result of the negotiations on services taking place in the Uruguay Round and in particular to ensure that under any provision of this Agreement a Party grants to the other Party a treatment no less favourable than that accorded under the provisions of a future General Agreement on Trade and Services (GATS).

3.   The exclusion of Community companies and nationals established in the Slovak Republic in accordance with the provisions of Chapter II of Title IV from public aid granted by the Slovak

Republic in the areas of public education services, health related and social services and cultural services shall, for the duration of the transitional period referred to in Article 7, be deemed compatible with the provisions of Title IV and with the competition rules referred to in Title V.

TITLE V
PAYMENTS, CAPITAL, COMPETITION AND OTHER ECONOMIC PROVISIONS, APPROXIMATION OF LAWS

CHAPTER I
Current payments and movement of capital

Article 60

The Contracting Parties undertake to authorize, in freely convertible currency, any payments on the current account of balance of payments to the extent that the transaction underlying the payments concern movements of goods, services or persons between the Parties which have been liberalized pursuant to this Agreement.

Article 61

1.   With regard to transactions on the capital account of balance of payments, from the entry into force of this Agreement, the Member States and the Slovak Republic respectively shall ensure the free movement of capital relating to direct investments made in companies formed in accordance with the laws of the host country and investments made in accordance with the provisions of Chapter II of Title IV, and the liquidation or repatriation of these investments and of any profit stemming therefrom. Notwithstanding the above provision, such free movement, liquidation and repatriation shall be ensured by the end of the fifth year following the entry into force of this Agreement for all investments linked to establishment of nationals establishing in the Slovak Republic as self-employed persons pursuant to Chapter II of Title IV.

2.   Without prejudice to paragraph 1, the Member States, as from the entry into force of this Agreement, and the Slovak Republic as from the end of the fifth year following the entry into force of this Agreement, shall not introduce any new foreign exchange restrictions on the movement of capital and current payments connected therewith between residents of the Community and the Slovak Republic and shall not make the existing arrangements more restrictive.

3.   The Parties shall consult each other with a view to facilitating the movement of capital between the Community and the Slovak Republic in order to promote the objectives of this Agreement.

Article 62

1.   During the five years following the date of entry into force of this Agreement, the Contracting Parties shall take measures permitting the creation of the necessary conditions for the further gradual application of Community rules on the free movement of capital.

2.   By the end of the fifth year from the entry into force of this Agreement, the Association Council shall examine ways of enabling Community rules on the movement of capital to be applied in full.

Article 63

With reference to the provisions of this Chapter, and notwithstanding the provisions of Article 65, until a full convertibility of the Slovak Republic currency within the meaning of Article VIII of the International Monetary Fund is introduced, the Slovak Republic may in exceptional circumstances apply exchange restrictions connected with the granting or taking up of short and medium-term credits to the extent that such restrictions are imposed on the Slovak Republic for the granting of such credits and are permitted according to the Slovak Republic's status under the IMF.

The Slovak Republic shall apply these restrictions in a non-discriminatory manner. They shall be applied in such a manner as to cause the least possible disruption to this Agreement. The Slovak Republic shall inform the Association Council promptly of the introduction of such measures and of any changes therein.

CHAPTER II
Competition and other economic provisions

Article 64

1.   The following are incompatible with the proper functioning of the Agreement, in so far as they may affect trade between the Community and the Slovak Republic:

   (i)   all agreements between undertakings, decisions by associations of undertakings and concerted practices between undertakings which have as their object or effect the prevention, restriction or distortion of competition;

   (ii)   abuse by one or more undertakings of a dominant position in the territories of the Community or of the Slovak Republic as a whole or in a substantial part thereof;

   (iii)   any public aid which distorts or threatens to distort competition by favouring certain undertakings or the production of certain goods.

2.   Any practices contrary to this Article shall be assessed on the basis of criteria arising from the application of the rules of Articles 85, 86 and 92 of the Treaty establishing the European Economic Community.

3.   The Association Council shall, within three years of the entry into force of this Agreement, adopt the necessary rules for the implementation of paragraphs 1 and 2. Until the implementing rules are adopted, practices incompatible with paragraph 1 shall be dealt with by the Contracting Parties on their respective territories according to their respective legislations. This is without prejudice to paragraph 6.

4.   (a)   For the purposes of applying the provisions of paragraph 1 (iii), the Parties recognize that during the first five years after the entry into force of this

Agreement, any public aid granted by the Slovak Republic shall be assessed taking into account the fact that the Slovak Republic shall be regarded as an area identical to those areas of the Community described in Article 92 (3) (a) of the Treaty establishing the European Economic Community. The Association Council shall, taking into account the economic situation of the Slovak Republic, decide whether that period should be extended by further periods of five years.

(b)   Each Party shall ensure transparency in the area of public aid, inter alia by reporting annually to the other Party on the total amount and the distribution of the aid given and by providing, upon request, information on aid schemes. Upon request by one Party, the other Party shall provide information on particular individual cases of public aid.

5.   With regard to products referred to in Chapters II and III of Title III:

- the provision of paragraph 1 (iii) does not apply,

- any practices contrary to paragraph 1 (i) should be assessed according to the criteria established by the Community on the basis of Articles 42 and 43 of the Treaty establishing the European Economic Community and in particular of those established in Council Regulation No 26/62.

6.   If the Community or the Slovak Republic considers that a particular practice is incompatible with the terms of paragraph 1, and:

- is not adequately dealt with under the implementing rules referred to in paragraph 3, or

- in the absence of such rules, and if such practice causes or threatens to cause serious prejudice to the interest of the other Party or material injury to its domestic industry, including its services industry, it may take appropriate measures after consultation within the Association Council or after 30 working days following referral for such consultation.

In the case of practices incompatible with paragraph 1 (iii), such appropriate measures may, where the General Agreement on Tariffs and Trade applies thereto, only be adopted in accordance with the procedures and under the conditions laid down by the General Agreement on Tariffs and Trade and any other relevant instrument negotiated under its auspices which are applicable between the Parties.

7.   Notwithstanding any provisions to the contrary adopted in accordance with paragraph 3, the Parties shall exchange information taking into account the limitations imposed by the requirements of professional and business secrecy.

8.   This Article shall not apply to the products covered by the Treaty establishing the European Coal and Steel Community which are the subject of Protocol 2.

Article 65

1.   Where one or more Member States of the Community or the Slovak Republic is in serious balance of payments difficulties, or under imminent threat thereof, the Community or the Slovak Republic, as the case may be, may, in accordance with the conditions established under the

General Agreement on Tariffs and Trade, adopt restrictive measures, including measures relating to imports, which shall be of limited duration and may not go beyond what is necessary to remedy the balance of payments situation. The measures shall be progressively relaxed as balance of payments conditions improve and they shall be eliminated when conditions no longer justify their maintenance. The Community or the Slovak Republic, as the case may be, shall inform the other Party forthwith of their introduction and, whenever practicable, of a time schedule for their removal.

2.   The Parties shall nevertheless endeavour to avoid the imposition of restrictive measures for balance of payments purposes.

3.   Any restrictive measures shall not apply to transfers related to investment and in particular to the repatriation of amounts invested or reinvested and of any kind of revenues stemming therefrom.

Article 66

With regard to public undertakings, and undertakings to which special or exclusive rights have been granted, the Association Council shall ensure that as from the third year following the date of entry into force of this Agreement, the principles of the Treaty establishing the European Economic Community, in particular Article 90, and the principles of the concluding document of the April 1990 Bonn meeting of the Conference on Security and Cooperation in Europe, in particular entrepreneurs' freedom of decision, are upheld.

Article 67

1.   The Slovak Republic shall continue to improve the protection of intellectual, industrial and commercial property rights in order to provide, by the end of the fifth year after the entry into force of this Agreement, a level of protection similar to that existing in the Community, including comparable means of enforcing such rights.

2.   Within the same time, the Slovak Republic shall apply to accede to the Munich Convention on the granting of European patents of 5 October 1973. The Slovak Republic shall also accede to the other multilateral conventions on intellectual, industrial and commercial property rights referred to in Annex XVII paragraph 1 to which Member States are Parties, or which are de facto applied by Member States.

Article 68

1.   The Contracting Parties consider the opening up of the award of public contracts on the basis of non-discrimination and reciprocity, in particular in the GATT context, to be a desirable objective.

2.   The Slovak Republic companies as defined in Article 49, shall be granted access to contract award procedures in the Community pursuant to Community procurement rules under a treatment no less favourable than that accorded to Community companies as of the entry into force of this Agreement.

Community companies as defined in Article 49 shall be granted access to contract award procedures in the Slovak Republic under a treatment no less favourable than that accorded to

Slovak Republic companies at the latest at the end of the transitional period referred to in Article 7.

Community companies established in the Slovak Republic under the provisions of Chapter II of Title IV shall have upon entry into force of this Agreement access to contract award procedures under a treatment no less favourable than that accorded to Slovak Republic companies.

The Association Council shall periodically examine the possibility for the Slovak Republic in introduce access to award procedures in the Slovak Republic for all Community companies prior to the end of the transitional period.

3.   As regards establishment, operations, supply of services between the Community and the Slovak Republic, as well as employment and movement of labour linked to the fulfilment of public contracts, the provisions of Articles 38 to 59 are applicable.

CHAPTER III
Approximation of laws

Article 69

The Contracting parties recognize that the major precondition for the Slovak Republic's economic integration into the Community is the approximation of the Slovak Republic's existing and future legislation to that of the Community. The Slovak Republic shall endeavour to ensure that its legislation will be gradually made compatible with that of the Community.

Article 70

The approximation of laws shall extend to the following areas in particular: customs law, company law, banking law, company accounts and taxes, intellectual property, protection of workers at the workplace, financial services, rules on competition, protection of health and life of humans, animals and plants, consumer protection, indirect taxation, technical rules and standards, nuclear law and regulation, transport and the environment.

Article 71

The Community shall provide the Slovak Republic with technical assistance for the implementation of these measures, which may include inter alia:

- the exchange of experts,

- the provision of early information especially on relevant legislation,

- organization of seminars,

- training activities,

- aid for the translation of Community legislation in the relevant sectors.

TITLE VI
ECONOMIC COOPERATION

Article 72

1.   The Community and the Slovak Republic shall establish economic cooperation aimed at contributing to the Slovak Republic's development and growth potential. Such cooperation shall strengthen existing economic links on the widest possible foundation, to the benefit of both Parties.

2.   Policies and other measures will be designed to bring about economic and social development of the Slovak Republic and will be guided by the principle of sustainable development. These policies should ensure that environmental considerations are also fully incorporated from the outset and that they are linked to the requirements of harmonious social development.

3.   To this end the cooperation should focus in particular on policies and measures related to industry including the mining sector, investment, agriculture, energy, transport, regional development and tourism.

4.   Special attention must be devoted to measures capable of fostering cooperation between the countries of central and Eastern Europe with a view to a harmonious development of the region.

Article 73
Industrial cooperation

1.   Cooperation shall aim at promoting the modernization and restructuring of Slovak Republic industry in both public and private sectors as well as industrial cooperation between economic operators of both sides, with the particular objective of strengthening the private sector.

2.   Particular attention shall be paid to:

- the restructuring of individual sectors; in this context, the Association Council will examine in particular the problems affecting the sectors of coal and steel and the conversion of the defence industry,

- the establishment of new undertakings in areas offering potential for growth.

3.   Industrial cooperation initiatives take into account priorities determined by the Slovak Republic. The initiatives should seek in particular to establish a suitable framework for undertakings, to improve management know-how and to promote transparency as regards markets and conditions for undertakings, and will include technical assistance where appropriate.

Article 74
Investment promotion and protection

1.   Cooperation shall aim to establish a favourable climate for private investment, both domestic and foreign, which is essential to economic and industrial reconstruction in the Slovak Republic.

2.   The particular aims of cooperation shall be:

- to improve the institutional framework for investments in the Slovak Republic,

- the extension by the Member States and the Slovak Republic of agreements for the promotion and protection of investment,

- to implement suitable arrangements for the transfer of capital,

- to proceed with deregulation and to improve economic infrastructure,

- to exchange information on investment opportunities in the form of trade fairs, exhibitions, trade weeks and other events.

ANNEX XVIa (Title IV, Chapter II)

ESTABLISHMENT: FINANCIAL SERVICES

Definitions

A financial service is any service of a financial nature offered by a financial service provider of a party. Financial services include the following activities:

A.   All insurance and insurance-related services

    1.   Direct insurance (including co-insurance).

      (i)   life

      (ii)   non-life.

    2.   Reinsurance and retrocession.

    3.   Insurance intermediation, such as brokerage and agency.

    4.   Services auxiliary to insurance, such as consultancy, actuarial, risk assessment and claim settlement services.

B.   Banking and other financial services (excluding insurance)

    1.   Acceptance of deposits and other repayable funds from the public.

2.   Lending of all types, including, inter-alia, consumer credit, mortgage credit, factoring and financing of commercial transaction.

3.   Financial leasing.

4.   All payment and money transmission services, including credit charge and debit cards, travellers cheques and bankers drafts.

5.   Guarantees and commitments.

6.   Trading for own account of customers, whether on an exchange, in an over the counter market or otherwise, the following:

   (a)   money market instruments (cheques, bills, certificates of deposits, etc.);

   (b)   foreign exchange;

   (c)   derivative products including, but not limited to, futures and options;

   (d)   exchange rates and interest rate instruments, including products such as swaps, forward rate agreements, etc.;

   (e)   transferable securities;

   (f)   other negotiable instruments and financial assets, including bullion.

7.   Participation in issues of all kinds of securities, including underwriting and placement as agent (whether publicly or privately) and provision of services related to such issues.

8.   Money broking.

9.   Asset management, such as cash or portfolio management, all forms of collective investment management, pension fund management, custodial depository and trust services.

10.   Settlement and clearing services for financial assets, including securities, derivative products, and other negotiable instruments.

11.   Advisory intermediation and other auxiliary financial services on all the activities listed in points 1 to 10 above, including credit reference and analysis, investment and portfolio research and advice, advice on acquisitions and on corporate restructuring and strategy.

12.   Provision and transfer of financial information, and financial data processing and related software by providers of other financial services.

Excluded from the definition of financial services are the following activities:

(a)   activities carried out by central banks or by any other public institution in pursuit of monetary and exchange rate policies;

(b)   activities conducted by central banks, government agencies or departments, or public institutions, for the account or with the guarantee of the government, except when those activities may be carried out by financial service providers in competition with such public entities;

(c)   activities forming part of a statutory system of social security or public retirement plans, except when those activities may be carried out by financial service providers in competition with public entities or private institutions.

ANNEX XVII

1.   Paragraph 2 of Article 67 concerns the following multilateral convention: Protocol relating to the Madrid Agreement concerning the International Registration of Marks (Madrid 1989).

2.   The Association Council may decide that paragraph 2 of Article 67 shall apply to other multilateral conventions.

3.   The Contracting Parties confirm the importance they attach to the obligations arising from the following multilateral conventions:

- Berne Convention for the protection of literary and artistic works (Paris Act, 1971),

- International Convention for the protection of performers, producers of phonograms and broadcasting organizations (Rome, 1961),

- Paris Convention for the protection of industrial property (Stockholm Act, 1967 and amended in 1979),

- Madrid Agreement concerning the international registration of marks (Stockholm Act, 1967 and amended in 1979),

- Nice Agreement concerning the international classification of goods and services for the purposes of the registration of marks (Geneva 1977, amended 1979),

- Budapest Treaty on the international recognition of the deposit of micro-organisms for the purposes of patent procedures (1977, modified in 1980),

- Patent Cooperation Treaty (Washington 1970, amended 1979 and modified in 1984).

4.   For the purposes of Paragraph 3 of this Annex and of the provisions of Article 76 (1) referring to intellectual property, Contracting Parties shall be the Slovak Republic, the European Economic Community and the Member States, each in, as far as they are respectively competent

for matters concerning industrial, intellectual and commercial property covered by these conventions or by Article 76 (1).

5.   The provisions of this Annex and those of Article 76 (1) referring to intellectual property are without prejudice to the competences of the European Economic Community and its Member States in matters of industrial, intellectual and commercial property.

*

EUROPE AGREEMENT ESTABLISHING AN ASSOCIATION BETWEEN THE EUROPEAN COMMUNITIES AND THEIR MEMBER STATES, OF THE ONE PART, AND THE REPUBLIC OF BULGARIA, OF THE OTHER PART*
[excerpts]

> The Europe Agreement Establishing an Association between the European Communities and Their Member States, of the One Part, and the Republic of Bulgaria, of the Other Part was signed on 8 March 1993. It entered into force on 1 February 1995. The member States of the European Communities are: Austria, Belgium, Denmark, Finland, France, Germany, Greece, Ireland, Italy, Luxembourg, the Netherlands, Portugal, Spain, Sweden and the United Kingdom.

TITLE IV
MOVEMENT OF WORKERS, ESTABLISHMENT, SUPPLY OF SERVICES

CHAPTER II
Establishment

Article 45

1.   Each Member State shall grant, from entry into force of the Agreement, for the establishment of Bulgarian companies and nationals and for the operation of Bulgarian companies and nationals established in its territory, a treatment no less favourable than that accorded to its own companies and nationals, save for matters referred to in Annex XVa.

2.   Bulgaria shall

    (i)   grant, from entry into force of the Agreement, for the establishment of Community companies and nationals a treatment no less favourable than that accorded to its own companies and nationals, save for the sectors and matters referred to in Annexes XVb and XVc, where such treatment shall be granted at the latest by the end of the transitional period referred to in Article 7;

    (ii)   grant, from entry into force of the Agreement, in the operation of Community companies and nationals established in Bulgaria a treatment no less favourable than that accorded to its own companies and nationals.

3.   The provisions contained in paragraph 2 of this Article shall not apply to the matters listed in Annex XVd.

---

*   *Source*: European Communities (1994). "Europe Agreement Establishing an Association between the European Communities and Their Member States, of the One Part, and the Republic of Bulgaria, of the Other Part", *Official Journal of the European Communities*, L 358, 31 December 1994 pp. 3 - 0222; available also on the Internet (http://www.europa.eu.int/eur-lex/en/lif/dat/1994/en_294A1231_24.html). [Note added by the editor.]

4.   Bulgaria shall, during the transitional period referred to in paragraph 2 (i), not adopt any new regulations or measures which introduce discrimination as regards the establishment of Community companies and nationals in its territory in comparison to its own companies and nationals.

5.   For the purposes of this Agreement

  (a)   'establishment' shall mean

      (i)   as regards nationals, the right to take up and pursue economic activities as self-employed persons and to set up and manage undertakings, in particular companies, which they effectively control. Self-employment and business undertakings by nationals shall not extend to seeking or taking employment in the labour market or confer a right of access to the labour market of the other Party. The provisions of this chapter do not apply to those who are not exclusively self-employed;

      (ii)   as regards companies, the right to take up and pursue economic activities by means of the setting up and management of subsidiaries, branches and agencies;

  (b)   'subsidiary' of a company shall mean a company which is effectively controlled by the first company;

  (c)   'economic activities' shall in particular include activities of an industrial character, activities of a commercial character, activities of craftsmen and activities of the professions.

6.   The Association Council shall, during the transitional period referred to in paragraph 2 (i), examine regularly the possibility of accelerating the granting of national treatment in the sectors referred to in Annexes XVb and XVc and the inclusion of areas or matters listed in Annex XVd within the scope of application of the provisions of paragraph 2 (i) of this Article. Amendments may be made to these Annexes by decision of the Association Council.

Following the expiration of the transitional period referred to in paragraph 2 (i), the Association Council may exceptionally, upon request by Bulgaria, and if the necessity arises, decide to prolong the duration of exclusion of certain areas or matters listed in Annexes XVb and XVc for a limited period of time.

Article 46

1.   Subject to the provisions of Article 45 with the exception of financial services described in Annex XVb, each Party may regulate the establishment and operation of companies and nationals on its territory, in so far as these regulations do not discriminate against companies and nationals of the other Party in comparison to its own companies and nationals.

2.   In respect of financial services, described in Annex XVb, this Agreement does not prejudice the right of the Parties to adopt measures necessry for the conduct of the Party's monetary policy, or for prudential grounds in order to ensure the protection of investors, depositors, policy holders, or persons to whom a fiduciary duty is owed, or to ensure the integrity

and stability of the financial system. These measures shall not discriminate on grounds of nationality against companies and nationals of the other Party in comparison to its own companies and nationals.

Article 47

In order to make it easier for Community nationals and Bulgarian nationals to take up and pursue regulated professional activities in Bulgaria and the Community respectively, the Association Council shall examine which steps are necessary to be taken to provide for the mutual recognition of qualifications. It may take all necessary measures to that end.

Article 48

The provisions of Article 46 do not preclude the application by a Party of particular rules concerning the establishment and operation in its territory of branches and agencies of companies of another Party not incorporated in the territory of the first Party, which are justified by legal or technical differences between such branches and agencies as compared to branches and agencies of companies incorporated in its territory, or, as regards financial services, for prudential reasons. The difference in treatment shall not go beyond what is strictly necessary as a result of such legal or technical differences, or, as regards financial services, described in Annex XVb, for prudential reasons.

Article 49

1.   A 'Community company' and a 'Bulgarian company' respectively shall, for the purpose of this Agreement, mean a company or a firm set up in accordance with the laws of a Member State or of Bulgaria respectively and having its registered office, central administration, or principle place of business in the territory of the Community or Bulgaria respectively. However, should the company or firm, set up in accordance with the laws of a Member State or of Bulgaria respectively, have only its registered office in the territory of the Community or Bulgaria respectively, its operations must possess a real and continuous link with the economy of one of the Member States or Bulgaria respectively.

2.   With regard to international maritime transport, a national or a shipping company of the Member States or of Bulgaria, respectively established outside the Community or Bulgaria respectively and controlled by nationals of a Member State, or Bulgarian nationals respectively, shall also be beneficiaries of the provisions of this chapter and Chapter III of this title, if their vessels are registered in that Member State or in Bulgaria respectively in accordance with their respective legislations.

3.   A 'Community national' and a 'Bulgarian national' respectively shall, for the purpose of this Agreement, mean a natural person who is a national of one of the Member States or of Bulgaria respectively.

4.   The provisions of this Agreement shall not prejudice the application by each Party of any measure necessary to prevent the circumvention of its measures concerning third country access to its market, through the provisions of this Agreement.

Article 50

For the purpose of this Agreement 'financial services' shall mean those activities described in Annex XVb. The Association Council may extend or modify the scope of Annex XVb.

Article 51

During the first five years following the date of entry into force of this Agreement, or for the sectors referred to in Annex XVb and XVc during the transitional period referred to in Article 7, Bulgaria may introduce measures which derogate from the provisions of this chapter as regards the establishment of Community companies and nationals if certain industries:

- are undergoing restructuring, or

- are facing serious difficulties, particularly where these entail serious social problems in Bulgaria, or

- face the elimination or a drastic reduction of the total market share held by Bulgarian companies or nationals in a given sector or industry in Bulgaria, or

- are newly emerging industries in Bulgaria.

Such measures:

(i)   shall cease to apply at the latest two years after the expiration of the fifth year following the date of entry into force of this Agreement; and

(ii)   shall be reasonable and necessary in order to remedy the situation; and

(iii) shall only relate to establishments in Bulgaria to be created after the entry into force of such measures and shall not introduce discrimination concerning the operations of Community companies or nationals already established in Bulgaria at the time of introduction of a given measure compared to Bulgarian companies or nationals.

The Association Council may exceptionally, upon request by Bulgaria, and if the necessity arises, decide to prolong the period referred to in indent (i) for a given sector for a limited period of time not exceeding the duration of the transitional period referred to in Article 7.

While devising and applying such measures, Bulgaria shall grant whenever possible to Community companies and nationals a preferential treatment, and in no case a treatment less favourable than that accorded to companies or nationals from any third country.

Prior to the introduction of these measures, Bulgaria shall consult the Association Council and shall not put them into effect before a one month period following the notification to the Association Council of the concrete measures to be introduced by Bulgaria, except where the threat of irreparable damage requires the taking of urgent measures in which case Bulgaria shall consult the Association Council immediately after their introduction.

Upon the expiration of the fifth year following the entry into force of the Agreement, or for the sectors referred to in Annexes XVb and XVc upon expiration of the transitional period referred to in Article 7, Bulgaria may introduce such measures only with the authorization of the Association Council and under conditions determined by the latter.

Article 52

1.   The provisions of this chapter shall not apply to air transport services, inland-waterways transport services and maritime cabotage transport services.

2.   The Association Council may make recommendations for improving establishment and operations in the areas covered by paragraph 1.

Article 53

1.   Notwithstanding the provisions of Chapter I of this title, the beneficiaries of the rights of establishment granted by Bulgaria and the Community respectively shall be entitled to employ, or have employed by one of their subsidiaries, in accordance with the legislation in force in the host country of establishment, in the territory of Bulgaria and the Community respectively, employees who are nationals of Community Member States and Bulgaria respectively, provided that such employees are key personnel as defined in paragraph 2, and that they are employed exclusively by such beneficiaries or their subsidiaries. The residence and work permits of such employees shall only cover the period of such employment.

2.   Key personnel of the beneficiaries of the rights of establishment, herein referred to as 'organization', are:

   (a)   senior employees of an organization who primarily direct the management of the organization, receiving general supervision or direction principally from the board of directors or shareholders of the business, including:

   -    directing the organization or a department or sub-division of the organization,

   -    supervising and controlling the work of other supervisory, professional or managerial employees,

   -    having the authority personally to engage and dismiss or recommend engaging, dismissing or other personnel actions.

   (b)   persons employed by an organization who possess high or uncommon:

   -    qualifications referring to a type of work or trade requiring specific technical knowledge,

   -    knowledge essential to the organization's service, research equipment, techniques or management.

These may include, but are not limited to, members of accredited professions.

Each such employee must have been employed by the organization concerned for at least one year preceding the detachment by the organization.

Article 54

1.   The provisions of this chapter shall be applied subject to limitations justified on grounds of public policy, public security or public health.

2.   They shall not apply to activities which in the territory of each party are connected, even occasionally, with the exercise of official authority.

Article 55

Companies which are controlled and exclusively owned jointly by Bulgarian companies or nationals and Community companies or nationals shall also be beneficiaries of the provisions of this chapter and Chapter III of this title.

CHAPTER III
Supply of services between the Community and Bulgaria

Article 56

1.   The Parties undertake in accordance with the provisions of this chapter to take the necessary steps to allow progressively the supply of services by Community or Bulgarian companies or nationals who are established in a Party other than that of the person for whom the services are intended taking into account the development of the services sectors in the Parties.

2.   In step with the liberalization process mentioned in paragraph 1, and subject to the provisions of Article 59 (1), the Parties shall permit the temporary movement of natural persons providing the service or who are employed by the service provider as key personnel as defined in Article 53 (2), including natural persons who are representatives of a Community or Bulgarian company or national and are seeking temporary entry for the purpose of negotiating for the sale of services or entering into Agreements to sell services for that service provider, where those representatives will not be engaged in making direct sales to the general public or in supplying services themselves.

3.   The Association Council shall take the measures necessary to implement progressively the provisions of paragraph 1 of this Article.

Article 57

With regard to supply of transport services between the Community and Bulgaria, the following replaces the provisions of Article 56:

1.   With regard to international maritime transport, the Parties undertake to apply effectively the principle of unrestricted access to the market and traffic on a commercial basis.

(a)   The above provision does not prejudice the rights and obligations under the United Nations Code of Conduct for Liner Conferences, as applied by one or the other Contracting Party to this Agreement.

Non-conference liners will be free to operate in competition with a conference as long as they adhere to the principle of fair competition on a commercial basis.

(b)   The Parties affirm their commitment to a freely competitive environment as being an essential feature of the dry and liquid bulk trade.

2.   In applying the principles of point 1, the Parties shall:

(a)   not introduce cargo sharing clauses in future bilateral agreements with third countries, other than in those exceptional circumstances where liner shipping companies from one or other Party to this Agreement would not otherwise have an effective opportunity to ply for trade to and from the third country concerned;

(b)   prohibit cargo sharing arrangements in future bilateral agreements concerning dry and liquid bulk trade;

(c)   abolish, upon entry into force of the Agreement, all unilateral measures, administrative, technical and other obstacles which could have restrictive or discriminatory effects on the free supply of services in international maritime transport.

3.   With a view to assuring a coordinated development and progressive liberalization of transport between the Parties adapted to their reciprocal commercial needs, the conditions of mutual market access in air transport and in inland transport shall be dealt with by special transport Agreements to be negotiated between the Parties after the entry into force of the Agreement.

4.   Prior to the conclusion of the Agreements referred to in paragraph 3, the Parties shall not take any measures or actions which are more restrictive or discriminatory as compared to the situation existing on the day preceding the day of entry into force of the Agreement.

5.   During the transitional period, Bulgaria shall progressively adapt its legislation including administrative, technical and other rules to that of the Community legislation existing at any time in the field of air and inland transport in so far as it serves liberalization purposes and mutual access to markets of the Parties and facilitates the movement of passengers and of goods.

6.   In step with the common progress in the achievement of the objectives of this chapter, the Association Council shall examine ways of creating the conditions necessary for improving freedom to provide air and inland transport services.

Article 58

The provisions of Article 54 shall apply to the matters covered by this chapter.

CHAPTER IV
General provisions

Article 59

1.   For the purpose of Title IV, nothing in the Agreement shall prevent the Parties from applying their laws and regulations regarding entry and stay, work, labour conditions and establishment of natural persons and supply of services, provided that, in so doing, they do not apply them in a manner as to nullify or impair the benefits accruing to any Party under the terms of a specific provision of the Agreement. The above provision does not prejudice the application of Article 54.

2.   The provisions of Chapters II, III and IV of Title IV shall be adjusted by decision of the Association Council in the light of the result of the negotiations on services taking place in the Uruguay Round and in particular to ensure that under any provision of this Agreement a Party grants to the other Party a treatment no less favourable than that accorded under the provisions of a future General Agreement on Trade and Services (GATS).

Pending Bulgaria's accession to a future GATS Agreement, and without prejudice to any decisions the Association Council may take,

(i)   the Community shall grant to Bulgarian companies and nationals a treatment no less favourable than that accorded under the provisions of a future GATS Agreement to companies and nationals of other members of that Agreement;

(ii)   Bulgaria shall grant Community companies and nationals a treatment no less favourable than that accorded by Bulgaria to companies and nationals from any third country.

3.   The exclusion of Community companies and nationals established in Bulgaria in accordance with the provisions of Chapter II of Title IV from public aid granted by Bulgaria in the areas of public education services, health-related and social services and cultural services shall, for the duration of the transitional period referred to in Article 7, be deemed compatible with the provisions of Title IV and with the competition rules referred to in Title V.

TITLE V
PAYMENTS, CAPITAL, COMPETITION AND OTHER
ECONOMIC PROVISIONS, APPROXIMATION OF LAWS

CHAPTER I
Current payments and movement of capital

Article 60

The Parties undertake to authorize, in freely convertible currency, any payments on the current account of balance of payments to the extent that the transactions underlying the payments concern movements of goods, services, or persons between the Parties which have been liberalized pursuant to this Agreement.

Article 61

1.   With regard to transactions on the capital account of balance of payments, from entry into force of the Agreement, the Member States and Bulgaria respectively shall ensure the free movement of capital relating to direct investments made in companies formed in accordance with the laws of the host country and investments made in accordance to the provisions of Chapter II of Title IV, and the liquidation or repatriation of these investments and of any profit stemming therefrom.

Notwithstanding the above provision, such free movement, liquidation and repatriation shall be ensured by the end of the first stage referred to in Article 7 for all investments linked to establishment of Community nationals establishing in Bulgaria as self-employed persons pursuant to Chapter II of Title IV.

2.   Without prejudice to paragraph 1, the Member States, as from the entry into force of the Agreement, and Bulgaria as from the end of the fifth year following the entry into force of the Agreement, shall not introduce any new foreign exchange restrictions on the movement of capital and current payments connected therewith between residents of the Community and Bulgaria and shall not make the existing arrangements more restrictive.

3.   The provisions of paragraphs 1 and 2 shall not prevent Bulgaria from applying restrictions on outward investments by Bulgarian nationals and companies. However, the liquidation or repatriation of investments made in Bulgaria and of any profit stemming therefrom shall not be affected.

4.   The Parties shall consult each other with a view to facilitating the movement of capital between the Community and Bulgaria in order to promote the objectives of this Agreement.

Article 62

1.   During the five years following the date of entry into force of the Agreement, the Parties shall take measures permitting the creation of the necessary conditions for the further gradual application of Community rules on the free movement of capital.

2.   By the end of the fifth year from the entry into force of the Agreement, the Association Council shall examine ways of enabling Community rules on the movement of capital to be applied in full.

Article 63

With reference to the provisions of this chapter, and notwithstanding the provisions of Article 65, until a full convertibility of Bulgarian currency in the meaning of Article VIII of the International Monetary Fund (IMF) is introduced, Bulgaria may in exceptional circumstances apply exchange restrictions connected with the granting or taking up of short and medium-term credits to the extent that such restrictions are imposed on Bulgaria for the granting of such credits and are permitted according to Bulgaria's status under the IMF.

Bulgaria shall apply these restrictions in a non-discriminatory manner. They shall be applied in such a manner as to cause the least possible disruption to this Agreement. Bulgaria shall inform the Association Council promptly of the introduction of such measures and of any changes therein.

CHAPTER II
Competition and other economic provisions

Article 64

1.   The following are incompatible with the proper functioning of this Agreement, in so far as they may affect trade between the Community and Bulgaria:

    (i)   all Agreements between undertakings, decisions by associations of undertakings and concerted practices between undertakings which have as their object or effect the prevention, restriction or distortion of competition;

    (ii)   abuse by one or more undertakings of a dominant position in the territories of the Community or of Bulgaria as a whole or in a substantial part thereof;

    (iii)   any public aid which distorts or threatens to distort competition by favouring certain undertakings or the production of certain goods.

2.   Any practices contrary to this Article shall be assessed on the basis of criteria arising from the application of the rules of Articles 85, 86, and 92 of the Treaty establishing the European Economic Community.

3.   The Association Council shall, within three years of the entry into force of the Agreement, adopt the necessary rules for the implementation of paragraphs 1 and 2.

4.   (a)   For the purposes of applying the provision of paragraph 1, point (iii), the Parties recognize that during the first five years after the entry into force of the Agreement, any public aid granted by Bulgaria shall be assessed taking into account the fact that Bulgaria shall be regarded as an area identical to those areas of the Community described in Article 92 (3) (a) of the Treaty establishing the European Economic Community. The Association Council shall, taking into account the economic situation of Bulgaria, decide whether that period should be extended by further periods of five years.

    (b)   Each Party shall ensure transparency in the area of public aid, inter alia by reporting annually to the other Party on the total amount and the distribution of the aid given and by providing, upon request, information on aid schemes. Upon request by one Party, the other Party shall provide information on particular individual cases of public aid.

5.   With regard to products referred to in Chapters II and III of Title III:

-       the provision of paragraph 1 (iii) does not apply,

-       any practices contrary to paragraph 1 (i) should be assessed according to the criteria established by the Community on the basis of Articles 42 and 43 of the

Treaty establishing the European Economic Community and in particular of those established in Council Regulation No 26/1962.

6.   If the Community or Bulgaria considers that a particular practice is incompatible with the terms of paragraph 1, and:

-      is not adequately dealt with under the implementing rules referred to in paragraph 3, or

-      in the absence of such rules, and if such practice causes or threatens to cause serious prejudice to the interest of the other Party or material injury to its domestic industry, including its services industry, it may take appropriate measures after consultation within the Association Council or after 30 working days following referral for such consultation.

In the case of practices incompatible with paragraph 1 (iii) of this Article, such appropriate measures may, where the General Agreement on Tariffs and Trade applies thereto, only be adopted in conformity with the procedures and under the conditions laid down by the General Agreement on Tariffs and Trade and any other relevant instrument negotiated under its auspices which are applicable between the Parties.

7.   Notwithstanding any provisions to the contrary adopted in conformity with paragraph 3, the Parties shall exchange information taking into account the limitations imposed by the requirements of professional and business secrecy.

8.   This Article shall not apply to the products covered by the Treaty establishing the European Coal and Steel Community which are the subject of Protocol 2.

Article 65

1.   The Parties shall endeavour to avoid the imposition of restrictive measures including measures relating to imports for balance of payments purposes. In the event of their introduction, the Party having introduced the same shall present to the other Party a time schedule for their removal.

2.   Where one or more Member States or Bulgaria is in serious balance of payments difficulties, or under imminent threat thereof, the Community or Bulgaria, as the case may be, may, in accordance with the conditions established under the General Agreement on Tariffs and Trade, adopt restrictive measures, including measures relating to imports, which shall be of limited duration and may not go beyond what is necessary to remedy the balance of payments situation. The Community or Bulgaria, as the case may be, shall inform the other Party forthwith.

3.   Any restrictive measures shall not apply to transfers related to investments and in particular to the repatriation of amounts invested or reinvested and of any kind of revenues stemming therefrom.

Article 66

With regard to public undertakings and undertakings to which special or exclusive rights have been granted, the Association Council shall ensure that, as from the third year from the date of entry into force of the Agreement, the principles of the Treaty establishing the European Economic Community, notably Article 90, and the principles of the concluding document of the April 1990 Bonn meeting of the Conference on Security and Cooperation in Europe (notably entrepreneurs' freedom of decision) are upheld.

Article 67

1.   Bulgaria shall continue to improve the protection of intellectual, industrial and commercial property rights in order to provide, by the end of the fifth year after the entry into force of the Agreement, for a level of protection similar to that existing in the Community, including comparable means of enforcing such rights.

2.   Within the same time, Bulgaria shall apply to accede to the Munich Convention on the Grant of European Patents of 5 October 1973. Bulgaria shall also accede to the other multilateral convention(s) on intellectual, industrial and commercial property rights (referred to in paragraph 1 of Annex XVI) to which Member States are Parties, or which are de facto applied by Member States.

Article 68

1.   The Parties consider the opening up of the award of public contracts on the basis of the principles of non-discrimination and reciprocity, in particular in the GATT context, to be a desirable objective.

2.   The Bulgarian companies as defined in Article 49 shall be granted access to contract award procedures in the Community pursuant to Community procurement rules under a treatment no less favourable than that accorded to Community companies as of the entry into force of the Agreement.

Community companies as defined in Article 49 shall be granted access to contract award procedures in Bulgaria under a treatment no less favourable than that accorded to Bulgarian companies at the latest at the end of the transitional period referred to in Article 7.

Community companies established in Bulgaria under the provisions of Chapter II of Title IV in the form of subsidiaries as described in Article 45 and in the forms described in Article 55 shall have upon entry into force of the Agreement access to contract award procedures under a treatment no less favourable than that accorded to Bulgarian companies. Community companies established in Bulgaria in the form of branches and agencies as described in Article 45 shall be granted such treatment at the latest by the end of the transitional period.

The Association Council shall periodically examine the possibility for Bulgaria to introduce access to award procedures in Bulgaria for all Community companies prior to the end of the transitional period.

3.   As regards establishment, operations, supply of services between the Community and Bulgaria, as well as employment and movement of labour linked to the fulfillment of public contracts, the provisions of Articles 38 to 59 are applicable.

CHAPTER III
Approximation of laws

Article 69

The Parties recognize that an important condition for Bulgaria's economic integration into the Community is the approximation of Bulgaria's existing and future legislation to that of the Community. Bulgaria shall endeavour to ensure that its legislation will be gradually made compatible with that of the Community.

Article 70

The approximation of laws shall extend to the following areas in particular: customs law, company law, banking law, company accounts and taxes, intellectual property, protection of workers at the workplace, financial services, rules on competition, protection of health and life of humans, animals and plants, consumer protection, indirect taxation, technical rules and standards, nuclear law and regulation, transport and the environment.

Article 71

The Community shall provide Bulgaria with technical assistance for the implementation of these measures, which may include inter alia:

- the exchange of experts,

- the provision of early information especially on relevant legislation,

- organization of seminars,

- training activities,

- aid for the translation of Community legislation in the relevant sectors.

TITLE VI
ECONOMIC COOPERATION

Article 72

1. The Community and Bulgaria shall establish economic cooperation aimed at contributing to Bulgaria's development and growth potential. Such cooperation shall strengthen existing economic links on the widest possible foundation, to the benefit of both Parties.

2. Policies and other measures will be designed to bring about economic and social development of Bulgaria and will be guided by the principle of sustainable development. These policies should ensure that environmental considerations are also fully incorporated from the outset and that they are linked to the requirements of harmonious social development.

3.   To this end, the cooperation should focus in particular on policies and measures related to industry including investment, agriculture and agro-industrial sector, energy, transport, telecommunications, regional development and tourism.

4.   Special attention shall be devoted to measures capable of fostering cooperation between the countries of central and Eastern Europe with a view to a harmonious development of the region.

Article 73
Industrial cooperation

1.   Cooperation shall seek to promote the following in particular:

-       industrial cooperation between economic operators of both sides, with the particular objective of strengthening the private sector,

-       Community participation in Bulgaria's efforts in both public and private sectors to modernize and restructure its industry, which will effect the transition from a centrally planned system to a market economy under conditions which ensure that the environment is protected,

-       the restructuring of individual sectors; in this context the Association Council will examine in particular the problems affecting the sector of coal and steel and the conversion of the defence industry,

-       the establishment of new undertakings in areas offering potential for growth, particularly in branches of light industry, consumer goods and market services,

-       transfer of technology and know-how.

2.   Industrial cooperation initiatives shall take into account priorities determined by Bulgaria. The initiatives should seek in particular to establish a suitable framework for undertakings, to improve management know-how and to promote transparency as regards markets and conditions for undertakings, and will include technical assistance where appropriate.

Article 74
Investment promotion and protection

1.   Cooperation shall aim at maintaining and, if necessary, improving a legal framework and a favourable climate for private investment and its protection, both domestic and foreign, which is essential to economic and industrial reconstruction and development in Bulgaria. The cooperation shall also aim to encourage and promote foreign investment and privatization in Bulgaria.

2.   The particular aims of cooperation shall be:

-       the conclusion, where appropriate, by the Member States and Bulgaria of agreements for the promotion and protection of investment,

- the conclusion, where appropriate, of agreements between Member States and Bulgaria to avoid double taxation,

- to implement suitable arrangements for the transfer of capital,

- to proceed with deregulation and to improve economic infrastructure,

- to exchange information on investment opportunities in the form of trade fairs, exhibitions, trade weeks and other events,

- to exchange information on laws, regulations and administrative practices in the field of investment.

3.   Bulgaria shall honour the rules on trade related aspects of investment measures (TRIMs), once these have been adopted within the GATT.

ANNEX XVb

Financial services

Definitions:

A financial service is any service of a financial nature offered by a financial service provider of a party. Financial services include the following activities:

A.   All insurance and insurance-related services.

     1.   Direct insurance (including co-insurance).

         (i)   life;

         (ii)   non-life.

     2.   Reinsurance and retrocession.

     3.   Insurance intermediation, such as brokerage and agency.

     4.   Services auxiliary to insurance, such as consultancy, actuarial, risk assessment and claim settlement services.

B.   Banking and other financial services (excluding insurance).

     1.   Acceptance of deposits and other repayable funds from the public.

     2.   Lending of all types, including, inter alia, consumer credit, mortgage credit, factoring and financing of commercial transaction.

     3.   Financial leasing.

4.   All payment and money transmission services, including credit charge and debit cards, travellers cheques and bankers drafts.

5.   Guarantees and commitments.

6.   Trading for own account of customers, whether on an exchange, in an over the counter market or otherwise, the following:

   (a)   money market instruments (cheques, bills, certificates of deposits, etc.);

   (b)   foreign exchange;

   (c)   derivative products including, but not limited to, futures and options;

   (d)   exchange rates and interest rate instruments, including products such as swaps, forward rate agreements, etc.;

   (e)   transferable securities;

   (f)   other negotiable instruments and financial assets, including bullion.

7.   Participation in issues of all kinds of securities, including underwriting and placement as agent (whether publicly or privately) and provision of services related to such issues.

8.   Money broking.

9.   Asset management, such as cash or portfolio management, all forms of collective investment management, pension fund management, custodial depository and trust services.

10.   Settlement and clearing services for financial assets, including securities, derivative products, and other negotiable instruments.

11.   Advisory intermediation and other auxiliary financial services on all the activities listed in Points 1 to 10, including credit reference and analysis, investment and portfolio research and advice, advice on acquisitions and on corporate restructuring and strategy.

12.   Provision and transfer of financial information, and financial data processing and related software by providers of other financial services.

The following activities are excluded from the definition of financial services:

   (a)   Activities carried out by central banks or by any other public institution in pursuit of monetary and exchange rate policies.

   (b)   Activities conducted by central banks, government agencies or departments, or public institutions, for the account or with the guarantee of the government, except when those activities may be carried out by financial service providers in competition with such public entities.

(c)   Activities forming part of a statutory system of social security of public retirement plans, except when those activities may be carried out by financial service providers in competition with public entities or private institutions.

ANNEX XVI

Intellecutal property

1.   Paragraph 2 of Article 67 concerns the following multilateral conventions:

- Protocol relating to the Madrid Agreement concerning the international registration of marks (Madrid 1989);

- International Convention for the protection of performers, producers of phonograms and broadcasting organizations (Rome, 1961);

2.   The Association Council may decide that paragraph 2 of Article 67 shall apply to other present or future multilateral conventions, in particular the GATT-TRIPS (trade related intellectual property right) agreement.

3.   The Contracting Parties confirm the importance they attach to the obligations arising from the following multilateral conventions:

- Berne Convention for the protection of literary and artistic works (Paris Act, 1971);

- Paris Convention for the protection of industrial property (Stockholm Act, 1967 and amended in 1979);

- Madrid Agreement concerning the international registration of marks (Stockholm Act, 1967 and amended in 1979);

- Budapest Treaty on the international recognition of the deposit of micro-organisms for the purposes of patent procedures (1977, modified in 1980);

- Patent Cooperation Treaty (Washington 1970, amended 1979 and modified in 1984).

4.   Before the end of the first stage, Bulgaria shall comply in its internal legislation with the substantial provisions of the Nice Agreement concerning the international classification of goods and services for the purposes of registration of marks (Geneva 1977, amended 1979).

5.   For the purposes of paragraph 3 of this Annex and the provisions of Article 76, paragraph 1 referring to intellectual property, Contracting Parties shall be Bulgaria, the European Economic Community and the Member States, each in as far as they are respectively competent for matters concerning industrial, intellectual and commercial property covered by these conventions or by Article 76, paragraph 1.

6.   The provisions of this Annex and of the provisions of Article 76, paragraph 1 referring to intellectual property are without prejudice to the competence of the European Economic Community and its Member States in matters of industrial, intellectual and commercial property.

*

PARTNERSHIP AND COOPERATION AGREEMENT ESTABLISHING A PARTNERSHIP BETWEEN THE EUROPEAN COMMUNITIES AND THEIR MEMBER STATES, OF THE ONE PART, AND THE REPUBLIC OF MOLDOVA, OF THE OTHER PART[*]
[excerpts]

The Partnership and Cooperation Agreement Establishing a Partnership between the European Communities and Their Member States, of the One Part, and the Republic of Moldova, of the Other Part was signed on 28 November 1994. It entered into force on 1 July 1998. The member States of the European Communities are: Austria, Belgium, Denmark, Finland, France, Germany, Greece, Ireland, Italy, Luxembourg, the Netherlands, Portugal, Spain, Sweden and the United Kingdom.

CHAPTER II
CONDITIONS AFFECTING THE ESTABLISHMENT AND OPERATION OF COMPANIES

Article 29

1. (a) The Community and its Member States shall grant for the establishment of Republic of Moldovan companies in their territories treatment no less favourable than that accorded to companies of any third country, and this in conformity with their legislation and regulations.

   (b) Without prejudice to the reservations listed in Annex IV, the Community and its Member States shall grant to subsidiaries of Moldovan companies established in their territories a treatment no less favourable than that granted to any Community companies, in respect of their operation, and this in conformity with their legislation and regulations.

   (c) The Community and its Member States shall grant to branches of Moldovan companies established in their territories treatment no less favourable than that accorded to branches of companies of any third country, in respect of their operation, and this in conformity with their legislation and regulations.

2. (a) Without prejudice to the reservations listed in Annex V, the Republic of Moldova shall grant for the establishment of Community companies in its territory, treatment no less favourable than that accorded to its own companies or to companies of any third country whichever is the better, and this in conformity with its legislation and regulations.

---

[*] *Source*: European Communities (1998). "Partnership and Cooperation Agreement Establishing a Partnership between the European Communities and Their Member States, of the One Part, and the Republic of Moldova, of the Other Part", *Official Journal of the European Communities*, L 181, 24 June 1998, pp. 33 - 48; available also on the Internet (http://www.europa.eu.int). [Note added by the editor.]

(b)   The Republic of Moldova shall grant to subsidiaries and branches of Community companies, established in its territory, treatment no less favourable than that accorded to its own companies or branches respectively or to companies or branches of any third country respectively, whichever is the better, in respect of their operations, and this in conformity with its legislation and regulations.

3.   The provisions of paragraphs 1 and 2 cannot be used so as to circumvent a Party's legislation and regulations applicable to access to specific sectors or activities by subsidiaries of companies of the other Party established in the territory of such first Party.

The treatment referred to in paragraph 1 and 2 shall benefit companies established in the Community and the Republic of Moldova respectively at the date of entry into force of this Agreement and companies established after that date once they are established.

Article 30

1.   The provisions of Article 29 shall not apply to air transport, inland waterways transport and maritime transport, without prejudice to the provisions of Article 101.

2.   However, in respect of activities undertaken by shipping agencies for the provision of international maritime transport services, including intermodal activities involving a sea leg, each Party shall permit to the companies of the other Party their commercial presence in its territory in the form of subsidiaries or branches, under conditions of establishment and operation no less favourable than those accorded to its own companies or to subsidiaries or branches of companies of any third country, whichever are the better.

Such activities include, but are not limited to:

(a)   marketing and sales of maritime transport and related services through direct contact with customers, from quotation to invoicing, whether these services are operated or offered by the service supplier itself or by service suppliers with which the service seller has established standing business arrangements;

(b)   purchase and use, on their own account or on behalf of their customers (and the resale to their customers) of any transport and related services, including inward transport services by any mode, particularly inland waterways, road and rail, necessary for the supply of an integrated service;

(c)   preparation of documentation concerning transport documents, customs documents, or other documents related to the origin and character of the goods transported;

(d)   provision of business information by any means, including computerised information systems and electronic data interchange (subject to any non-discriminatory restrictions concerning telecommunications);

(e)   setting up of any business arrangement, including participation in the company's stock and the appointment of personnel recruited locally (or, in the case of foreign personnel, subject to the relevant provisions of this Agreement), with any locally established shipping agency;

(f)   acting on behalf of the companies, organising the call of the ship or taking over cargoes when required.

Article 31

For the purposes of this Agreement:

(a)   a 'Community company` or a 'Moldovan company` respectively shall mean a company set up in accordance with the laws of a Member State or of the Republic of Moldova respectively and having its registered office or central administration or principal place of business in the territory of the Community or the Republic of Moldova respectively. However, should the company, set up in accordance with the laws of a Member State or the Republic of Moldova respectively, have only its registered office in the territory of the Community or the Republic of Moldova respectively, the company shall be considered a Community or Moldovan company respectively if its operations possess a real and continuous link with the economy of one of the Member States or the Republic of Moldova respectively;

(b)   'subsidiary` of a company shall mean a company which is effectively controlled by the first company;

(c)   'branch` of a company shall mean a place of business not having legal personality which has the appearance of permanency, such as the extension of a parent body, has a management and is materially equipped to negotiate business with third parties so that the latter, although knowing that there will if necessary be a legal link with the parent body, the head office of which is abroad, do not have to deal directly with such parent body but may transact business at the place of business constituting the extension;

(d)   'establishment` shall mean the right of Community or Moldovan companies as referred to in point (a) to take up economic activities by means of the setting up of subsidiaries and branches in the Republic of Moldova or in the Community respectively;

(e)   'operation` shall mean the pursuit of economic activities;

(f)   'economic activities` shall mean activities of an industrial, commercial and professional character.

With regard to international maritime transport, including intermodal operations involving a sea leg, nationals of the Member States or of the Republic of Moldova established outside the Community or the Republic of Moldova respectively, and shipping companies established outside the Community or the Republic of Moldova and controlled by nationals of a Member State or Moldovan nationals respectively shall also be beneficiaries of the provisions of this Chapter and Chapter III, if their vessels are registered in that Member State or in the Republic of Moldova respectively in accordance with their respective legislations.

Article 32

1.　Notwithstanding any other provisions of the Agreement, a Party shall not be prevented from taking measures for prudential reasons, including for the protection of investors, depositors, policy holders or persons to whom a fiduciary duty is owned by a financial service supplier, or to ensure the integrity and stability of the financial system. Where such measures do not conform with the provisions of the Agreement, they shall not be used as a means of avoiding the obligations of a Party under the Agreement.

2.　Nothing in the Agreement shall be construed to require a Party to disclose information relating to the affairs and accounts of individual customers or any confidential or proprietary information in the possession of public entities.

Article 33

The provisions of this Agreement shall not prejudice the application by each Party of any measure necessary to prevent the circumvention of its measures concerning third country access to its market, through the provisions of this Agreement.

Article 34

1.　Notwithstanding the provisions of Chapter I, a Community company or a Moldovan company established in the territory of the Republic of Moldova or the Community respectively shall be entitled to employ, or have employed by one of its subsidiaries or branches, in accordance with the legislation in force in the host country of establishment, in the territory of the Republic of Moldova and the Community respectively, employees who are nationals of Community Member States and the Republic of Moldova respectively, provided that such employees are key personnel as defined in paragraph 2, and that they are employed exclusively by companies, subsidiaries or branches. The residence and work permits of such employees shall only cover the period of such employment.

2.　Key personnel of the abovementioned companies herein referred to as 'organisations' are 'intra-corporate transferees' as defined in (c) in the following categories, provided that the organisation is a legal person and that the persons concerned have been employed by it or have been partners in it (other than as majority shareholders), for at least the year immediately preceding such movement:

> (a)　persons working in a senior position with an organisation, who primarily direct the management of the establishment, receiving general supervision or direction principally from the board of directors or stockholders of the business or their equivalent, including:
>
> - directing the establishment or a department or subdivision of the establishment,
>
> - supervising and controlling the work of other supervisory, professional or managerial employees,
>
> - having the authority personally to engage and dismiss or recommend engaging, dismissing or other personnel actions;

(b)   persons working within an organisation who possess uncommon knowledge essential to the establishment's service, research equipment, techniques or management. The assessment of such knowledge may reflect, apart from knowledge specific to the establishment, a high level of qualification referring to a type of work or trade requiring specific technical knowledge, including membership of an accredited profession;

(c)   an 'intra-corporate transferee` is defined as a natural person working within an organisation in the territory of a Party, and being temporarily transferred in the context of pursuit of economic activities in the territory of the other Party; the organisation concerned must have its principal place of business in the territory of a Party and the transfer be to an establishment (branch, subsidiary) of that organisation, effectively pursuing like economic activities in the territory of the other Party.

Article 35

1.   The Parties shall use their best endeavours to avoid taking any measures or actions which render the conditions for the establishment and operation of each other's companies more restrictive than the situation existing on the day preceding the date of signature of the Agreement.

2.   The provisions of this Article are without prejudice to those of Article 43: the situations covered by such Article 43 shall be solely governed by its provisions to the exclusion of any other.

3.   Acting in the spirit of partnership and cooperation and in light of provisions contained in Article 50, the Government of the Republic of Moldova shall inform the Community of its intentions to submit new legislation or adopt new regulations which may render the conditions for the establishment or operation in the Republic of Moldova of subsidiaries and branches of Community companies more restrictive than the situation existing on the day preceding the date of signature of the Agreement. The Community may request the Republic of Moldova to communicate the drafts of such legislation or regulations and to enter into consultations about those drafts.

4.   Where new legislation or regulations introduced in the Republic of Moldova would result in rendering the conditions for establishment of Community companies into its territory and for the operation of subsidiaries and branches of Community companies established in the Republic of Moldova more restrictive than the situation existing on the day of signature of the Agreement, such respective legislation or regulations shall not apply during three years following the entry into force of the relevant act to those subsidiaries and branches already established in the Republic of Moldova at the time of entry into force of the relevant act.

CHAPTER III
CROSS-BORDER SUPPLY OF SERVICES BETWEEN
THE COMMUNITY AND THE REPUBLIC OF MOLDOVA

Article 36

1.   The Parties undertake in accordance with the provisions of this Chapter to take the necessary steps to allow progressively the cross-border supply of services by Community or Moldovan companies which are established in a Party other than that of the person for whom the services are intended, taking into account the development of the services sectors in the Parties.

2. The Cooperation Council shall make recommendations for the implementation of paragraph 1.

Article 37

The Parties shall cooperate with the aim of developing a market-oriented service sector in the Republic of Moldova.

Article 38

1.   The Parties undertake to apply effectively the principle of unrestricted access to the international maritime market and traffic on a commercial basis.

(a)   The above provision does not prejudice the rights and obligations arising from the United Nations Convention on a code of conduct for liner conferences, as applicable to one or other Contracting Party to this Agreement. Non-conference lines will be free to operate in competition with a conference as long as they adhere to the principle of fair competition on a commercial basis.

(b)   The Parties affirm their commitment to a freely competitive environment as being an essential feature of the dry and liquid bulk trade.

2.   In applying the principles of paragraph 1, the Parties shall:

(a)   not apply, as from entry into force of this Agreement, any cargo-sharing provisions of bilateral agreements between any Member State of the Community and the former Soviet Union;

(b)   not introduce cargo sharing clauses in future bilateral agreements with third countries, other than in those exceptional circumstances where liner shipping companies from one or other Party to the present Agreement would not otherwise have an effective opportunity to ply for trade to and from the third country concerned;

(c)   prohibit cargo sharing arrangements in future bilateral agreements concerning dry and liquid bulk trade;

(d)   abolish, upon entry into force of this Agreement, all unilateral measures, administrative, technical and other obstacles which could have restrictive or discriminatory effects on the free supply of services in international maritime transport.

Each Party shall grant, inter alia, no less favourable treatment for the ships operated by nationals or companies of the other Party, than that accorded to a Party's own ships with regard to access to ports open to international trade, the use of infrastructure and auxiliary maritime services of the ports, as well as related fees and charges, customs facilities and the assignment of berths and facilities for loading and unloading.

3.   Nationals and companies of the Community providing international maritime transport services shall be free to provide international sea-river services in the inland waterways of the Republic of Moldova and vice versa.

Article 39

With a view to assuring a coordinated development of transport between the Parties, adapted to their commercial needs, the conditions of mutual market access and provision of services in transport by road, rail and inland waterways and, if applicable, in air transport may be dealt with by specific agreements where appropriate negotiated between the Parties as defined in Article 96 after entry into force of this Agreement.

CHAPTER IV
GENERAL PROVISIONS

Article 40

1.   The provisions of this Title shall be applied subject to limitations justified on grounds of public policy, public security or public health.

2.   They shall not apply to activities which in the territory of either Party are connected, even occasionally, with the exercise of official authority.

Article 41

For the purpose of this Title, nothing in this Agreement shall prevent the Parties from applying their laws and regulations regarding entry and stay, work, labour conditions and establishment of natural persons and supply of services, provided that - in so doing - they do not apply them in a manner as to nullify or impair the benefits accruing to any Party under the terms of a specific provision of the Agreement. The above provision does not prejudice the application of Article 40.

Article 42

Companies which are controlled and exclusively owned by Moldovan companies and Community companies jointly shall also be beneficiaries of the provisions of Chapters II, III and IV.

Article 43

Treatment granted by either Party to the other hereunder shall, as from the day one month prior to the date of entry into force of the relevant obligations of the General Agreement on Trade in Services (GATS), in respect of sectors or measures covered by the GATS, in no case be more favourable than that accorded by such first Party under the provisions of GATS and this in respect of each service sector, subsector and mode of supply.

Article 44

For the purposes of Chapters II, III and IV, no account shall be taken of treatment accorded by the Community, its Member States or the Republic of Moldova pursuant to commitments entered into in economic integration agreements in accordance with the principles of Article V of the GATS.

Article 45

1.   The most-favoured-nation treatment granted in accordance with the provisions of this Title shall not apply to the tax advantages which the Parties are providing or will provide in the future on the basis of agreements to avoid double taxation, or other tax arrangements.

2.   Nothing in this Title shall be construed to prevent the adoption or enforcement by the Parties of any measure aimed at preventing the avoidance or evasion of taxes pursuant to the tax provisions of agreements to avoid double taxation and other tax arrangements, or domestic fiscal legislation.

3.   Nothing in this Title shall be construed to prevent Member States or the Republic of Moldova from distinguishing, in the application of the relevant provisions of their fiscal legislation, between taxpayers who are not in identical situations, in particular as regards their place of residence.

Article 46

Without prejudice to Article 34, no provision of Chapters II, III and IV hereof shall be interpreted as giving the right to:

  - nationals of the Member States or of the Republic of Moldova respectively to enter, or stay in, the territory of the Republic of Moldova or the Community respectively in any capacity whatsoever, and in particular as a shareholder or partner in a company or manager or employee thereof or supplier or recipient of services,

  - Community subsidiaries or branches of Moldovan companies to employ or have employed in the territory of the Community nationals of the Republic of Moldova,

  - Moldovan subsidiaries or branches of Community companies to employ or have employed in the territory of Moldova nationals of the Member States,

  - Moldovan companies or Community subsidiaries or branches of Moldovan companies to supply Moldovan persons to act for and under the control of other persons by temporary employment contracts,

- Community companies or Moldovan subsidiaries or branches of Community companies to supply workers who are nationals of the Member States by temporary employment contracts.

TITLE V
CURRENT PAYMENTS AND CAPITAL

Article 47

1.   The Parties undertake to authorise in freely convertible currency, any payments on the current account of balance of payments between residents of the Community and of the Republic of Moldova connected with the movement of goods, services or persons made in accordance with the provisions of this Agreement.

2.   With regard to transactions on the capital account of balance of payments, from entry into force of the Agreement, the free movement of capital relating to direct investments made in companies formed in accordance with the laws of the host country and investments made in accordance with the provisions of Chapter II of Title IV, and the liquidation or repatriation of these investments and of any profit stemming therefrom, shall be ensured.

3.   Without prejudice to paragraph 2 or to paragraph 5, as from entry into force of this Agreement, no new foreign exchange restrictions on the movement of capital and current payments connected therewith between residents of the Community and the Republic of Moldova shall be introduced and the existing arrangements shall not become more restrictive.

4.   The Parties shall consult each other with a view to facilitating the movement of forms of capital other than those referred to in paragraph 2 between the Community and the Republic of Moldova, in order to promote the objectives of this Agreement.

5.   With reference to the provisions of this Article, until a full convertibility of the Moldovan currency within the meaning of Article VIII of the Articles of Agreement of the International Monetary Fund (IMF) is introduced, the Republic of Moldova may in exceptional circumstances apply exchange restrictions connected with the granting or taking up of short and medium-term financial credits to the extent that such restrictions are imposed on the Republic of Moldova for the granting of such credits and are permitted according to the Republic of Moldova's status under the IMF. The Republic of Moldova shall apply these restrictions in a non-discriminatory manner. They shall be applied in such a manner as to cause the least possible disruption to this Agreement. The Republic of Moldova shall inform the Cooperation Council promptly of the introduction of such measures and of any changes therein.

6.   Without prejudice to paragraphs 1 and 2, where, in exceptional circumstances, movements of capital between the Community and the Moldova cause, or threaten to cause, serious difficulties for the operation of exchange rate policy or monetary policy in the Community or the Republic of Moldova, the Community and the Republic of Moldova, respectively, may take safeguard measures with regard to movements of capital between the Community and the Republic of Moldova for a period not exceeding six months if such measures are strictly necessary.

TITLE VI
COMPETITION, INTELLECTUAL, INDUSTRIAL AND COMMERCIAL PROPERTY PROTECTION AND LEGISLATIVE COOPERATION

Article 48

1.   The Parties agree to work to remedy or remove through the application of their competition laws or otherwise, restrictions on competition by enterprises or caused by State intervention insofar as they may affect trade between the Community and the Republic of Moldova.

2.   In order to attain the objectives mentioned in paragraph 1:

2.1.   The Parties shall ensure that they have and enforce laws addressing restrictions on competition by enterprises within their jurisdiction.

2.2.   The Parties shall refrain from granting State aids favouring certain undertakings or the production of goods other than primary products as defined in the GATT, or the provision of services, which distort or threaten to distort competition insofar as they affect trade between the Community and the Republic of Moldova.

2.3.   Upon request by one Party, the other Party shall provide information on its aid schemes or on particular individual cases of State aid. No information needs to be provided which is covered by legislative requirements of the Parties on professional or commercial secrets.

2.4.   In the case of State monopolies of a commercial character, the Parties declare their readiness, as from the fourth year from the date of entry into force of their Agreement, to ensure that there is no discrimination between nationals of the Parties regarding the conditions under which goods are procured or marketed.

2.5.   In the case of public undertakings or undertakings to which Member States or the Republic of Moldova grant exclusive rights, the Parties declare their readiness, as from the fourth year from the date of entry into force of this Agreement, to ensure that there is neither enacted nor maintained any measure distorting trade between the Community and the Republic of Moldova to an extent contrary to the Parties' respective interests. This provision shall not obstruct the performance, in law or fact, of the particular tasks assigned to such undertakings.

2.6.   The period defined in paragraphs 2.4 and 2.5 may be extended by agreement of the Parties.

3.   Consultations may take place within the Cooperation Committee at the request of the Community or the Republic of Moldova on the restrictions or distortions of competition referred to in paragraphs 1 and 2 and on the enforcement of their competition rules, subject to limitations imposed by laws regarding disclosure of information, confidentiality and business secrecy. Consultations may also comprise questions on the interpretation of paragraphs 1 and 2.

4.   The Parties with experience in applying competition rules shall give full consideration to providing other Parties, upon request and within available resources, technical assistance for the development and implementation of competition rules.

5.   The above provisions in no way affect the Parties' rights to apply adequate measures, notably those referred to in Article 18, in order to address distortions of trade in goods or services.

Article 49

1.   Pursuant to the provisions of this Article and of Annex III, the Republic of Moldova shall continue to improve the protection of intellectual, industrial and commercial property rights in order to provide, by the end of the fifth year after the entry into force of the Agreement for a level of protection similar to that existing in the Community, including effective means of enforcing such rights.

2.   By the end of the fifth year after entry into force of the Agreement, the Republic of Moldova shall accede to the multilateral conventions on intellectual, industrial and commercial property rights referred to in paragraph 1 of Annex III to which Member States of the Community are parties or which are de facto applied by Member States according to the relevant provisions contained in these conventions.

Article 50

1.   The Parties recognise that an important condition for strengthening the economic links between the Republic of Moldova and the Community is the approximation of the Republic of Moldova's existing and future legislation to that of the Community. The Republic of Moldova shall endeavour to ensure that its legislation will be gradually made compatible with that of the Community.

2.   The approximation of laws shall extend to the following areas in particular: customs law, company law, banking law, company accounts and taxes, intellectual property, protection of workers at the workplace, financial services, rules on competition, public procurement, protection of health and life of humans, animals and plants, the environment, consumer protection, indirect taxation, technical rules and standards, nuclear laws and regulations, transport.

3.   The Community shall provide the Republic of Moldova with technical assistance as appropriate for the implementation of these measures, which may include, inter alia:

- the exchange of experts,

- the provision of early information especially on relevant legislation,

- organisation of seminars,

- training activities,
- aid for translation of Community legislation in the relevant sectors.

TITLE VII
ECONOMIC COOPERATION

Article 51

1.   The Community and the Republic of Moldova shall establish economic cooperation aimed at contributing to the process of economic reform and recovery and sustainable development of the Republic of Moldova. Such cooperation shall strengthen existing economic links, to the benefit of both parties.

2.   Policies and other measures will be designed to bring about economic and social reforms and restructuring of the economic system in the Republic of Moldova and will be guided by the requirements of sustainability and harmonious social development; they will also fully incorporate environmental considerations.

3.   To this end the cooperation will concentrate on industrial cooperation, investment promotion and protection, public procurement, standards and conformity assessment, mining and raw materials, science and technology, education and training, agriculture and the agro-industrial sector, energy, environment, transport, telecommunications, financial services, money laundering, monetary policy, regional development, social cooperation, tourism, small and medium-sized enterprises, information and communication, consumer protection, customs, statistical cooperation, economics and drugs.

4.   Special attention shall be devoted to measures capable of fostering cooperation between the Independent States with a view to stimulating a harmonious development of the region.

5.   Where appropriate, economic cooperation and other forms of cooperation provided for in this Agreement may be supported by technical assistance from the Community, taking into account the Community's relevant Council regulation applicable to technical assistance in the Independent States, the priorities agreed upon in the indicative programme related to Community technical assistance to the Republic of Moldova and its established coordination and implementation procedures.

6.   The Cooperation Council shall make recommendations as to the development of cooperation in fields identified in paragraph 3.

Article 52 Industrial cooperation

1.   Cooperation shall aim at promoting the following in particular:

- the development of business links between economic operators of both sides, e.g. in view of the transfer of technologies and know-how,

- Community participation in the Republic of Moldova's efforts to restructure and technically upgrade its industry,

- the improvement of management,

- the development of appropriate commercial rules and practices, including product marketing,

- environmental protection,

- adaptation of the structure of industrial production to the standards of an advanced market economy,

- the conversion of the military-industrial complex.

2.   The provisions of this Article shall not affect the enforcement of Community competition rules applicable to undertakings.

Article 53 Investment promotion and protection

1.   Bearing in mind the respective powers and competences of the Community and the Member States, cooperation shall aim to establish a favourable climate for investment, both domestic and foreign, especially through better conditions for investment protection, the transfer of capital and the exchange of information on investment opportunities.

2.   The particular aims of cooperation shall be:

- the conclusion, where appropriate, between the Member States and the Republic of Moldova, of agreements for the promotion and protection of investment,

- the conclusion, where appropriate, between the Member States and the Republic of Moldova, of agreements to avoid double taxation,

- the creation of favourable conditions for attracting foreign investments into the Moldovan economy,

- to establish stable and adequate business law and conditions, and to exchange information on laws, regulations and administrative practices in the field of investment,

- to exchange information on investment opportunities in the form of, inter alia, trade fairs, exhibitions, trade weeks and other events.

Article 54 Public procurement

The Parties shall cooperate to develop conditions for open and competitive award of contracts for goods and services in particular through calls for tenders.

ANNEX III

INTELLECTUAL, INDUSTRIAL AND COMMERCIAL PROPERTY RIGHTS CONVENTIONS REFERRED TO IN ARTICLE 49(2)

1.   Paragraph 2 of Article 49 concerns the following multilateral conventions:

- Berne Convention for the Protection of Literary and Artistic Works (Paris Act, 1971),

- International Convention for the Protection of Performers, Producers of Phonograms and Broadcasting Organisations (Rome, 1961),

- Protocol relating to the Madrid Agreement concerning the International Registration of Marks (Madrid, 1989),

- Nice Agreement concerning the International Classification of Goods and Services for the purposes of the Registration of Marks (Geneva 1977, amended 1979),

- International Convention for the Protection of New Varieties of Plants (UPOV) (Geneva Act, 1991).

2.   The Cooperation Council may recommend that paragraph 2 of Article 49 shall apply to other multilateral conventions. If problems in the area of intellectual, industrial, and commercial property affecting trading conditions were to occur, urgent consultation shall be undertaken, at the request of either Party, with a view to reaching mutually satisfactory solutions.

3.   The Parties confirm the importance they attach to the obligations arising from the following multilateral conventions:

- Budapest Treaty on the International Recognition of the Deposit of Micro-organisms for the purposes of Patent Procedures (1977, modified in 1980),

- Paris Convention for the Protection of Industrial Property (Stockholm Act, 1967 and amended in 1979),

- Madrid Agreement concerning the International Registration of Marks (Stockholm Act, 1967, and amended in 1979),

- Patent Cooperation Treaty (Washington 1970, amended and modified in 1984).

4.   From the entry into force of this Agreement the Republic of Moldova shall grant to Community companies and nationals, in respect of the recognition and protection of intellectual, industrial and commercial property, treatment no less favourable than that granted by it to any third country under bilateral agreements.

5.   The provisions of paragraph 4 shall not apply to advantages granted by the Republic of Moldova to any third country on an effective reciprocal basis or to advantages granted by the Republic of Moldova to another country of the former USSR.

*

AGREEMENT ON PARTNERSHIP AND CO-OPERATION ESTABLISHING A PARTNERSHIP BETWEEN THE EUROPEAN COMMUNITIES AND THEIR MEMBER STATES, OF ONE PART, AND THE RUSSIAN FEDERATION, OF THE OTHER PART*
[excerpts]

> The Agreement on Partnership and Co-operation Establishing a Partnership between the European Communities and Their Member States, of One Part, and the Russian Federation, of the Other Part was signed on 24 June 1994. It entered into force on 1 December 1997. The member States of the European Communities are: Austria, Belgium, Denmark, Finland, France, Germany, Greece, Ireland, Italy, Luxembourg, the Netherlands, Portugal, Spain, Sweden and the United Kingdom.

TITLE IV
PROVISIONS ON BUSINESS AND INVESTMENT

CHAPTER II
CONDITIONS AFFECTING THE ESTABLISHMENT AND OPERATION OF COMPANIES

Article 28

1.   The Community and its Member States of the one part and Russia of the other part, shall grant to each other treatment no less favourable than that accorded to any third country, with regard to conditions affecting the establishment of companies in their territories and this in conformity with the legislation and regulations applicable in each Party.

2.   Without prejudice to the reservations listed in Annex 3, the Community and its Member States shall grant to Community subsidiaries of Russian companies a treatment no less favourable than that granted to other Community companies or to Community companies which are subsidiaries of any third country companies whichever is the better, in respect of their operation and this in conformity with their legislation and regulations.

3.   Without prejudice to the reservations listed in Annex 4, Russia shall grant to Russian subsidiaries of Community companies a treatment no less favourable than that granted to other Russian companies or to Russian companies which are subsidiaries of any third country companies whichever is the better, in respect of their operation and this in conformity with its legislation and regulations.

4.   The Community and its Member States of the one part and Russia of the other part shall grant to branches of Russian and Community companies respectively a treatment no less

---

* *Source*: European Communities (1997). "Agreement on Partnership and Co-operation Establishing a Partnership between the European Communities and Their Member States, of One Part, and the Russian Federation, of the Other Part", *Official Journal of the European Communities*, L 327, 28 November 1997, pp. 3 - 69; available also on the Internet (http://www.europa.eu.int). [Note added by the editor.]

favourable than that accorded to branches of companies of any third country, in respect of their operation and this in conformity with their legislation and regulations.

5.   The provisions of paragraphs 2 and 3 cannot be used so as to circumvent a Party's legislation and regulations applicable to access to specific sectors or activities by subsidiaries of companies of the other Party established in the territory of such first Party.

The treatment referred to in paragraphs 2 and 3 shall benefit companies established in the Community and Russia respectively at the date of entry into force of this Agreement and companies established after that date once they are established.

Article 29

The provisions of Article 28 of this Agreement together with the following provisions shall apply in respect of banking and insurance services referred to in Annex 6.

1.   In respect of banking services referred to in Annex 6, Part B, the nature of the treatment accorded by Russia pursuant to Article 28 (1), with regard to establishment by means of the setting up of subsidiaries only and pursuant to Article 28 (3), is set out in Annex 7, Part A.

In respect of insurance services referred to in Annex 6, Part A (1) and (2), the nature of the treatment accorded by Russia pursuant to Article 28 (1) is set out in Annex 7, Part B.

2.   Notwithstanding any other provisions of this Agreement, a Party shall not be prevented from taking measures for prudential reasons, including for the protection of investors, depositors, policy holders or persons to whom a fiduciary duty is owed by a financial service supplier, or to ensure the integrity and stability of the financial system. Such measures shall not be used as a means of avoiding the Party's obligations under the Agreement.

Nothing in the Agreement shall be construed to require a Party to disclose information relating to the affairs and accounts of individual customers or any confidential or proprietary information in the possession of public entities.

3.   Without prejudice to the provisions of Part A (1) (d) and (e) of Annex 7, the Community and the Member States of the one part and Russia of the other part shall not adopt any new regulations or measures which would introduce or worsen discrimination as compared to the situation existing on the date of the signature of the Agreement as regards conditions affecting the establishment of the other Party's companies in their respective territories in comparison to their own companies.

The parties agree that the terms 'worsen discrimination` include the aggravation of discriminatory conditions or their extension or reintroduction after the current period of application.

4.   For the purposes of this Agreement, as regards banking activities a company shall be regarded as a Russian subsidiary of a Community company when more than fifty percent (50 %) of its share capital is held by the Community company.

Article 30

For the purpose of this Agreement:

(a)   'establishment` shall mean the right of Community or Russian companies as referred to in paragraph (h) of this Article to take up economic activities by means of the setting up of subsidiaries and branches in Russia or in the Community respectively.

In respect of financial services mentioned in Article 29, 'establishment` shall mean the right of Community or Russian companies as referred to in paragraph (h) of this Article to take up economic activities by means of the setting up of subsidiaries and branches in Russia or in the Community respectively after receiving a licence from the competent authorities in conformity with the legislation and regulations applicable in each Party;

(b)   'subsidiary` of a company shall mean a company which is controlled by the first company;

(c)   'economic activities` shall mean activities of an industrial, commercial or professional character, including financial services;

(d)   'branch` of a company shall mean a place of business not having legal personality which has the appearance of permanency, such as the extension of a parent body, has a management and is materially equipped to negotiate business with third parties so that the latter, although knowing that there will if necessary be a legal link with the parent body, the head office of which is abroad, do not have to deal directly with such parent body but may transact business at the place of business constituting the extension;

(e)   'Community subsidiary` or 'Russian subsidiary` respectively shall mean a 'Community company` or a 'Russian company` respectively, as hereafter defined, which is also a subsidiary of a 'Russian company` or a 'Community company` respectively;

(f)   a national of a Member State or of Russia respectively shall mean a natural person who is a national of one of the Member States or of Russia respectively in accordance with their respective legislation;

(g)   'operation` shall mean the pursuit of economic activities;
In respect of financial services mentioned in Article 29, 'operation` shall mean the pursuit of all the economic activities authorized by the licence granted to the company by the competent authorities in conformity with the laws and regulations applicable in each Party;

(h)   a 'Community company` or a 'Russian company` respectively shall mean a company set up in accordance with the laws of a Member State or of Russia respectively and having its registered office or central administration, or principal place of business in the territory of the Community or Russia respectively. However, should the company, set up in accordance with the laws of a Member State or Russia respectively, have only its registered office in the territory of the Community or Russia respectively, the company shall be considered a Community or Russian company respectively if its operations possess a real and continuous link with the economy of one of the Member States or Russia respectively.

With regard to international maritime transport, shall also be beneficiaires of the provisions of this chapter and Chapter III, shipping companies established outside the Community or Russia and controlled by nationals of a Member State or of Russia respectively, if their vessels are registered in that Member State or in Russia in accordance with their respective legislation.

For the purposes of this provision, international maritime transport shall be considered to include intermodal transport operations involving a sea leg without prejudice to applicable nationality restrictions concerning the carriage of goods and passengers by other transport modes;

(i)   For the purpose of Article 29 and Annex 7, with regard to banking services referred to in Annex 6, Part B, 'Russian subsidiary` or 'Community subsidiary` as defined in paragraph (e), shall refer to such a subsidiary which is a bank in accordance with the laws of Russia or a Member State respectively.

For the purpose of Article 29 and Annex 7, with regard to banking services referred to in Annex 6, Part B, 'Community company` or 'Russian company` as defined in paragraph (h), shall refer to such a company which is a bank in accordance with the laws of a Member State or Russia respectively.

Article 31

Notwithstanding Article 100, the provisions of this Title shall not prejudice the application by each Party of any measure necessary to prevent the circumvention, through the provisions of this Agreement, of its measures concerning third country access to its market.

Article 32

1.   Notwithstanding the provisions of Chapter I of this Title, a Community company and a Russian company established in the territory of Russia or the Community respectively shall be entitled to employ, or have employed by one of its subsidiaries, branches or joint ventures, in accordance with the legislation in force in the host country of establishment, in the territory of Russia and the Community respectively, employees who are nationals of Member States and Russia respectively, provided that such employees are key personnel as defined in paragraph 2 of this Article, and that they are employed exclusively by companies, subsidiaries, branches or joint ventures. The residence and work permits of such employees shall only cover the period of such employment.

2.   Key personnel of the abovementioned companies herein referred to as 'organizations` are 'intra-corporate transferees` as defined in paragraph (c) in the following categories, provided that the organization is a legal person and that the persons concerned have been employed by it or have been partners in it (other than as majority shareholders), for at least the year immediately preceding such movement:

(a)   persons working in a senior position with an organization, who primarily direct the management of the establishment (branch, subsidiary or joint venture), receiving general supervision or direction principally from the board of directors or stockholders of the business or their equivalent, including:

- directing the establishment or a department or subdivision of the establishment,

        - supervising and controlling the work of other supervisory, professional or managerial employees,

        - having the authority personally to engage and dismiss or recommend engaging, dismissing or other personnel actions;

(b)   persons working within an organization who possess uncommon knowledge essential to the establishment's service, research equipment, techniques or management. The assessment of such knowledge may reflect, apart from knowledge specific to the establishment, a high level of qualification referring to a type of work or trade requiring specific technical knowledge, including membership of an accredited profession;

(c)   an 'intra-corporate transferee` is defined as a natural person working within an organization in the territory of a Party, and being temporarily transferred in the context of pursuit of economic activities in the territory of the other Party; the organization concerned must have its principal place of business in the territory of a Party and the transfer must be to an establishment of that organization, effectively pursuing like economic activities in the territory of the other Party.

Article 33

The Parties recognize the importance of granting each other national treatment with regard to the establishment and, where not so foreseen herein, operation of each other's companies in their territories and agree to consider the possibility of movement towards this end on a mutually satisfactory basis, and in the light of any recommendations by the Cooperation Council.

Article 34

1.   The Parties shall use their best endeavours to avoid taking any measures or actions which render the conditions for the establishment and operation of each other's companies more restrictive than the situation existing on the day preceding the date of signature of the Agreement.

2.   By the end of the third year after signature of the Agreement at the latest, and thereafter at annual intervals the Parties shall examine within the Cooperation Council:

- measures introduced by either Party since the signature of the Agreement which affect the establishment or operation of companies of one Party in the territory of the other Party, and which are the subject of commitments assumed in Article 28, and

- whether it is possible for the Parties to assume:

- the obligation not to take any measures or actions which may render the conditions for the establishment and operation of each other's companies more restrictive than the situation existing at the time of such examination, where not already foreseen herein, or

- other obligations affecting their freedom of action in areas agreed between the Parties in respect of the commitments assumed in Article 28.

If after such examination one Party is of the view that measures introduced by the other Party since the signature of the Agreement result in a situation which is significantly more restrictive in respect of establishment or operation of companies of the first Party in the territory of the other Party as compared with the situation existing at the date of signature of the Agreement, such Party may request the other Party to enter into consultations. In such case the provisions of Part A of Annex 8 shall apply.

3.   In furtherance of the aims of this Article, measures shall be taken as indicated in Part B of Annex 8.

4.   The provisions of this Article are without prejudice to those of Article 51. The situations covered by such Article 51 shall be solely governed by its provisions to the exclusion of any other.

Article 35

1.   Article 28 shall not apply to air transport, inland waterways transport and maritime transport.

2.   However, in respect of activities, as indicated below, undertaken by shipping agencies for the provision of services to international maritime transport, including intermodal transport operations involving a sea-leg, each Party shall permit the companies of the other Party to have a commercial presence in its territory in the form of subsidiaries or branches, under conditions of establishment and operation no less favourable than those accorded to its own companies or to subsidiaries or branches of companies of any third country, whichever are the better, and this in conformity with the legislation and regulations applicable in each Party.

3.   Such activities include:

(a)   marketing and sales of maritime transport and related services through direct contact with customers, from quotation to invoicing;

(b)   purchase and resale of any transport and related services, including transport services by any inland mode, necessary for the supply of an intermodal service;

(c)   preparation of documentation concerning transport documents, customs documents, or other documents related to the origin and character of the goods transported;

(d)   provision of business information by any means, including computerized information systems and electronic data interchange (subject to any non-discriminatory restrictions concerning telecommunications);

(e)   setting up of any business arrangement with other shipping agencies;

(f)   acting on behalf of the companies, inter alia in organizing the call of the vessel or taking over cargoes when required.

CHAPTER III
CROSS-BORDER SUPPLY OF SERVICES

Article 36

For the sectors listed in Annex 5 to this Agreement, the Parties shall grant each other treatment no less favourable than that accorded to any third country with regard to the conditions affecting the cross-border supply of services, by Community or Russian companies into the territory of Russia or the Community respectively, pursuant to the legislation and regulations applicable in each Party.

Article 37

Subject to the provisions of Article 48 of this Agreement, the Parties shall permit for the sectors list in Annex 5 to this Agreement the temporary movement of natural persons, who are representatives of a Community or a Russian company and are seeking temporary entry for the purpose of negotiating for the sales of cross-border services or entering into agreements to sell cross-border services for that company, where those representatives will not be engaged in making direct sales to the general public or in supplying services themselves.

Article 38

1.   For the sectors listed in Annex 5, each Party may regulate the conditions of cross-border supply of services into its territory. In so far as these regulations are of general application they shall be administered in a reasonable, objective and impartial manner.

2.   Paragraph 1 is without prejudice to the provisions of Articles 36 and 50.

3.   By the end of the third year after signature of the Agreement and the latest, the Parties shall examine within the Cooperation Council:

>   - measures introduced by either Party since the signature of the Agreement which affect the cross-border supply of services covered by Article 36, and

>   - whether it is possible for the Parties to assume:

>   - the obligation not to take any measures or actions which may render the conditions for the cross-border supply of services covered by Article 36 more restrictive than the situation existing at the time of such examination, or

>   - other obligations affecting their freedom of action in areas agreed between the Parties in respect of the commitments assumed in Article 36.

If after such examination one Party is of the view that measures introduced by the other Party since the signature of the Agreement result in a situation which is significantly more restrictive in respect of cross-border supply of services covered by Article 36 as compared with the situation existing at the date of signature of the Agreement, such first Party may request the other Party to enter into consultations. In such case the provisions of Part A of Annex 8 shall apply.

4.   In furtherance of the aims of this Article, measures shall be taken as indicated in Part B of Annex 8.

5.   The provisions of this Article are without prejudice to those of Article 51. The situations covered by such Article 51 shall be solely governed by its provisions to the exclusion of any other.

Article 39

1.   With regard to maritime transport, the Parties undertake to apply effectively the principle of unrestricted access to the international market and traffic on a commercial basis.

    (a)   The above provision does not prejudice the rights and obligations arising under the United Nations Convention on a code of conduct for liner conferences, as applicable to the Parties to this Agreement. Non-conference lines shall be free to operate in competition with a conference as long as they adhere to the principle of fair competition on a commercial basis.

    (b)   The Parties affirm their commitment to a freely competitive environment as being an essential feature of the dry and liquid bulk trade.

2.   In applying the principles of paragraph 1, the Parties shall:

    (a)   not apply, in their mutual trade, as from entry into force of this Agreement, any cargo sharing provisions of bilateral agreements between any Member State and the former USSR;

    (b)   not introduce cargo sharing arrangements in future bilateral agreements with third countries concerning dry and liquid bulk and liner trade. However, this does not exclude the possibility of such arrangements concerning liner cargo in those exceptional circumstances where liner shipping companies from one or other Party to this Agreement would not otherwise have an effective opportunity to ply for trade to and from the third country concerned;

    (c)   abolish, upon entry into force of this Agreement, all unilateral measures, administrative, technical and other obstacles which could constitute a disguised restriction or have discriminatory effects on the free supply of services in international maritime transport.

Each Party shall grant, inter alia, a treatment no less favourable than that accorded to a Party's own vessels, for vessels used for the transport of goods, passengers or both, and flying the flag of the other Party, with respect to access to ports open to foreign vessels, the use of infrastructure and auxiliary maritime services of those ports, as well as related fees and charges, customs facilities and the assignment of berths and facilities for loading and unloading.

3.   The Parties agree that, following the entry into force of this Agreement and not later than 31 December 1996, they will conduct negotiations on the stage-by-stage opening of the inland waterways of each Party to the nationals and shipping companies of the other Party, in respect of the freedom to provide international sea-river services.

Article 40

For the purpose of establishing favourable conditions for rail transport between the Parties, it is agreed that both Parties will, in the framework of this Agreement and through appropriate bilateral and multilateral mechanisms, promote:

- the facilitation of customs and other border clearance procedures for freight and for rolling stock,

- cooperation in the creation of suitable rolling stock meeting the requirements of international traffic,

- the approximation of regulations and procedures which govern international transport,

- the safeguarding and development of international passenger traffic between the Member States and Russia.

Article 41

Cooperation shall ensure fair, balanced and competitive conditions for the space launching and transportation market based on sound economic factors and, in particular, steps will be taken to promote the negotiation and implementation of multilateral rules regarding international trade in space launching and transportation services.

During the transnational period to the year 2000, conditions for the supply of space launch services shall be agreed upon.

Article 42

The Parties shall endeavour to provide each other every assistance possible as regards measures promoting cross-border trade in mobile satellite communications on their respective territories, in conformity with their respective legislation, practices and conditions. In 1996, the Parties will meet to consider the possibilities of granting to each other most-favoured-nation treatment for mobile satellite services.

Article 43

With a view to assuring a coordinated development of transport between the Parties, adapted to their commercial needs, the Parties may, after the entry into force of this Agreement, conclude specific Agreements regarding the conditions of mutual market access and of provision of services in the transport sector, to the extent that these conditions are not already addressed by this Agreement. Such Agreements may apply to more than one or to a single mode of transport.

CHAPTER IV
GENERAL PROVISIONS

Article 44

For the purposes of Chapters II, III and of Title V, no account shall be taken of treatment accorded by the Community, its Member States or Russia pursuant to commitments entered into in economic integration agreements.

Article 45

Companies which are controlled and exclusively owned by Community companies and Russian companies jointly shall also be beneficiaries of the provisions of Chapters II and III of this Title and those of Title V.

Article 46

1.   The provisions of this Title shall be applied subject to limitations justified on grounds of public policy, public security or public health.

2.   They shall not apply to activities which in the territory of either Party are connected, even occasionally, with the exercise of official authority.

Article 47

The Cooperation Council shall make recommendations for the further liberalization of trade in services, taking into account the development of the services sectors in the Parties and the other international commitments entered into by the Parties, in particular in the light of the final results of the negotiations of the General Agreement on Trade in Services, hereinafter referred to as 'GATS`.

Article 48

For the purpose of this Title, nothing in the Agreement shall prevent the Parties from applying their laws and regulations regarding entry and stay, work, labour conditions and establishment of natural persons and supply of services, provided that, in so doing, they do not apply them in a manner as to nullify or impair the benefits accruing to any Party under the terms of a specific provision of the Agreement. The above provision does not prejudice the application of Article 46.

Article 49

1.   The most-favoured-nation treatment granted in accordance with the provisions of this Title or of Title V shall not apply to the tax advantages which the Parties are providing or will provide in the future on the basis of agreements to avoid double taxation, or other tax arrangements.

2.   Nothing in this Title or in Title V shall be construed to prevent the adoption or enforcement by the Parties of any measure aimed at preventing the avoidance or evasion of taxes

pursuant to the tax provisions of agreements to avoid double taxation and other tax arrangements, or domestic fiscal legislation.

3.   Nothing in this Title or in Title V shall be construed to prevent Member States or Russia from distinguishing, in the application of the relevant provisions of their fiscal legislation, between taxpayers who are not in identical situations, in particular as regards their place of residence.

Article 50

Without prejudice to Articles 32 and 37, no provision of Chapters II, III and IV hereof shall be interpreted as giving the right to:

- nationals of the Member States or of Russia respectively to enter, or stay in, the territory of Russia or the Community respectively in any capacity whatsoever, and in particular as a shareholder or partner in a company or manager or employed thereof or supplier or recipient of services,

- Community subsidiaries or branches of Russian companies to employ or have employed in the territory of the Community nationals of Russia,

- Russian subsidiaries or branches of Community companies to employ or have employed in the territory of Russia nationals of the Member States,

- Russian companies or Community subsidiaries or branches of Russian companies to supply workers who are Russian nationals to act for and under the control of other persons by temporary employment contracts,

- Community companies or Russian subsidiaries or branches of Community companies to supply workers who are nationals of the Member States to act for and under the control of other persons by temporary employment contracts.

Article 51

1.   Treatment granted by either Party to the other hereunder shall, has from the day one month prior to the date of entry into force of the relevant obligations of the GATS, in respect of sectors or measures covered by the GATS, in no case be more favourable than that accorded by such first Party under the provisions of the GATS, and this, in respect of each service sector, sub-sector and mode of supply.

2.   Without prejudice to the automatic nature of the provisions of paragraph 1, the Party which has assumed obligations under the GATS shall inform the other of the appropriate provisions and the adaptations resulting therefrom for this Agreement.

3.   Within one month of receipt from the Party, which has assumed obligations under the GATS, of the information referred to in paragraph 2, the other Party may notify the first Party of its intention to make adjustments to its obligations under this Title, and make those adjustments as follows:

- where a service sector, sub-sector or mode of supply of a service has been excluded from the Agreement, its scope reduced or made subject to the fulfilment of conditions pursuant to paragraph 1, the identical sector, sub-sector or mode of supply may be excluded or its scope reduced in the same way or made subject to the fulfilment of identical or similar conditions.

4.   These adjustments made by the second Party should lead to the re-establishment of a balance of obligations between the Parties.

5.   In the case that a Party considers that the adjustments made under paragraph 3 have not led to the re-establishment of the balance of obligations between the Parties, such Party may request the other Party, to enter into consultations within 30 days in order to find a satisfactory solution by means of any other appropriate adjustment of its obligations under this Title.

6.   If within 30 days of the opening of such consultations no satisfactory solution has been found, the procedures of Article 101 will be applicable at the request of either Party.

TITLE V
PAYMENTS AND CAPITAL

Article 52

1.   The Parties undertake to authorize, in freely convertible currency, any current payments between residents of the Community and of Russia connected with the movement of goods, services or persons made in accordance with the provisions of the present Agreement.

2.   The free movement of capital between residents of the Community and of Russia in the form of direct investment made in companies formed in accordance with the laws of the host country and investments made in accordance with the provisions of Chapter II of Title IV, and the transfer abroad of this investment, including any compensation payments arising from measures such as expropriation, nationalization or measures of equivalent effect, and of any profit stemming therefrom shall be ensured.

3.   The provisions of Part 2 shall not prevent Russia from applying restrictions on outward direct investment by Russian residents. Five years after the entry into force of this Agreement the Parties agree to consult over the maintenance of these restrictions, taking into account all the relevant monetary, fiscal and financial considerations.

4.   Transfers in respect of capital movements covered under paragraph 2 shall be made on the same exchange rate conditions as those relating to current transactions.

5.   Without prejudice to paragraphs 6 and 7, after a transitional period of five years as from entry into force of this Agreement, the Parties shall not introduce any new restrictions on the movement of capital and current payments connected therewith between resident of the Community and Russia and shall not make the existing arrangements more restrictive. However, the introduction of restrictions during the transitional period referred to in the first sentence of this paragraph shall not affect the rights and obligations of the Parties under paragraphs 2, 3, 4 and 9 of this Article.

6.   After the prohibition in paragraph 5 has come into effect and without prejudice to paragraphs 1 and 2, where, in exceptional circumstances, movements of capital between the Community and Russia cause, or threaten to cause, serious difficulties for the operation of exchange rate policy or monetary policy in the Community or Russia, the Community and Russia, respectively, may take safeguard measures with regard to movements of capital between the Community and Russia for a period not exceeding six months if such measures are strictly necessary.

7.   With reference to the provisions of this Article, until a full convertibility of the Russian currency within the meaning of Article VIII of the Articles of Agreement of the International Monetary Fund (IMF) is introduced, Russia may apply exchange restrictions connected with the granting or taking up of short and medium-term financial credits to the extent that such restrictions are imposed on Russia for the granting of such credits and are permitted according to Russia's status under the IMF.

Russia shall apply these restrictions in a non-discriminatory manner. They shall be applied in such a manner as to cause the least possible disruption to this Agreement. Russia shall inform the Cooperation Council promptly of the introduction of such measures and of any changes therein.

8.   The Parties shall consult each other with a view to facilitating the movement of capital between the Community and Russia in order to promote the objectives of the present Agreement. The Parties shall particularly endeavour to further liberalize movements of capital related to portfolio investment and commercial credits, and movements of capital related to financial loans and credits granted by Community residents to Russian residents. The Cooperation Council shall make appropriate recommendations within the first five years after entry into force of this Agreement.

9.   The Parties shall accord to one another most-favoured-nation treatment in respect of freedom of current payments and capital movements and in respect of methods of payment.

TITLE VI
COMPETITION; INTELLECTUAL, INDUSTRIAL AND COMMERCIAL PROPERTY PROTECTION; LEGISLATIVE COOPERATION

Article 53 Competition

1.   The Parties agree to work to remedy or remove through the application of their competition laws or otherwise, restrictions on competition by enterprises or caused by State intervention in so far as they may affect trade between the Community and Russia.

2.   In order to attain the objectives mentioned in paragraph 1:

   2.1.   The Parties shall ensure that they have and enforce laws addressing restrictions on competition by enterprises within their jurisdiction.

   2.2.   The Parties shall refrain from granting export aids favouring certain undertakings or the production of products other than primary products. The Parties also declare their readiness, as from the third year from the date of entry into force of this Agreement, to establish for other aids which distort or threaten to distort competition in so far as they affect trade between the Community and Russia, strict disciplines, including the outright prohibition of certain aids. These categories of aids and the disciplines applicable to each shall be defined jointly within a period of three years after entry into force of this Agreement.

Upon request by one Party, the other Party shall provide information on its aid schemes or in particular individual cases of State aid.

2.3.   During a transitional period expiring five years after the entry into force of the Agreement, Russia may take measures inconsistent with paragraph 2.2, second sentence, provided that these measures are introduced and applied in the circumstances referred to in Annex 9.

2.4.   In the case of State monopolies of a commercial character, the Parties declare their readiness, as from the third year from the date of entry into force of this Agreement, to ensure that there is no discrimination between nationals and companies of the Parties regarding the conditions under which goods are procured or marketed.

In the case of public undertakings or undertakings to which Member States or Russia grant exclusive rights, the Parties declare their readiness, as from the third year from the date of entry into force of this Agreement, to ensure that there is neither enacted nor maintained any measure distorting trade between the Community and Russia to an extent contrary to the Parties' respective interests. This provision shall not obstruct the performance, in law or fact, of the particular tasks assigned to such undertakings.

2.5.   The period defined in paragraphs 2.2 and 2.4 may be extended by agreement of the Parties.

3.   Consultations may take place within the Cooperation Committee at the request of the Community or Russia on the restrictions or distortions of competition referred to in paragraphs 1 and 2 and on the enforcement of their competition rules, subject to limitations imposed by laws regarding disclosure of information, confidentiality and business secrecy. Consultations may also comprise questions on the interpretation of paragraphs 1 and 2.

4.   The Party with experience in applying competition rules shall give full consideration to providing the other Party, upon request and within available resources, technical assistance for the development and implementation of competition rules.

5.   The above provisions in no way affect a Party's rights to apply adequate measures, notably those referred to in Article 18, in order to address distortions of trade.

Article 54 Intellectual, industrial and commercial property protection

1.   Pursuant to the provisions of this Article and Annex 10, the Parties confirm the importance they attach to ensure adequate and effective protection and enforcement of intellectual, industrial and commercial property rights.

2.   The Parties confirm the importance they attach to the obligations arising from the following multilateral conventions:

- Paris Convention for the protection of industrial property (Stockholm Act, 1967 and amended in 1979),

- Madrid Agreement concerning the international registration of marks (Stockholm Act, 1967, and amended in 1979),

- Nice Agreement concerning the international classification of goods and services for the purposes of the registration of marks (Geneva, 1977, and amended in 1979),

- Budapest Treaty on the international recognition of the deposit of microorganisms for the purposes of patent procedure (1977, modified in 1980),

- Patent Cooperation Treaty (Washington 1970, amended and modified in 1979 and 1984),

- Protocol relating to the Madrid Agreement concerning the international registration of marks (Madrid, 1989).

3.   The implementation of the provisions of this Article and Annex 10 shall be regularly reviewed by the Parties in accordance with Article 90. If problems in the area of intellectual, industrial and commercial property affecting trading conditions were to occur, urgent consultations shall be undertaken, at the request of either Party, with a view to reaching mutually satisfactory solutions.

Article 55 Legislative cooperation

1.   The Parties recognize that an important condition for strengthening the economic links between Russia and the Community is the approximation of legislation. Russia shall endeavour to ensure that its legislation will be gradually made compatible with that of the Community.

2.   The approximation of laws shall extend to the following areas in particular: company law, banking law, company accounts and taxes, protection of workers at the workplace, financial services, rules on competition, public procurement, protection of health and life of humans, animals and plants, the environment, consumer protection, indirect taxation, customs law, technical rules and standards, nuclear laws and regulations, transport.

TITLE VII
ECONOMIC COOPERATION

Article 56

1.   The Community and Russia shall foster economic cooperation of wide scope in order to contribute to the expansion of their respective economies, to the creation of a supportive international economic environment and to the integration between Russia and a wider area of cooperation in Europe. Such cooperation shall strengthen and develop economic links to the benefit of both Parties.

2.   Policies and other measures of the Parties related to this Title shall in particular be designed to bring about economic and social reforms and restructuring in Russia and shall be guided by the requirements of sustainability and harmonious social development; they shall also fully incorporate environmental considerations.

3.   The cooperation shall, inter alia, cover:

- development of their respective industries and transport,

- exploration of new sources of supply and of new markets,

- encouragement of technological and scientific progress,

- encouragement of a stable social and human resources development and of local employment development,

- promotion of the regional cooperation with the aim of its harmonious and sustainable development.

4.   The Parties consider it essential that, alongside with establishing a relationship of partnership and cooperation with each other, they maintain and develop cooperation with other European States and with the other countries of the former USSR with a view to a harmonious development of the region and shall make every effort to encourage this process.

5.   As far as applicable economic and other forms of cooperation provided for in this Agreement may be supported by the Community on the basis of the relevant Council Regulations on technical assistance to the countries of the former USSR, taking into account the priorities agreed upon by the Parties. Support may also be provided through such other relevant Community instruments as may be available.

Special attention shall be devoted by the Parties to measures capable of fostering cooperation with the other countries of the former USSR.

6.   The provisions of this Title shall not affect the enforcement of the Parties' competition rules and of the specific competition provisions of this Agreement applicable to undertakings.

Article 57 Industrial cooperation

1.   Cooperation shall aim at promoting the following in particular:

- the development of business links between economic operators, including small and medium-size enterprises,

- the improvement of management on enterprise level,

- the process of privatization in the context of economic restructuring, and the strengthening of the private sector,

- efforts in both public and private sector, to restructure and modernize the industry, during the transition period leading towards a market economy and under conditions ensuring environment protection and sustainable development,

- the conversion of defence industries,

- the development of appropriate market-based commercial rules and practices as well as transfer of know-how.

2.   Industrial cooperation initiatives shall take into account priorities determined by the Community and by Russia. The initiatives should seek in particular to establish a suitable framework for undertakings, to improve management know-how and to promote transparency as regards markets and conditions for undertakings.

Article 58 Investment promotion and protection

1.   Bearing in mind the respective powers and competences of the Community and the Member States, cooperation shall aim to establish a favourable climate for investment, both domestic and foreign, especially through better conditions for investment protection, the transfer of capital and the exchange of information on investment opportunities.

2.   The aims of this cooperation shall be in particular:

- the conclusion, where appropriate, between the Member States and Russia of agreements for the promotion and protection of investment,

- the conclusion, where appropriate, between the Member States and Russia of agreements to avoid double taxation,

- to exchange information on investment opportunities in the form of inter alia trade fairs, exhibitions, trade weeks and other events,

- to exchange information on laws, regulations and administrative practices in the field of investment.

Article 59 Public procurement

The Parties shall cooperate to develop conditions for open and competitive award of public procurement contracts in particular through calls for tenders.

ANNEX 5

CROSS-BORDER SUPPLY OF SERVICES LIST OF SERVICES FOR WHICH THE PARTIES SHALL GRANT MOST-FAVOURED-NATION (MFN) TREATMENT

(a)   Sectors to be covered, according to the provisional Central Product Classification (CPC) of the United Nations Organization:

Consultancy services relating to accounting review services: part of CPC 86212 other than 'auditing services`

Consultancy services relating to bookkeeping services CPC 86220

Engineering services CPC 8672

Integrated engineering services CPC 8673

Advisory and pre-design architectural services CPC 86711

Architectural design services CPC 86712

Urban planning and landscape architectural services CPC 8674

Computer and related services:

Consultancy services related to the installation of computer hardware CPC 841

Software implementation services CPC 842

Database services CPC 844

Advertising CPC 871

Market research and opinion polling CPC 864

Management consulting services CPC 866

Technical testing and analysis services CPC 8676

Advisory and consulting services relating to agriculture, hunting and forestry

Advisory and consulting services relating to fishing

Advisory and consulting services relating to mining

Printing and publishing CPC 88442

Convention services

Translation services CPC 87905

Interior design services CPC 87907

Telecommunications:

Value-added services including (but not limited to) electronic mail, voice mail, on-line information and database retrieval, data processing, EDI, code and protocol conversion Packet and circuit switched data services

Construction and related engineering services: site investigation work CPC 5111

Franchising CPC 8929

Adult education services by correspondence part of CPC 924

News and press agency services CPC 962

Rental/leasing services without operators related to other transport equipment (CPC 83101 private cars, 83102 goods transport vehicles, 83105) and relating to other machinery and equipment (CPC 83106, 83107, 83108, 83109)

Commission agents services and wholesale trade services related to import-export trade (part of CPC 621 and 622)

Research and development in software

Reinsurance and retrocession and the services auxiliary to insurance, such as consultancy, actuarial, risk assessment and claim settlement services

Insurance of risks relating to:

(i) maritime shipping and commercial aviation and space launching and freight (including satellites), with such insurance to cover any or all of the following: persons being transported, the goods being exported from or imported to, the same vehicle transporting the goods and any liability arising therefrom;

(ii) goods in international transit; and

(iii) accident and health insurance; and personal motor liability insurance in the case of cross-border movement.

(b) Data processing services CPC 843
Provision and transfer of financial information and financial data processing (see paragraphs B.11 and B.12 of Annex 6):

For the services listed under paragraph (b) MFN subject to Article 38 will be applied, without paragraph A of Annex 8.

ANNEX 6

DEFINITIONS IN RELATION TO FINANCIAL SERVICES

A financial service is any service of a financial nature offered by a financial service supplier of one of the Parties. Financial services include the following activities:

A. All insurance and insurance-related services

1. Direct insurance (including co-insurance)

    (i)   life;

    (ii)   non-life.

2. Reinsurance and retrocession.

3. Insurance intermediation, such as brokerage and agency.

4. Services auxiliary to insurance, such as consultancy, actuarial, risk assessment and claim settlement services.

B. Banking and other financial services (excluding insurance)

1. Acceptance of deposits and other repayable funds from the public.

2. Lending of all types, including consumer credit, mortgage credit, factoring and financing of commercial transactions.

3. Financial leasing.

4. All payment and money transmission services, including credit charge and debit cards, travellers cheques and bankers drafts.

5. Guarantees and commitments.

6. Trading for own account or for the account of customers, whether on an exchange, in an over the counter market or otherwise, the following:

    (a)   money market instruments (including cheques, bills, certificates of deposits, etc.);

    (b)   foreign exchange;

    (c)   derivative products including, but not limited to, futures and options;

    (d)   exchange rates and interest rate instruments, including products such as swaps, forward rate agreements, etc.;

    (e)   transferable securities;

    (f)   other negotiable instruments and financial assets, including bullion.

7. Participation in issues of all kinds of securities, including underwriting and placement as agent (whether publicly or privately) and provision of services related to such issues.

8. Money broking.

9.   Asset management, such as cash or portfolio management, all forms of collective investment management, pension fund management, custodial depository and trust services.

10.   Settlement and clearing services for financial assets, including securities, derivative products, and other negotiable instruments.

11.   Provision and transfer of financial information, and financial data processing and related software by suppliers of other financial services.

12.   Advisory intermediation and other auxiliary financial services on all the activities listed in points 1 to 11 above, including credit reference and analysis, investment and portfolio research and advice, advice on acquisitions and on corporate restructuring and strategy.

The following activities are excluded from the definition of financial services:

(a)   activities carried out by central banks or by any other public institution in pursuit of monetary and exchange rate policies;

(b)   activities conducted by central banks, government agencies or departments, or public institutions, for the account or with the guarantee of the government, except when those activities may be carried out by financial service suppliers in competition with such public entities;

(c)   activities forming part of a statutory system of social security or public retirement plans, except when those activities may be carried out by financial service suppliers in competition with public entities or private institutions.

ANNEX 7

FINANCIAL SERVICES

A.   In respect of banking services referred to in Annex 6, Part B, the most-favoured-nation treatment granted pursuant to Article 28 (1), with regard to establishment by means of the setting up of a subsidiary only (excluding therefore establishment by means of the setting up of a branch), and the national treatment granted pursuant to Article 28 (3), by Russia means treatment no less favourable than the treatment granted by Russia to its own companies with the following exceptions:

1.   Russia reserves the right:

(a)   to continue to apply to Russian subsidiaries and branches of Community companies the ceiling limiting the overall share of foreign capital in the Russian banking system which is in operation on the date of signature of the Agreement;

(b)   to apply to Russian subsidiaries of Community companies a minimum capital requirement higher than that applied to its own companies provided that this minimum capital requirement is not raised as compared with the one in force on the date of signature of the Agreement before national treatment is applied in respect of the minimum capital requirement;

(c)   to restrict the number of branches of Russian subsidiaries of Community companies;

(d)   to set a minimum level not higher than ECU 55 000 for balances on accounts of each physical person with Russian subsidiaries of Community companies;

(e)   to prohibit Russian subsidiaries of Community companies from carrying out transactions with shares and instruments convertible into shares of Russian joint stock companies;

(f)   to prohibit Russian subsidiaries of Community companies from carrying out transactions with Russian residents.

2.   The exceptions in paragraph 1 may only apply under the following conditions:

(i)   provided that they are applied to subsidiaries of companies of every country; and

(ii)   for the exceptions mentioned in paragraph 1, subparagraphs (c), (d) and (e):

    (a)   until the expiry of five years from signature of the Agreement at the latest for the exceptions mentioned in subparagraphs (c) and (d) and three years for the exception mentioned in subparagraph (e); and

    (b)   where the proportion of the share capital of the Russian subsidiary of the Community company held by Russian nationals or companies does not exceed fifty percent (50 %); and

    (c)   to Russian subsidiaries of Community companies established after the entry into force of these exceptions;

(iii)   for the exception mentioned in paragraph 1, subparagraph (f), until 1 January 1996 and only to Russian subsidiaries of Community companies established after 15 November 1993 or which have not commenced their operations with Russian residents before 15 November 1993.

3.   (a)   After the expiry of five years from the date of signature of the Agreement, Russia will consider the possibility of:

    (i)   increasing the ceiling limiting the overall share of foreign capital in the Russian banking system which is in operation on the date of the signature of this Agreement, mentioned in subparagraph (a) of paragraph 1, taking into consideration all the relevant monetary, fiscal, financial and balance of payments considerations and the state of the banking system of Russia;
    (ii)   reducing the minimum capital requirement, mentioned in subparagraph (b) of paragraph 1, taking into consideration all the relevant monetary, fiscal, financial and balance of payments considerations and the state of the banking system of Russia.

(b) After the expiry of three years from the signature of this Agreement, Russia will consider the softening of restrictions mentioned in subparagraphs (c) and (d) of paragraph 1, taking into consideration all the relevant monetary, fiscal, financial and balance of payments considerations and the state of the banking system of Russia.

B.   In respect of insurance services referred to in Annex 6, Part A, paragraphs 1 and 2 the most-favoured-nation treatment granted pursuant to Article 28 (1) with regard to establishment by means of the setting up of a subsidiary only authorized for the insurance operations is set out in the legislation and regulations applicable in Russia on the day of establishment taking into account the following conditions:

1.   upon the expiry of five years from signature of the Agreement at the latest, Russia shall abolish the maximum foreign shareholding limit of 49 % in company capital;

2.   during the transitional period of five years the abolition of the maximum foreign shareholding limit does not prevent Russia from introducing measures for granting licences to Community companies in some classes of insurance. These measures could be taken only in the field of compulsory insurance schemes in the social security, or for public procurement, or for the reasons described in Article 29 (2), and shall not nullify or substantially impair the effects of the abolition of the maximum foreign shareholding limit of 49 %.

ANNEX 10

PROTECTION OF INTELLECTUAL, INDUSTRIAL AND COMMERCIAL PROPERTY REFERRED TO IN ARTICLE 54

1.   Russia shall continue to improve the protection of intellectual, industrial and commercial property rights in order to provide, by the end of the fifth year after the entry into force of the Agreement, for a level of protection similar to that existing in the Community, including effective means of enforcing such rights.

2.   By the end of the fifth year following entry into force of the Agreement, Russia shall accede to the multilateral conventions on intellectual, industrial and commercial property rights to which Member States are parties or which are de facto applied by Member States, according to the relevant provisions contained in these conventions:

- Berne Convention for the Protection of Literary and Artistic Works (Paris Act, 1971),

- International Convention for the Protection of Performers, Producers of Phonograms and Broadcasting Organizations (Rome, 1961),

- International Convention for the Protection of New Varieties of Plants (UPOV) (Geneva Act, 1978).

3.   The Cooperation Council may recommend that paragraph 2 of this Annex shall apply to other multilateral conventions.

4.   From the entry into force of this Agreement, Russia shall grant to Community companies and nationals, in respect of the recognition and protection of intellectual, industrial and commercial property, treatment no less favourable than that granted by it to any third country under bilateral agreements.

5.   The provisions of paragraph 4 shall not apply to advantages granted by Russia to any third country on an effective reciprocal basis and to advantages granted by Russia to another country of the former USSR.

*

FREE TRADE AGREEMENT BETWEEN THE EFTA STATES AND ESTONIA[*]
[excerpts]

The Free Trade Agreement between the EFTA States and Estonia was signed on 7 December 1995. It entered into force on 1 October 1997 for Estonia, Iceland, Norway and Switzerland. For Liechtenstein it entered into force on 1 January 1998.

ARTICLE 14
Public procurement

1.   The State Parties to this Agreement consider the effective liberalization of their respective public procurement markets on the basis of non-discrimination and reciprocity, in particular on the basis of the Agreement on Government Procurement at Annex IV to the Agreement Establishing the WTO, as an integral objective of this Agreement.

2.   To this effect, the Parties shall, within one year after the entry into force of this Agreement, elaborate rules within the framework of the Joint Committee with a view to ensuring such liberalization.

3.   The States Parties to this Agreement concerned shall endeavour to accede to the WTO Agreement on Government Procurement.

ARTICLE 15
Protection of intellectual property

1.   The States Parties to this Agreement shall grant and ensure adequate, effective and non-discriminatory protection of intellectual property rights, including measures for the enforcement of such rights against infringement thereof, counterfeiting and piracy. Particular obligations of the States Parties to this Agreement are contained in Annex IV.

2.   In accordance with the substantive provisions of the TRIPS Agreement, in particular Articles 4 and 5 thereof, the States Parties to this Agreement shall grant to each others' nationals treatment no less favourable than that accorded to nationals of any other State. In accordance with Article 4, paragraph (d) of the TRIPS Agreement, any advantage, favour, privilege or immunity deriving from international agreements in force for a State Party to this Agreement at the entry into force of this Agreement and notified to the other States Parties at the latest six months after the entry into force of this Agreement, shall be exempted from this obligation, provided that it does not constitute an arbitrary or unjustifiable discrimination of nationals of the other States Parties.

3.   Two or more States Parties to this Agreement may conclude further agreements exceeding the requirements of this Agreement, provided that such agreements shall be open to all other

---

[*]   *Source*: European Free Trade Association Secretariat (1995). "Free Trade Agreement between the EFTA States and Estonia", available on the Internet (http://secretariat.efta.int). [Note added by the editor.]

States Parties to this Agreement on terms equivalent to those under the agreements and that they shall be ready to enter into good faith negotiations to this end.

4.   The States Parties to this Agreement agree, upon request of an EFTA State or Estonia, to review the provisions on the protection of intellectual property rights contained in the present Article and in Annex IV, with a view to further improve levels of protection and to avoid or remedy trade distortions caused by actual levels of protection of intellectual property rights.

ARTICLE 16
Rules of competition concerning undertakings

1.   The following are incompatible with the proper functioning of this Agreement in so far as they may affect trade between an EFTA State and Estonia:

(a)   all agreements between undertakings, decisions by associations of undertakings and concerted practices between undertakings which have as their object or effect the prevention, restriction or distortion of competition;

(b)   abuse by one or more undertakings of a dominant position in the territories of the States Parties to this Agreement as a whole or in a substantial part thereof.

2.   The provisions of paragraph 1 shall also apply to the activities of public undertakings, and undertakings for which the States Parties to this Agreement grant special or exclusive rights, in so far as the application of these provisions does not obstruct the performance, in law or in fact, of the particular public tasks assigned to them.

3.   If a State Party to this Agreement considers that a given practice is incompatible with the provisions of paragraphs 1 and 2, it may take appropriate measures under the conditions and in accordance with the procedures laid down in Article 24 (Procedure for the application of safeguard measures).

ARTICLE 29
Services and Investment

1.   The States Parties to this Agreement recognize the growing importance of certain areas, such as services and investments. In their efforts to gradually develop and broaden their co-operation, in particular in the context of European integration, they will co-operate with the aim of achieving a gradual liberalization and mutual opening of markets for investments and trade in services, taking into account the results of the Uruguay Round as well as any relevant work under the auspices of the WTO. They will endeavour to accord to each others' operators treatment no less favourable than that accorded to other foreign operators in their territories on condition that a balance of rights and obligations as well as a balance of operating conditions exist between the individual States Parties to this Agreement.

2.   The EFTA States and Estonia will discuss this co-operation in the Joint Committee with the aim of developing and deepening their relations under this Agreement.

ANNEX IV

REFERRED TO IN ARTICLE 15
PROTECTION OF INTELLECTUAL PROPERTY

ARTICLE 1
DEFINITION AND SCOPE OF PROTECTION

"Intellectual property protection" includes in particular protection of copyright and neighbouring rights, including computer programmes and databases, trademarks for goods and services, geographical indications, including appellations of origin, industrial designs, patents, topographies of integrated circuits, as well as undisclosed information on know-how.

Article 2
International conventions

(1)   The States Parties to this Agreement agree to comply with the substantive standards of the following multilateral agreements:

- WTO Agreement of 15 April 1994 on Trade-Related Aspects of Intellectual Property Rights (TRIPS Agreement);

- Paris Convention of 20 March 1883 for the Protection of Industrial Property (Stockholm Act, 1967);

- Berne Convention of 9 September 1886 for the Protection of Literary and Artistic Works (Paris Act, 1971);

(2)   The States Parties to this Agreement shall adhere to the following agreements:

- Budapest Treaty of 28 April 1977 on the International Recognition of the Deposit of Micro-organisms for the Purposes of Patent Procedure;

- International Convention of 26 October 1961 for the Protection of Performers, Producers of Phonograms and Broadcasting Organisations (Rome Convention);

(3)   The States Parties to this Agreement shall furthermore make best endeavours to adhere to other multilateral agreements facilitating co-operation in the field of protection of intellectual property rights.

(4)   The States Parties to this Agreement agree to promptly hold expert consultations, upon request of any State Party, on activities relating to the identified or to future international conventions on harmonization, administration and enforcement of intellectual property rights and on activities in international organizations, such as the World Trade Organization (WTO), the World Intellectual Property Organization (WIPO), as well as relations of the States Parties with third countries on matters concerning intellectual property.

Article 3
Additional substantive standards

The States Parties to this Agreement shall ensure in their national laws at least the following:

- adequate and effective protection of copyright, including computer programmes and databases, as well as of neighbouring rights;

- adequate and effective protection of trademarks for goods and services, in particular of internationally well-known trademarks;

- adequate and effective means to protect geographical indications, including appellations of origin, with regard to all products and services;

- adequate and effective protection of industrial designs by providing in particular a period of protection of five years from the date of application with a possibility of renewal for two consecutive periods of five years each;

- adequate and effective patent protection for inventions in all fields of technology on a level similar to that prevailing in the European Patent Convention of 5 October 1973, and in particular a term of protection of 20 years from the date of filing;

- adequate and effective protection of topographies of integrated circuits;

- adequate and effective protection of undisclosed information on know-how;

- compulsory licensing of patents shall be non-exclusive, non-discriminatory, subject to compensation commensurate with the market value for the licence of the patent and to judicial review. The scope and duration of such licence shall be limited to the purpose for which it was granted. Licences granted on the grounds of non-working shall be used only to the extent necessary to satisfy the local market on reasonable commercial terms and under the conditions of Article 31 of the TRIPS Agreement.

Article 4
Acquisition and maintenance of intellectual property rights

Where the acquisition of an intellectual property right is subject to the right being granted or registered, the States Parties to this Agreement shall ensure that the procedures for grant or registration are of the same level as that provided in the TRIPS Agreement, in particular Article 62.

Article 5
Enforcement of intellectual property rights

The States Parties to this Agreement shall provide for enforcement provisions under their national laws of the same level as that provided in the TRIPS Agreement, in particular Articles 41 to 61.

Article 6

Technical co-operation

The States Parties to this Agreement shall agree upon appropriate modalities for technical assistance and co-operation of respective authorities of the States Parties. To this end, they shall co-ordinate efforts with relevant international organizations.

*

PARTNERSHIP AND COOPERATION AGREEMENT ESTABLISHING A PARTNERSHIP BETWEEN THE EUROPEAN COMMUNITIES AND THEIR MEMBER STATES, OF THE ONE PART, AND THE KYRGYZ REPUBLIC, OF THE OTHER PART[*]
[excerpts]

The Partnership and Cooperation Agreement Establishing a Partnership between the European Communities and Their Member States, of the One Part, and the Kyrgyz Republic, of the Other Part was signed on 9 February 1995. It entered into force on 1 July 1999. The member States of the European Communities are: Austria, Belgium, Denmark, Finland, France, Germany, Greece, Ireland, Italy, Luxembourg, the Netherlands, Portugal, Spain, Sweden and the United Kingdom.

TITLE IV

PROVISIONS AFFECTING BUSINESS AND INVESTMENT

CHAPTER II

CONDITIONS AFFECTING THE ESTABLISHMENT AND OPERATION OF COMPANIES

Article 23

1.   The Community and its Member States shall grant treatment no less favourable than that accorded to any third country for the establishment of Kyrgyz companies as defined in Article 25 by means of the setting up of subsidiaries and branches and shall grant to subsidiaries and branches of Kyrgyz companies established in their territory treatment no less favourable than that accorded to any third country company or branch respectively, in respect of their operations, and this in conformity with their legislation and regulations.

2.   Without prejudice to the provisions of Articles 35 and 84, the Kyrgyz Republic shall grant to Community companies and their branches treatment no less favourable than that accorded to Kyrgyz companies and their branches or to any third country companies and their branches whichever is the better, in respect of their establishment and operations, as defined in Article 25, on its territory, and this in conformity with its legislation and regulations.

Article 24

The provisions of Article 23 shall not apply to air transport, inland waterways and maritime transport.

---

[*]   *Source*: European Communities (1999). "Partnership and Cooperation Agreement Establishing a Partnership between the European Communities and Their Member States, of the One Part, and the Kyrgyz Republic, of the Other Part", *Official Journal of the European Communities*, L 196, 28 July 1999, pp. 48 - 89; available also on the Internet (http://www.europa.eu.int). [Note added by the editor.]

Article 25

For the purpose of this Agreement:

(a)   a "Community company" or a "Kyrgyz company" respectively shall mean a company set up in accordance with the laws of a Member State or of the Kyrgyz Republic respectively and having its registered office or central administration, or principal place of business in the territory of the Community or the Kyrgyz Republic respectively. However, should the company, set up in accordance with the laws of a Member State or the Kyrgyz Republic respectively, the company shall be considered a Community or Kyrgyz company respectively if its operations possess a real and continuous link with the economy of one of the Member States or the Kyrgyz Republic respectively;

(b)   "subsidiary" of a company shall mean a company which is effectively controlled by the first company;

(c)   "branch" of a company shall mean a place of business not having legal personality which has the appearance of permanency, such as the extension of a parent body, has a management and is materially equipped to negotiate business with third parties so that the latter, although knowing that there will if necessary be a legal link with the parent body, the head office of which is abroad, do not have to deal directly with such parent body but may transact business at the place of business constituting the extension;

(d)   "establishment" shall mean the right of Community or Kyrgyz companies as referred to in point (a), to take up economic activities by means of the setting up and management of subsidiaries and branches in the Kyrgyz Republic or in the Community respectively;

(e)   "operation" shall mean the pursuit of economic activities;

(f)   "economic activities" shall mean activities of an industrial, commercial and professional character.

With regard to international maritime transport, including intermodal operations involving a sea leg, nationals of the Member States or of the Kyrgyz Republic established outside the Community or the Kyrgyz Republic respectively, and shipping companies established outside the Community or the Kyrgyz Republic and controlled by nationals of a Member State or Kyrgyz nationals respectively, shall also be beneficiaries of the provisions of this Chapter and Chapter III if their vessels are registered in that Member State or in the Kyrgyz Republic respectively in accordance with their respective legislation.

Article 26

1.   Notwithstanding any other provisions of the Agreement, a Party shall not be prevented from taking measures for prudential reasons, including for the protection of investors, depositors, policy holders or persons to whom a fiduciary duty is owed by a financial service supplier, or to ensure the integrity and stability of the financial system. Where such measures do not conform with the provisions of the Agreement, they shall not be used as a means of avoiding the obligations of a Party under the Agreement.

2.   Nothing in the Agreement shall be construed to require a Party to disclose information relating to the affairs and accounts of individual customers or any confidential or proprietary information in the possession of public entities.

Article 27

The provisions of this Agreement shall not prejudice the application by each Party of any measure necessary to prevent the circumvention of its measures concerning third-country access to its market, through the provisions of this Agreement.

Article 28

1.   Notwithstanding the provisions of Chapter I of this Title, a Community company or a Kyrgyz company established in the territory of the Kyrgyz Republic or the Community respectively shall be entitled to employ, or have employed by one of its subsidiaries or branches, in accordance with the legislation in force in the host country of establishment, in the territory of the Kyrgyz Republic and the Community respectively, employees who are nationals of Community Member States and the Kyrgyz Republic respectively, provided that such employees are key personnel as defined in paragraph 2, and that they are employed exclusively by companies, or branches. The residence and work permits of such employees shall only cover the period of such employment.

2.   Key personnel of the abovementioned companies herein referred to as "organisations" are "intra-corporate transferees" as defined in (c) in the following categories, provided that the organisation is a legal person and that the persons concerned have been employed by it or have been partners in it (other than majority shareholders), for at least the year immediately preceding such movement:

(a)   persons working in a senior position with an organisation, who primarily direct the management of the establishment, receiving general supervision or direction principally from the board of directors or stockholders of the business or their equivalent, including:

- directing the establishment or a department or subdivision of the establishment,

- supervising and controlling the work of other supervisory, professional or managerial employees,

- having the authority personally to hire and fire or recommend hiring, firing or other personnel actions;

(b)   persons working within an organisation who possess uncommon knowledge essential to the establishment's service, research equipment, techniques or management. The assessment of such knowledge may reflect, apart from knowledge specific to the establishment, a high level of qualification referring to a type of work or trade requiring specific technical knowledge, including membership of an accredited profession;

(c)   an "intra-corporate transferee" is defined as a natural person working within an organisation in the territory of a Party, and being temporarily transferred in the context of pursuit of economic activities in the territory of the other Party; the organisation concerned must have its principal place of business in the territory of a Party and the transfer be to an establishment (branch, subsidiary) of that organisation, effectively pursuing like economic activities in the territory of the other Party.

Article 29

The Parties recognise the importance of granting each other national treatment with regard to the establishment and operation of each other's companies in their territories and agree to consider the possibility of movement towards this end on a mutually satisfactory basis, and in the light of any recommendations by the Cooperation Council.

Article 30

1.   The Parties shall use their best endeavours to avoid taking any measures or actions which render the conditions for the establishment and operation of each other's companies more restrictive than the situation existing on the day preceding the date of signature of the Agreement.

2.   The provisions of this Article are without prejudice to those of Article 38: the situations covered by such Article 38 shall be solely governed by its provisions to the exclusion of any other.

3.   Acting in the spirit of partnership and cooperation and in the light of the provisions of Article 44 the Government of the Kyrgyz Republic shall inform the Community of its intentions to submit new legislation or adopt new regulations which may render the conditions for the establishment or operation in the Kyrgyz Republic of subsidiaries and branches of Community companies more restrictive than the situation existing on the day preceding the date of signature of the Agreement. The Community may request the Kyrgyz Republic to communicate the drafts of such legislation or regulations and to enter into consultations about those drafts.

4.   Where new legislation or regulations introduced in the Kyrgyz Republic would result in rendering the conditions for operation of subsidiaries and branches of Community companies established in the Kyrgyz Republic more restrictive than the situation existing on the day of signature of the Agreement, such respective legislation or regulations shall not apply during three years following the entry into force of the relevant act to those subsidiaries and branches already established in the Kyrgyz Republic at the time of entry into force of the relevant act.

CHAPTER III

CROSS-BORDER SUPPLY OF SERVICES BETWEEN THE COMMUNITY AND THE KYRGYZ REPUBLIC

Article 31

1.   The Parties undertake in accordance with the provisions of this Chapter to take the necessary steps to allow progressively the supply of services by Community or Kyrgyz

companies which are established in a Party other than that of the person for whom the services are intended taking into account the development of the service sectors in the Parties.

2.   The Cooperation Council shall make recommendations for the implementation of paragraph 1.

Article 32

The Parties shall cooperate with the aim of developing a market-oriented service sector in the Kyrgyz Republic.

Article 33

1.   The Parties undertake to apply effectively the principle of unrestricted access to the international maritime market and traffic on a commercial basis:

(a)   the above provision does not prejudice the rights and obligations arising from the United Nations Convention on a Code of Conduct for Liner Conferences, as applicable to one or other Contracting Party to this Agreement. Non-conference lines will be free to operate in competition with a conference as long as they adhere to the principle of fair competition on a commercial basis;

(b)   the Parties affirm their commitment to a freely competitive environment as being an essential feature of the dry and liquid bulk trade.

2.   In applying the principles of paragraph 1, the Parties shall:

(a)   not apply, as from entry into force of this agreement, any cargo-sharing provisions of bilateral agreements between any Member States of the Community and the former Soviet Union;

(b)   not introduce cargo-sharing clauses into future bilateral agreements with third countries, other than in those exceptional circumstances where liner shipping companies from one or other Party to this Agreement would not otherwise have an effective opportunity to ply for trade to and from the third country concerned;

(c)   prohibit cargo sharing arrangements in future bilateral agreements concerning dry and liquid bulk trade;

(d)   abolish upon entry into force of this Agreement, all unilateral measures, administrative, technical and other obstacles which could have restrictive or discriminatory effects on the free supply of services in international maritime transport.

Article 34

With a view to assuring a coordinated development of transport between the Parties, adapted to their commercial needs, the conditions of mutual market access and provision of services in transport by road, rail and inland waterways and, if applicable, in air transport may be dealt with by specific agreements where appropriate negotiated between the Parties after entry into force of this Agreement.

CHAPTER IV

GENERAL PROVISIONS

Article 35

1.   The provisions of this Title shall be applied subject to limitations justified on grounds of public policy, public security or public health.

2.   They shall not apply to activities which in the territory of either Party are connected, even occasionally, with the exercise of official authority.

Article 36

For the purpose of this Title, nothing in the Agreement shall prevent the Parties from applying their laws and regulations regarding entry and stay, work, labour conditions and establishment of natural persons and supply of services, provided that, in so doing, they do not apply them in a manner as to nullify or impair the benefits accruing to any Party under the terms of a specific provision of the Agreement. The above provision does not prejudice the application of Article 35.

Article 37

Companies which are controlled and exclusively owned by Kyrgyz companies and Community companies jointly shall also be beneficiaries of the provisions of Chapters II, III and IV.

Article 38

Treatment granted by either Party to the other thereunder shall, as from the day one month prior to the date of entry into force of the relevant obligations of the General Agreement on Trade in Services (GATS), in respect of sectors or measures covered by the GATS, in no case be more favourable than that accorded by such first Party under the provisions of GATS and this in respect of each service sector, sub-sector and mode of supply.

Article 39

For the purposes of Chapters II, III and IV, no account shall be taken of treatment accorded by the Community, its Member States or the Kyrgyz Republic pursuant to commitments entered into in economic integration agreements in accordance with the principles of Article V of the GATS.

Article 40

1.   The most-favoured-nation treatment granted in accordance with the provisions of this Title shall not apply to the tax advantages which the Parties are providing or will provide in the future on the basis of agreements to avoid double taxation, or other tax arrangements.

2.   Nothing in this Title shall be construed to prevent the adoption or enforcement by the Parties of any measure aimed at preventing the avoidance or evasion of taxes pursuant to the tax provisions of agreements to avoid double taxation and other tax arrangements, or domestic fiscal legislation.

3.   Nothing in this Title shall be construed to prevent Member States or the Kyrgyz Republic from distinguishing, in the application of the relevant provisions of their fiscal legislation, between tax payers who are not in identical situtations, in particular as regards their place of residence.

Article 41

Without prejudice to Article 28, no provision of Chapters II, III and IV shall be interpreted as giving the right to:

- nationals of the Member States or of the Kyrgyz Republic respectively to enter, or stay in, the territory of the Kyrgyz Republic or the Community respectively in any capacity whatsoever, and in particular as a shareholder or partner in a company or manager or employee thereof or supplier or recipient of services,

- Community subsidiaries or branches of Kyrgyz companies to employ or have employed in the territory of the Community nationals of the Kyrgyz Republic,

- Kyrgyz subsidiaries or branches of Community companies to employ or have employed in the territory of the Kyrgyz Republic nationals of the Member States,

- Kyrgyz companies or Community subsidiaries or branches of Kyrgyz companies to supply Kyrgyz persons to act for and under the control of other persons by temporary employment contracts,

- Community companies or Kyrgyz subsidiaries or branches of Community companies to supply workers who are nationals of the Member States by temporary employment contracts.

CHAPTER V

CURRENT PAYMENTS AND CAPITAL

Article 42

1.   The Parties undertake to authorise in freely convertible currency, any payments on the current account of balance of payments between residents of the Community and of the Kyrgyz Republic connected with the movement of goods, services or persons made in accordance with the provisions of this Agreement.

2.   With regard to transactions on the capital account of balance of payments, from entry into force of the Agreement, the free movement of capital relating to direct investments made in companies formed in accordance with the laws of the host country and investments made in

accordance with the provisions of Chapter II, and the liquidation or repatriation of these investments and of any profit stemming therefrom shall be ensured.

3. Without prejudice to paragraph 2 or to paragraph 5, as from entry into force of this Agreement, no new foreign exchange restrictions on the movement of capital and current payments connected therewith between residents of the Community and the Kyrgyz Republic shall be introduced and the existing arrangements shall not become more restrictive.

4. The Parties shall consult each other with a view to facilitating the movement of forms of capital other than those referred to in paragraph 2 above between the Community and the Kyrgyz Republic in order to promote the objectives of this Agreement.

5. With reference to the provisions of this Article, until a full convertibility of the Kyrgyz currency within the meaning of Article VIII of the Articles of Agreement of the International Monetary Fund (IMF) is introduced, the Kyrgyz Republic may in exceptional circumstances apply exchange restrictions connected with the granting or taking up of short and medium-term financial credits to the extent that such restrictions are imposed on the Kyrgyz Republic for the granting of such credits and are permitted according to the Kyrgyz Republic's status under the IMF. The Kyrgyz Republic shall apply these restrictions in a non-discriminatory manner. They shall be applied in such a manner as to cause the least possible disruption to this Agreement. The Kyrgyz Republic shall inform the Cooperation Council promptly of the introduction of such measures and of any changes therein.

6. Without prejudice to paragraphs 1 and 2, where, in exceptional circumstances, movement of capital between the Community and the Kyrgyz Republic causes, or threaten to cause, serious difficulties for the operation of exchange rate policy or monetary policy in the Community or the Kyrgyz Republic, the Community and the Kyrgyz Republic, respectively, may take safeguard measures with regard to movements of capital between the Community and the Kyrgyz Republic for a period not exceeding six months if such measures are strictly necessary.

CHAPTER VI

INTELLECTUAL, INDUSTRIAL AND COMMERCIAL PROPERTY PROTECTION

Article 43

1. Pursuant to the provisions of this Article and of Annex II, the Kyrgyz Republic shall continue to improve the protection of intellectual, industrial and commercial property rights in order to provide, by the end of the fifth year after the entry into force of the Agreement, for a level of protection similar to that existing in the Community, including effective means of enforcing such rights. The Cooperation Council may decide to extend the above period, in the light of particular circumstances prevailing in the Kyrgyz Republic.

2. By the end of the fifth year after entry into force of the Agreement, the Kyrgyz Republic shall accede to the multilateral conventions on intellectual, industrial and commercial property rights referred to in paragraph 1 of Annex II to which Member States are parties or which are de facto applied by Member States, according to the relevant provisions contained in these conventions.

TITLE V

LEGISLATIVE COOPERATION

Article 44

1.   The Parties recognise that an important condition for strengthening the economic links between the Kyrgyz Republic and the Community is the approximation of Kyrgyz Republic's existing and future legislation to that of the Community. The Kyrgyz Republic shall endeavour to ensure that its legislation will be gradually made compatible with that of the Community.

2.   The approximation of laws shall extend to the following areas in particular: customs law, company law, banking law, company accounts and taxes, intellectual property, protection of workers at the workplace, financial services, rules on competition, public procurement, protection of health and life of humans, animals and plants, the environment, consumer protection, indirect taxation, technical rules and standards, nuclear laws and regulations and transport.

3.   The Community shall provide the Kyrgyz Republic with technical assistance for the implementation of these measures, which may include, inter alia:

- the exchange of experts,
- the provision of early information especially on relevant legislation,
- organisation of seminars,
- training activities,
- aid for translation of Community legislation in the relevant sectors.

4.   The Parties agree to examine ways to apply their respective competition laws on a concerted basis in such cases where trade between them is affected.

TITLE VI

ECONOMIC COOPERATION

Article 45

1.   The Community and the Kyrgyz Republic shall establish economic cooperation aimed at contributing to the process of economic reform and recovery and sustainable development of the Kyrgyz Republic. Such cooperation shall strengthen existing economic links, to the benefit of both parties.

2.   Policies and other measures will be designed to bring about economic and social reforms and restructuring of the economic system in the Kyrgyz Republic and will be guided by the requirements of sustainability and harmonious social development; they will also fully incorporate environmental considerations.

3.   To this end the cooperation will concentrate, in particular, on economic and social development, human resources development, support for enterprises (including privatisation,

investment and development of financial services), agriculture and food, energy and civil nuclear safety, transport, tourism, environmental protection and regional cooperation.

4.   Special attention shall be devoted to measures capable of fostering cooperation between the Independent States with a view to stimulating a harmonious development of the region.

5.   Where appropriate, economic cooperation and other forms of cooperation provided for in this Agreement may be supported by technical assistance from the Community, taking into account the Community's relevant Council regulation applicable to technical assistance in the Independent States, the priorities agreed upon in the indicative programme related to Community technical assistance to the Kyrgyz Republic and its established coordination and implementation procedures.

Article 46
Industrial cooperation

1.   Cooperation shall aim at promoting the following in particular:

- the development of business links between economic operators of both sides,
- Community participation in Kyrgyzstan's efforts to restructure its industry,
- the improvement of management,
- the development of appropriate commercial rules and practices,
- environmental protection.

2.   The provisions of this Article shall not affect the enforcement of Community competition rules applicable to undertakings.

Article 47
Investment promotion and protection

1.   Bearing in mind the respective powers and competences of the Community and the Member States, cooperation shall aim to establish a favourable climate for private investment, both domestic and foreign, especially through better conditions for investment protection, the transfer of capital and the exchange of information on investment opportunities.

2.   The aims of cooperation shall be in particular:

- the conclusion, where appropriate, between the Member States and the Kyrgyz Republic of agreements for the promotion and protection of investment,

- the conclusion, where appropriate, between the Member States and the Kyrgyz Republic of agreements to avoid double taxation,

- the creation of favourable conditions for attracting foreign investments into the Kyrgyz economy,

- to establish stable and adequate business law and conditions, and to exchange information on laws, regulations and administrative practices in the field of investment,

- to exchange information on investment opportunities in the form of, inter alia, trade fairs, exhibitions, trade weeks and other events.

Article 48
Public procurement

The Parties shall cooperate to develop conditions for open and competitive award of contracts for goods and services in particular through calls for tenders.

Article 50
Mining and raw materials

1.   The Parties shall aim at increasing investment and trade in mining and raw materials.

2.   The cooperation shall focus in particular on the following areas:

- exchange of information on the prospects of the mining and non-ferrous metals sectors,
- the establishment of a legal framework for cooperation,
- trade matters,
- the adoption and implementation of environmental legislation,
- training,
- safety in the mining industry.

Article 51
Cooperation in science and technology

1.   The Parties shall promote cooperation in civil scientific research and technological development (RTD) on the basis of mutual benefit and, taking into account the availability of resources, adequate access to their respective programmes and subject to appropriate levels of effective protection of intellectual, industrial and commercial property rights (IPR).

2.   Science and technology cooperation shall cover:

- the exchange of scientific and technical information,

- joint RTD activities,

- training activities and mobility programmes for scientists, researchers and technicians engaged in RTD on both sides.

Where such cooperation takes the form of activities involving education and/or training, it should be carried out in accordance with the provisions of Article 52.

The Parties, on the basis of mutual agreement, can engage in other forms of cooperation in science and technology.

In carrying out such cooperation activities, special attention shall be devoted to the redeployment of scientists, engineers, researchers and technicians which are or have been engaged in research and/or production of weapons of mass destruction.

3.   The Cooperation covered by this Article shall be implemented according to specific arrangements to be negotiated and concluded in accordance with the procedures adopted by each Party, and which shall set out, inter alia, appropriate IPR provisions.

Article 53
Agriculture and the agro-industrial sector

The purpose of cooperation in this area shall be the pursuance of agrarian reform, the modernisation, privatisation and restructuring of agriculture, the agro-industrial and service sectors in the Kyrgyz Republic, development of domestic and foreign markets for the Kyrgyz products, in conditions that ensure the protection of the environment, taking into account the necessity to improve security of food supply as well as the development of agri-business, the processing and distribution of agricultural products. The Parties shall also aim at the gradual approximation of Kyrgyz standards to Community technical regulations concerning industrial and agricultural food products including sanitary and phytosanitary standards.

Article 54
Energy

1.   Cooperation shall take place within the principles of the market economy and the European Energy Charter, against a background of the progressive integration of the energy markets in Europe.

2.   The cooperation shall include among others the following areas:

- the environmental impact of energy production supply and consumption, in order to prevent or minimise the environmental damage resulting from these activities,

- improvement of the quality and security of energy supply, including diversification of supply, in an economic and environmentally sound manner,

- formulation of energy policy,
- improvement in management and regulation of the energy sector in line with a market economy,

- the introduction of the range of institutional, legal, fiscal and other conditions necessary to encourage increased energy trade and investment,

- promotion of energy saving and energy effectiveness,

- modernisation of energy infrastructure,

- improvement of energy technologies in supply and end use across the range of energy types,

- management and technical training in the energy sector,

- security in energy supply, transportation and transit of energy and energy materials.

Article 56
Transport

The Parties shall develop and strengthen their cooperation in the field of transport.

This cooperation shall, inter alia, aim at restructuring and modernising transport systems and networks in the Kyrgyz Republic, and developing and ensuring, where appropriate, compatibility of transportation systems in the context of achieving a more global transport system.
The cooperation shall include, inter alia:

- the modernising of management and operations of road transport, railways, ports and airports,

  - modernisation and development of railways, waterways, roads, ports, airports and air navigation infrastructure including the modernisation of major routes of common interest and the trans-European links for the above modes,

  - promotion and development of multi-modal transport,

  - the promotion of joint research and development programmes,

  - preparation of the legislative and institutional framework for policy development and implementation including privatisation of the transport sector.

Article 57
Postal services and telecommunications

Within their respective powers and competences the Parties shall expand and strengthen cooperation in the following areas:

  - the establishment of policies and guidelines for the development of the telecommunications sector and postal services,

  - development of principles of a tariff policy and marketing in telecommunications and postal services,

  - carry out transfer of technology and know-how, including on European technical standards and certification systems,

  - encouraging the development of projects for telecommunications and postal services and attracting investment,

  - enhancing efficiency and quality of the provision of telecommunications and postal services, amongst others through liberalisation of activities of sub-sectors,

  - advanced application of telecommunications, notably in the area of electronic funds transfer,

  - management of telecommunications networks and their "optimisation",

- an appropriate regulatory basis for the provision of telecommunication and postal services and for the use of the radio frequency spectrum,

- training in the field of telecommunications and postal services for operations in market conditions.

Article 58
Financial services

Cooperation shall in particular aim at facilitating the involvement of the Kyrgyz Republic in universally accepted systems of mutual settlements. Technical assistance shall focus on:

- the development of banking and financial services, the development of a common market of credit resources, the involvement of the Kyrgyz Republic in a universally accepted system of mutual settlements,

- the development of fiscal system and its institutions in the Kyrgyz Republic, exchange of experience and personnel training,

- the development of insurance services, which would, inter alia, create a favourable framework for Community companies participation in the establishment of joint ventures in the insurance sector in the Kyrgyz Republic, as well as the development of export credit insurance.

This cooperation shall in particular contribute to foster the development of relations between the Kyrgyz Republic and the Member States in the financial services sector.

Article 59
Money laundering

1.	The Parties agree on the necessity of making efforts and cooperating in order to prevent the use of their financial systems for laundering of proceeds from criminal activities in general and drug offences in particular.

2.	Cooperation in this area shall include administrative and technical assistance with the purpose of establishing suitable standards against money laundering equivalent to those adopted by the Community and international forums in this field, including the Financial Action Task Force (FATF).

Article 63
Small and medium-sized enterprises

1.	The Parties shall aim to develop and strengthen small and medium-sized enterprises and their associations and cooperation between SMEs in the Community and the Kyrgyz Republic.

2.	Cooperation shall include technical assistance, in particular in the following areas:

- the development of a legislative framework for SMEs,

- the development of an appropriate infrastructure (an agency to support SMEs, communications, assistance to the creation of a fund for SMEs),

- the development of technology parks.

ANNEX II

INTELLECTUAL, INDUSTRIAL AND COMMERCIAL PROPERTY CONVENTIONS REFERRED TO IN ARTICLE 43

1.   Paragraph 2 of Article 43 concerns the following multilateral conventions:

- Berne Convention for the Protection of Literary and Artistic Works (Paris Act, 1971),

- International Convention for the Protection of Performers, Producers of Phonograms and Broadcasting Organisations (Rome, 1961),

- Protocol relating to the Madrid Agreement concerning the International Registration of Marks (Madrid, 1989),

- Nice Agreement concerning the International Classification of Goods and Services for the purposes of the Registration of Marks (Geneva 1977, and amended in 1979),

- Budapest Treaty on the International Recognition of the Deposit of Micro-organisms for the purposes of Patent Procedures (1977, modified in 1980),

- International Convention for the Protection of New Varieties of Plants (UPOV) (Geneva Act, 1991).

2.   The Cooperation Council may recommend that paragraph 2 of Article 43 shall apply to other multilateral conventions. If problems in the area of intellectual, industrial and commercial property affecting trading conditions were to occur, urgent consultations will be undertaken, at the request of either party, with a view to reaching mutually satisfactory solutions.

3.   The Parties confirm the importance they attach to the obligations arising from the following multilateral conventions:

- Paris Convention for the Protection of Industrial Property (Stockholm Act, 1967 and amended in 1979),

- Madrid Agreement concerning the International Registration of Marks (Stockholm Act, 1967, and amended in 1979),

- Patent Cooperation Treaty (Washington, 1970, amended in 1979 and modified in 1984).

4.   From the entry into force of this Agreement, the Kyrgyz Republic shall grant to Community companies and nationals, in respect of the recognition and protection of intellectual, industrial and commercial property, treatment no less favourable than that granted by it to any third country under bilateral agreements.

5.   The provisions of paragraph 4 shall not apply to advantages granted by the Kyrgyz Republic to any third country on an effective reciprocal basis and to advantages granted by the Kyrgyz Republic to another country of the former USSR.

*

EUROPE AGREEMENT ESTABLISHING AN ASSOCIATION BETWEEN THE EUROPEAN COMMUNITIES AND THEIR MEMBER STATES, OF THE ONE PART, AND THE REPUBLIC OF LITHUANIA, OF THE OTHER PART*
[excerpts]

The Europe Agreement Establishing an Association between the European Communities and Their Member States, of the One Part, and the Republic of Lithuania, of the Other Part was signed on 12 June 1995. It entered into force on 1 February 1998. The member States of the European Communities are: Austria, Belgium, Denmark, Finland, France, Germany, Greece, Ireland, Italy, Luxembourg, the Netherlands, Portugal, Spain, Sweden and the United Kingdom.

TITLE IV
MOVEMENT OF WORKERS, ESTABLISHMENT, SUPPLY OF SERVICES

CHAPTER II
ESTABLISHMENT

Article 44

1.   The Community and its Member States shall grant, except for the sectors included in Annex XVI, from entry into force of this Agreement:

(i)   treatment no less favourable than that accorded by Member States to their own companies or to any third country company, whichever is the better, with regard to the establishment of Lithuanian companies;

(ii)   to subsidiaries and branches of Lithuanian companies, established in their territory, treatment no less favourable than that accorded by Member States to their own companies and branches or to subsidiaries and branches of any third country company established in their territory, whichever is the better, in respect of their operation.

2.   Lithuania shall facilitate the setting up of operations on its territory by Community companies and nationals. To that end, it shall, except for the sectors included in Annex XVIIa:

(i)   grant, from entry into force of the Agreement, for the establishment of Community companies, treatment no less favourable than that accorded to its own companies or to companies of any third country, whichever is the better, save for the sectors

---

*   *Source*: European Communities (1998). "Europe Agreement Establishing an Association between the European Communities and Their Member States, of the One Part, and the Republic of Lithuania, of the Other Part", *Official Journal of the European Communities*, L 051, 20 February 1998 pp. 3 - 242; available also on the Internet (http://www.europa.eu.int/eur-lex/en/lif/dat/1998/en_298A0220_01.html). [Note added by the editor.]

referred to in Annex XVIIb, where national treatment shall be granted at the latest by the end of the transitional period referred to in Article 3;

(ii)   grant, from entry into force of this Agreement, for the operation of branches and subsidiaries of Community companies, established in Lithuania, treatment no less favourable than that accorded to its own companies or to subsidiaries and branches of any third country company established in its territory, whichever is the better.

3.   Lithuania shall, during the transitional period referred to in paragraph 2 (i) not adopt any measures or actions which introduce discrimination as regards the establishment and operations of Community companies and nationals in its territory in comparison with its own companies and nationals.

4.   The Association Council shall examine regularly the possibility of accelerating the granting of national treatment in the sectors referred to in Annex XVIIb and the inclusion of areas or matters listed in Annex XVIIa within the scope of application of paragraph 2 of this Article. Amendments may be made to these Annexes by decision of the Association Council.

Following the expiration of the transitional period referred to in Article 3, the Association Council may exceptionally, on request of Lithuania, and if the necessity arises, decide to prolong the duration of exclusion of certain areas or matters listed in Annex XVIIb for a limited period of time.

5.   The treatment described in paragraphs 1 and 2 shall be applicable for the establishment and operation of nationals as from the end of the transitional period referred to in Article 3.

6.   Notwithstanding the provisions of Article 44(2), Lithuanian subsidiaries and branches of Community companies shall have, from entry into force of this Agreement, the right to acquire, use, rent and sell real property, and as regards natural resources, agricultural land and forestry, the right to lease, where these are directly necessary for the conduct of economic activities for which they are established.

By the end of the transitional period referred to in Article 3 Lithuania shall grant these rights to Community nationals established in Lithuania.

Article 45

1.   The provisions of Article 44 shall not apply to air transport, inland waterways and maritime cabotage transport services.

2.   The Association Council may make recommendations for improving establishment and operations in the areas covered by paragraph 1.

Article 46

For the purposes of this Agreement:

(a)   a 'Community company` or a 'Lithuanian company` respectively shall mean a company set up in accordance with the laws of a Member State or of Lithuania respectively and having its registered office or central administration or principal place of business within the Community or in the territory of Lithuania respectively.

However, should the company, set up in accordance with the laws of a Member State or Lithuania respectively, have only its registered office within the Community or in the territory of Lithuania respectively, the company shall be considered a Community or Lithuanian company respectively if its operations possess a real and continuous link with the economy of one of the Member States or Lithuania respectively;

(b)   'subsidiary` of a company shall mean a company which is effectively controlled by the first company,

(c)   'branch` of a company shall mean a place of business not having legal personality which has the appearance of permanency, such as the extension of a parent body, has a management and is materially equipped to negotiate business with third parties so that the latter, although knowing that there will, if necessary, be a legal link with the parent body, the head office of which is abroad, do not have to deal directly with such parent body but may transact business at the place of business constituting the extension.

(d)   'establishment` shall mean:

(i)   as regards nationals, the right to take up economic activities as self-employed persons and to set up undertakings, in particular companies, which they effectively control. Self-employment and business undertakings by nationals shall not extend to seeking or taking employment in the labour market or confer a right of access to the labour market of another Party. The provisions of this Chapter do not apply to those who are not exclusively self-employed;

(ii)   as regards Community or Lithuanian companies, the right to take up economic activities by means of the setting up of subsidiaries and branches in Lithuania or in the Community respectively;

(e)   'operation` shall mean the pursuit of economic activities;

(f)   'economic activities` shall in principle include activities of an industrial, commercial and professional character and activities of craftsmen;

(g)   'Community national` and 'Lithuanian national` shall mean respectively a natural person who is a national of one of the Member States or of Lithuania;

(h)   with regard to international maritime transport, including intermodal operations involving a sea leg, nationals of the Member States or of Lithuania established outside the Community or Lithuania respectively, and shipping companies established outside the Community or Lithuania and controlled by nationals of a Member State or Lithuanian nationals respectively, shall also be beneficiaries of the provisions of Chapter II and Chapter III, if their vessels are registered in that Member State or in Lithuania respectively in accordance with their respective legislation.

Article 47

1.   Subject to the provisions of Article 44, with the exception of financial services described in Annex XVIII, each Party may regulate the establishment and operation of companies and nationals on its territory, in so far as these regulations do not discriminate against companies and nationals of the other Party in comparison with its own companies and nationals.

2.   In respect of financial services, notwithstanding any other provisions of this Agreement, a Party shall not be prevented from taking measures for prudential reasons, including for the protection of investors, depositors, policyholders or persons to whom a fiduciary duty is owed by a financial service supplier, or to ensure the integrity and stability of the financial system. Such measures shall not be used as a means of avoiding the Party's obligations under the Agreement.

3.   Nothing in the Agreement shall be construed to require a Party to disclose information relating to the affairs and accounts of individual customers or any confidential or proprietary information in the possession of public entities.

Article 48

1.   The provisions of Articles 44 and 47 do not preclude the application by a Party of particular rules concerning the establishment and operation in its territory of branches of companies of another Party not incorporated in the territory of the first Party, which are justified by legal or technical differences between such branches as compared with branches of companies incorporated in its territory or, as regards financial services, for prudential reasons.

2.   The difference in treatment shall not go beyond what is strictly necessary as a result of such legal or technical differences or, as regards financial services, for prudential reasons.

Article 49

1.   A 'Community company` or a 'Lithuanian company` established in the territory of Lithuania or the Community respectively shall be entitled to employ, or have employed by one of its subsidiaries or branches, in accordance with the legislation in force in the host country of establishment, in the territory of Lithuania and the Community respectively, employees who are nationals of Community Member States and Lithuania respectively, provided that such employees are key personnel as defined in paragraph 2 of this Article, and that they are employed exclusively by companies, subsidiaries or branches.

The residence and work permits of such employees shall only cover the period of such employment.

2.   Key personnel of the abovementioned companies herein referred to as 'organisations` are 'intracorporate transferees` as defined in (c) of this paragraph in the following categories, provided that the organisation is a juridical person and that the persons concerned have been employed by it or have been partners in it (other than as majority shareholders), for at least the year immediately preceding such movement:

(a)   persons working in a senior position with an organisation, who primarily direct the management of the establishment, receiving general supervision or direction principally from the board of directors or stockholders of the business or their equivalent, including:

- directing the establishment or a department or sub-division of the establishment,

- supervising and controlling the work of other supervisory, professional or managerial employees,

- having the authority personally to recruit and dismiss or recommend recruiting, dismissing or other personnel actions;

(b) persons working within an organisation who possess uncommon knowledge essential to the establishment's service, research equipment, techniques or management. The assessment of such knowledge may reflect, apart from knowledge specific to the establishment, a high level of qualification referring to a type of work or trade requiring specific technical knowledge, including membership of an accredited profession;

(c) an 'intracorporate transferee` is defined as a natural person working within an organisation in the territory of a Party, and being temporarily transferred in the context of pursuit of economic activities in the territory of the other Party; the organisation concerned must have its principal place of business in the territory of a Party and the transfer be to an establishment (branch, subsidiary) of that organisation, effectively pursuing like economic activities in the territory of the other Party.

3. The entry into and the temporary presence within the territory of the Community or Lithuania of Lithuanian and Community nationals respectively shall be permitted, when these representatives of companies are persons working in a senior position, as defined in paragraph 2

(a), within a company, and are responsible for the setting up of a Community subsidiary or branch of a Lithuanian company or of a Lithuanian subsidiary or branch of a Community company in a Community Member State or Lithuania respectively, when:

- those representatives are not engaged in making direct sales or supplying services, and

- the company has its principal place of business outside the Community or Lithuania, respectively, and has no other representative, office, branch or subsidiary in that Community Member State or Lithuania respectively.

Article 50

In order to make it easier for the Community nationals and Lithuanian nationals to take up and pursue regulated professional activities in Lithuania and the Community respectively, the Association Council shall examine which steps are necessary to be taken to provide for the mutual recognition of qualifications. It may take all necessary measures to that end.

Article 51

During the transitional period referred to in Article 3, Lithuania may introduce measures which derogate from the provisions of this Chapter as regards the establishment of Community companies and nationals if certain industries:

- are undergoing restructuring, or

- are facing serious difficulties, particularly where these entail serious social problems in Lithuania, or

- face the elimination or a drastic reduction of the total market share held by Lithuanian companies or nationals in a given sector or industry in Lithuania, or

- are newly emerging industries in Lithuania.
Such measures:

- shall cease to apply at the latest on the expiration of the transitional period referred to in Article 3,

- shall be reasonable and necessary in order to remedy the situation, and

- shall only relate to establishments in Lithuania to be created after the entry into force of such measures and shall not introduce discrimination concerning the operations of Community companies or nationals already established in Lithuania at the time of introduction of a given measure compared with Lithuanian companies or nationals.

While devising and applying such measures, Lithuania shall grant whenever possible to Community companies and nationals a preferential treatment, and in no case a treatment less favourable than that accorded to companies or nationals from any third country.

Prior to the introduction of these measures, Lithuania shall consult the Association Council and shall not put them into effect before a one-month period following the notification of the Association Council of the concrete measures to be introduced by Lithuania, except where the threat of irreparable damage requires the taking of urgent measures in which case Lithuania shall consult the Association Council immediately after their introduction.

On expiration of the transitional period referred to in Article 3, Lithuania may introduce such measures only with the authorisation of the Association Council and under conditions determined by the latter.

CHAPTER III
SUPPLY OF SERVICES

Article 52

1.   The Parties undertake in accordance with the following provisions to take the necessary steps to allow progressively the supply of services by Community or Lithuanian companies or

nationals which are established in a Party other than that of the person for whom the services are intended.

2.   In step with the liberalisation process mentioned in paragraph 1, and subject to the provisions of Article 56, the Parties shall permit the temporary movement of natural persons providing the service or who are employed by the service provider as key personnel as defined in Article 49(2), including natural persons who are representatives of a Community or Lithuanian company or national and are seeking temporary entry for the purpose of negotiating for the sale of services or entering into agreements to sell services for that service provider, where those representatives will not be engaged in making direct sales to the general public or in supplying services themselves.

3.   At the latest eight years after the entry into force of this Agreement, the Association Council shall take the measures necessary to implement progressively the provisions of paragraph 1. Account shall be taken of the progress achieved by the Parties in the approximation of their laws.

Article 53

1.   The Parties shall not take any measures or actions which render the conditions for the supply of services by Community and Lithuanian nationals or companies which are established in a Party other than that of the person for whom the services are intended significantly more restrictive as compared with the situation existing on the day preceding the day of entry into force of the Agreement.

2.   If one Party is of the view that measures introduced by the other Party since the signature of the Agreement result in a situation which is significantly more restrictive in respect of supply of services as compared with the situation existing at the date of signature of the Agreement, such first Party may request the other Party to enter into consultations.

Article 54

1.   With regard to international maritime transport, the Parties undertake to apply effectively the principle of unrestricted access to the market and traffic on a commercial basis.

    (a)   The above provision does not prejudice the rights and obligations arising from the United Nations Code of Conduct for Liner Conferences, as applicable to one or other Party to the present Agreement. Non-conference lines will be free to operate in competition with a conference as long as they adhere to the principle of fair competition on a commercial basis.

    (b)   The Parties affirm their commitment to a freely competitive environment as being an essential feature of the dry and liquid bulk trade.

2.   In applying the principles of paragraph 1, the Parties shall:

    (a)   not apply, as from entry into force of this Agreement, any cargo-sharing provisions of bilateral agreements between any Member State of the Community and the former Soviet Union;

(b)   not introduce cargo-sharing clauses into future bilateral agreements with third countries, other than in those exceptional circumstances where liner shipping companies from one or other Party to the present Agreement would not otherwise have an effective opportunity to ply for trade to and from the third country concerned;

(c)   prohibit cargo-sharing arrangements in future bilateral agreements concerning dry and liquid bulk trade;

(d)   abolish on entry into force of this Agreement all unilateral measures, administrative, technical and other obstacles which could have restrictive or discriminatory effects on the free supply of services in international maritime transport.

Each Party shall grant, inter alia, no less favourable treatment for the ships operated by nationals or companies of the other Party than that accorded to a Party's own ships with regard to access to ports open to international trade, the use of infrastructure and auxiliary maritime services of the ports, as well as related fees and charges, customs facilities and the assignment of berths and facilities for loading and unloading.

3.   Nationals and companies of the Community providing international maritime transport services shall be free to provide international sea-river services in the inland waterways of Lithuania and vice versa.

4.   With a view to ensuring the transit of goods through the territory of each Party, the Parties undertake to conclude an agreement as soon as possible and before the end of 1999 on the transit of intermodal traffic through each other's territory.

5.   With a view to assuring a coordinated development and progressive liberalisation of transport between the Parties, adapted to their reciprocal commercial needs, the conditions of mutual market access and provision of services in transport by road, rail and inland waterways and, if applicable, in air transport shall be dealt with by specific transport agreements where appropriate, negotiated between the Parties after entry into force of this Agreement.

6.   Prior to the conclusion of the agreements referred to in paragraph 5, the Parties shall not take any measures or actions which are more restrictive or discriminatory as compared with the situation existing on the day preceding the day of entry into force of the Agreement.

7.   During the transitional period, Lithuania shall progressively adapt its legislation including administrative, technical and other rules to that of the Community legislation existing at any time in the field of road, rail, inland waterway and air transport in so far as it serves liberalisation purposes and mutual access to markets of the Parties and facilitates the movement of passengers and of goods.

8.   In step with the common progress in the achievement of the objectives of this Chapter, the Association Council shall examine ways of creating the conditions necessary for improving freedom to provide road, rail, inland waterway and air transport services.

CHAPTER IV
GENERAL PROVISIONS

Article 55

1.   The provisions of this Title shall be applied subject to limitations justified on grounds of public policy, public security or public health.

2.   They shall not apply to activities which in the territory of either Party are connected, even occasionally, with the exercise of official authority.

Article 56

For the purpose of this Title nothing in the Agreement shall prevent the Parties from applying their laws and regulations regarding entry and stay, work, labour conditions and establishment of natural persons and supply of services, provided that, in so doing, they do not apply them in a manner as to nullify or impair the benefits accruing to any Party under the terms of a specific provision of the Agreement.

Article 57

Companies which are controlled and exclusively owned by Lithuanian companies or nationals and Community companies or nationals jointly shall also be beneficiaries of the provisions of Chapters II, III and IV of this Title.

Article 58

1.   The most-favoured-nation treatment granted in accordance with the provisions of this Title shall not apply to the tax advantages which the Parties are providing or will provide in the future on the basis of agreements to avoid double taxation, or other tax arrangements.

2.   Nothing in this Title shall be construed to prevent the adoption or enforcement by the Parties of any measure aimed at preventing the avoidance or evasion of taxes pursuant to the tax provisions of agreements to avoid double taxation and other tax arrangements, or domestic fiscal legislation.

3.   Nothing in this Title shall be construed to prevent Member States or Lithuania from distinguishing, in the application of the relevant provisions of their fiscal legislation, between taxpayers who are not in identical situations, in particular as regards their place of residence.

Article 59

The provisions of this Title shall be progressively adjusted by the Parties. In formulating recommendations to this effect, the Association Council shall take into account the respective obligations of the Parties under the General Agreement on Trade in Services (GATS), and in particular of its Article V.

Article 60

The provisions of this Agreement shall not prejudice the application by each Party of any measure necessary to prevent the circumvention of its measures concerning third country access to its market through the provisions of this Agreement.

TITLE V
PAYMENTS, CAPITAL, COMPETITION AND OTHER
ECONOMIC PROVISIONS, APPROXIMATION OF LAWS

CHAPTER I
CURRENT PAYMENTS AND MOVEMENT OF CAPITAL

Article 61

The Parties undertake to authorise, in freely convertible currency, any payments on the current account of balance of payments to the extent that the transaction underlying the payments concerns movements of goods, services, or persons between the Parties which have been liberalised pursuant to the present Agreement.

Article 62

1.   With regard to transactions on the capital account of balance of payments, from entry into force of the Agreement, the Member States and Lithuania respectively shall ensure the free movement of capital relating to direct investments made in companies formed in accordance with the provisions of Chapter II of Title IV, and the liquidation or repatriation of these investments and of any profit stemming therefrom.

The liquidation or repatriation of investments linked to establishment of Community nationals establishing in Lithuania as self-employed persons pursuant to Chapter II of Title IV shall be liberalised from entry into force of this Agreement. Notwithstanding the above provision, complete free movement of capital for all of these investments shall be ensured by the end of the transitional period referred to in Article 3.

2.   With regard to transactions on the capital account of balance of payments, from entry into force of this Agreement the Member States and Lithuania respectively shall ensure the free movement of capital relating to portfolio investment. This shall also apply to the free movement of capital relating to credits related to commercial transactions or the provision of services in which a resident of one of the Parties is participating and to financial loans.

3.   Without prejudice to paragraph 1, the Member States, as from the entry into force of the Agreement, and Lithuania as from the end of the transitional period referred to in Article 3, shall be introduce any new restrictions on the movement of capital and current payments connected therewith between residents of the Community and Lithuania and shall not make the existing arrangements more restrictive.

4.   The provisions of paragraphs 1 and 2 shall not prevent Lithuania from applying restrictions on outward investments by Lithuanian nationals and companies. However, the liquidation or repatriation of investments made in Lithuania and of any profit stemming

therefrom shall not be affected. Five years after the entry into force of this Agreement the Parties agree to consult over the maintenance of any such restrictions, taking into account all the relevant monetary, fiscal and financial considerations.

5.   The Parties shall consult each other with a view to facilitating the movement of capital between the Community and Lithuania in order to promote the objective of the present Agreement.

Article 63

1.   During the transitional period referred to in Article 3, the Parties shall take measures permitting the creation of the necessary conditions for the further gradual application of Community rules on the free movement of capital.

2.   By the end of the transitional period referred to in Article 3, the Association Council shall examine ways of enabling Community rules on the movement of capital to be applied in full.

CHAPTER II
COMPETITION AND OTHER ECONOMIC PROVISIONS

Article 64

1.   The following are incompatible with the proper functioning of this Agreement, in so far as they may affect trade between the Community and Lithuania:

    (i)   all agreements between undertakings, decisions by associations of undertakings and concerted practices between undertakings which have as their object or effect the prevention, restriction or distortion of competition;

    (ii)   abuse by one or more undertakings of a dominant position in the territories of the Community or of Lithuania as a whole or in a substantial part thereof;

    (iii)   any public aid, which distorts or threatens to distort competition by favouring certain undertakings or the production of certain goods.

2.   Any practices contrary to this Article shall be assessed on the basis of criteria arising from the application of the rules of Articles 85, 86 and 92 of the Treaty establishing the European Community or, for products covered by the ECSC Treaty, on the basis of corresponding rules of the ECSC Treaty including secondary legislation.

3.   The Association Council shall, by 31 December 1997, adopt by decision the necessary rules for the implementation of paragraphs 1 and 2.

Until these rules are adopted, the provisions of the Agreement on interpretation and application of Articles VI, XVI and XXIII of the GATT shall be applied as the rules for the implementation of paragraph 1 point (iii) and related parts of paragraph 2.

4.   (a)   For the purposes of applying the provisions of paragraph 1(iii), the Parties recognise that until 31 December 1999, any public aid granted by Lithuania shall

be assessed taking into account the fact that Lithuania shall be regarded as an area identical to those areas of the Community described in Article 92(3)(a) of the Treaty establishing the European Community. The Association Council shall, taking into account the economic situation of Lithuania, decide whether that period should be extended by further periods of five years.

    (b)   Each Party shall ensure transparency in the area of public aid, inter alia, by reporting annually to the other Party on the total amount and the distribution of the aid given and by providing, on request, information on aid schemes. On request by one Party, the other Party shall provide information on particular individual cases of public aid.

5.   With regard to products referred to in Chapters II and III of Title III:

- the provision of paragraph 1(iii) does not apply,

- any practices contrary to paragraph 1(i) should be assessed according to the criteria established by the Community on the basis of Articles 42 and 43 of the Treaty establishing the European Community and in particular of those established in Council Regulation No 26/1962.

6.   If the Community or Lithuania considers that a particular practice is incompatible with the terms of the first paragraph of this Article, and

- is not adequately dealt with under the implementing rules referred to in paragraph 3, or

- in the absence of such rules, and if such practice causes or threatens to cause serious prejudice to the interests of the other Party or material injury to its domestic industry, including its services industry, it may take appropriate measures after consultation within the Association Council or after 30 working days following referral for such consultation.

In the case of practices incompatible with paragraph 1(iii) of this Article, such appropriate measures may, where the GATT applies thereto, only be adopted in conformity with the procedures and under the conditions laid down by the GATT and any other relevant instrument negotiated under its auspices which are applicable between the Parties.

7.   Notwithstanding any provisions to the contrary adopted in conformity with paragraph 3, the Parties shall exchange information taking into account the limitations imposed by the requirements of professional and business secrecy.

Article 65

1.   The Parties shall endeavour to avoid the imposition of restrictive measures including measures relating to imports for balance of payments purposes. In the event of their introduction, the Party having introduced the same shall present to the other Party, as soon as possible, a time schedule for their removal.

2.   Where one or more Member States or Lithuania is in serious balance of payments difficulties, or under imminent threat thereof, the Community or Lithuania, as the case may be, may, in accordance with the conditions established under the GATT, adopt restrictive measures,

including measures relating to imports, which shall be of limited duration and may not go beyond what is necessary to remedy the balance of payments situation. The Community or Lithuania, as the case may be, shall inform the other Party forthwith.

3.   Any restrictive measures shall not apply to transfers related to investments and in particular to the repatriation of amounts invested or reinvested and of any kind of revenues stemming therefrom.

Article 66

With regard to public undertakings, and undertakings to which special or exclusive rights have been granted, the Association Council shall ensure that as from 1 January 1998, the principles of the Treaty establishing the European Community, notably Article 90, and the principles of the concluding document of the April 1990 Bonn meeting of the CSCE, notably entrepreneurs' freedom of decision, are upheld.

Article 67

1.   Pursuant to the provisions of this Article and of Annex XIX, the Parties confirm the importance that they attach to ensure adequate and effective protection and enforcement of intellectual, industrial and commercial property rights.

2.   Lithuania shall continue to improve the protection of intellectual, industrial and commercial property rights in order to provide, by the end of the transitional period referred to in Article 3, for a level of protection similar to that existing in the Community, including effective means of enforcing such rights.

3.   By the end of the transitional period referred to in Article 3, Lithuania shall accede to the multilateral conventions on intellectual, industrial and commercial property rights referred to in paragraph 1 of Annex XVII to which Member States of the Community are parties or which are, de facto, applied by Member States according to the relevant provisions contained in these conventions.

4.   If problems in the area of intellectual, industrial and commercial property affecting trading conditions were to occur, urgent consultations will be undertaken, at the request of either Party, with a view to reaching mutually satisfactory solutions.

Article 68

1.   The Parties consider the opening up of the award of public contracts on the basis of non-discrimination and reciprocity, in particular in the GATT and WTO context, to be a desirable objective.

2.   The Lithuanian companies as defined in Article 46 of this Agreement, shall be granted access to contract award procedures in the Community pursuant to Community procurement rules under a treatment no less favourable than that accorded to Community companies as of the entry into force of this Agreement.

Community companies in the sense of Article 46 of this Agreement shall be granted access to contract award procedures in Lithuania under a treatment no less favourable than that accorded to Lithuanian companies at the latest by the end of the transitional period referred to in Article 3. Community companies established in Lithuania under the provisions of Chapter II of Title IV in the form of subsidiaries as described in Article 46 and in the forms described in Article 57 shall have on entry into force of this Agreement access to contract award procedures under a treatment no less favourable than that accorded to Lithuanian companies. Community companies established in Lithuania in the form of branches and agencies as described in Article 46 shall be granted such treatment at the latest by the end of the transitional period referred to in Article 3.

The provisions in this paragraph shall also apply to public contracts covered by Directive 93/38/EEC of 14 June 1993 once Lithuania has introduced the appropriate legislation.

The Association Council shall periodically examine the possibility for Lithuania to introduce access to contract award procedures in Lithuania for all Community companies prior to the end of the transitional period.

3.   As regards establishment, operations, supply of services between the Community and Lithuania, as well as employment and movement of labour linked to the fulfilment of public contracts, the provisions of Articles 37 to 60 of this Agreement are applicable.

TITLE VI
ECONOMIC COOPERATION

Article 73 Industrial cooperation

1.   Cooperation shall seek to promote the following in particular:

- industrial cooperation between the economic operators of the two Parties, with the particular aim of strengthening the private sector in Lithuania,

- Community participation in Lithuania's efforts in both public and private sectors to modernise and restructure its industry, which will effect the transition from a centrally planned system to a market economy under conditions which ensure that the environment is protected,

- the restructuring of individual sectors,

- the establishment of new undertakings in areas offering potential for growth, particularly in branches of light industry, consumer goods and market services.

2.   Industrial cooperation initiatives shall take into account priorities determined by Lithuania. The initiatives should seek in particular to establish a suitable framework for undertakings, to improve management know-how and to promote transparency as regards markets and conditions for undertakings. Technical assistance will be included where appropriate.

Article 74 Investment promotion and protection

1.   Cooperation shall aim at maintaining and, if necessary, improving a legal framework and a favourable climate for private investment and its protection, both domestic and foreign, which is essential to economic and industrial reconstruction and development in Lithuania. The cooperation shall also aim to encourage and promote foreign investment and privatisation in Lithuania.

2.   The particular aims of cooperation shall be:

- for Lithuania to establish a legal framework which favours and protects investment,

- the conclusion, where appropriate, with Member States of bilateral agreements for the promotion and protection of investment,

- to proceed with deregulation and to improve economic infrastructure,

- to exchange information on investment opportunities in the context of trade fairs, exhibitions, trade weeks and other events.

Assistance from the Community could be granted in the initial stage to agencies which promote inward investment.

3.   Lithuania shall honour the rules on Trade-Related Aspects of Investment Measures (TRIMs).

ANNEX XVIII Concerning Article 47

Financial services

DEFINITIONS

A financial service is any service of a financial nature offered by a financial service provider of a Party. Financial services include the following activities:

A.   All insurance and insurance-related services

1.   Direct insurance (including co-insurance)

(i)   life

(ii)   non-life.

2.   Reinsurance and retrocession.

3.   Insurance intermediation, such as brokerage and agency.

4.   Services auxiliary to insurance, such as consultancy, actuarial, risk assessment and claim settlement services.

B.   Banking and other financial services (excluding insurance):

1.   acceptance of deposits and other repayable funds from the public;

2.   lending of all types, including, inter alia, consumer credit, mortgage credit, factoring and financing of commercial transactions;

3.   financial leasing;

4.   all payment and money transmission services, including credit charge and debit cards, travellers cheques and bankers drafts;

5.   guarantees and commitments;

6.   trading for own account of customers, whether on an exchange, in an over the counter market or otherwise, the following:

    (a)   money market instruments (cheques, bills, certificates of deposits, etc.),

    (b)   foreign exchange,

    (c)   derivative products including, but not limited to, futures and options,

    (d)   exchange rates and interest rate instruments, including products such as swaps, forward rate agreements, etc.,

    (e)   transferable securities,

    (f)   other negotiable instruments and financial assets, including bullion;

7.   participation in issues of all kinds of securities, including underwriting and placement as agent (whether publicly or privately) and provision of services related to such issues;

8.   money broking;

9.   asset management, such as cash or portfolio management, all forms of collective investment management, pension fund management, custodial depository and trust services;

10.   settlement and clearing services for financial assets, including securities, derivative products, and other negotiable instruments;

11.   advisory intermediation and other auxiliary financial services on all the activities listed in Points 1 to 10, including credit reference and analysis, investment and portfolio research and advice, advice on acquisitions and on corporate restructuring and strategy;

12.   provision and transfer of financial information, and financial data processing and related software by providers of other financial services.

The following activities are excluded from the definition of financial services:

(a)   activities carried out by central banks or by any other public institution in pursuit of monetary and exchange rate policies;

(b)   activities conducted by central banks, government agencies or departments, or public institutions, for the account or with the guarantee of the government, except when those activities may be carried out by financial service providers in competition with such public entities;

(c)   activities forming part of a statutory system of social security or public retirement plans, except when those activities may be carried out by financial service providers in competition with public entities or private institutions.

ANNEX XIX Concerning Article 67

Intellectual, industrial and commercial property protection

1.   Article 67(3) concerns the following multilateral Conventions:

- International Convention for the Protection of Performers, Producers of Phonograms and Broadcasting Organisations (Rome, 1961);

- Madrid Agreement concerning the International Registration of Marks (Stockholm Act, 1967 and amended in 1979);

- Nice Agreement concerning the International Classification of Goods and Services for the purposes of the Registration of Marks (Geneva, 1977 and amended in 1979);

- Protocol relating to the Madrid Agreement concerning the International Registration of Marks (Madrid 1989);

- Budapest Treaty on the International Recognition of the Deposit of Micro-organisms for the purposes of Patent Procedures (1977, modified 1980);

- International Convention for the Protection of New Varieties of Plants (UPOV) (Geneva Act, 1991).

The Association Council may decide that Article 67(3) shall apply to other multilateral conventions.

2.   The Parties confirm the importance they attach to the obligations arising from the following multilateral conventions:

- Berne Convention for the Protection of Literary and Artistic Works (Paris Act, 1971);

- Paris Convention for the Protection of Industrial Property (Stockholm Act, 1967 and amended in 1979);

- Patent Cooperation Treaty (Washington, 1970, amended in 1979 and modified in 1984).

3.   From entry into force of this Agreement, Lithuania shall grant to Community companies and nationals, in respect of the recognition and protection of intellectual, industrial and commercial property, treatment no less favourable than that granted by it to any third country under bilateral agreements.

4.   The provisions of paragraph 3 shall not apply to advantages granted by Lithuania to any third country on an effective reciprocal basis.

*

PARTNERSHIP AND COOPERATION AGREEMENT BETWEEN THE EUROPEAN COMMUNITIES AND THEIR MEMBER STATES, OF THE ONE PART, AND THE REPUBLIC OF ARMENIA, OF THE OTHER PART*
[excerpts]

The Partnership and Cooperation Agreement between the European Communities and Their Member States, of the One Part, and the Republic of Armenia, of the Other Part was signed on 22 April 1996. It entered into force on 1 July 1999. The member States of the European Communities are: Austria, Belgium, Denmark, Finland, France, Germany, Greece, Ireland, Italy, Luxembourg, the Netherlands, Portugal, Spain, Sweden and the United Kingdom.

TITLE IV

PROVISIONS AFFECTING BUSINESS AND INVESTMENT

CHAPTER II

CONDITIONS AFFECTING THE ESTABLISHMENT AND OPERATION OF COMPANIES

Article 23

1. The Community and its Member States shall grant treatment no less favourable than that accorded to any third country for the establishment of Armenian companies as defined in Article 25(d).

2. Without prejudice to the reservations listed in Annex IV, the Community and its Member States shall grant to subsidiaries of Armenian companies established in their territories a treatment no less favourable than that granted to any Community companies, in respect of their operation.

3. The Community and its Member States shall grant to branches of Armenian companies established in their territories treatment no less favourable than that accorded to branches of companies of any third country, in respect of their operations.

4. The Republic of Armenia shall grant for the establishment of Community companies as defined in Article 25(d) treatment no less favourable than that accorded to Armenian companies or to any third-country companies, whichever is the better, and shall grant to subsidiaries and branches of Community companies established in its territory treatment no less favourable than

---

* *Source*: European Communities (1999). "Partnership and Cooperation Agreement between the European Communities and Their Member States, of the One Part, and the Republic of Armenia, of the Other Part", *Official Journal of the European Communities*, L 239, 09 Septmber 1999, pp. 3 - 50; available also on the Internet (http://www.europa.eu.int). [Note added by the editor.]

that accorded to its own companies or branches or to any third-country company or branch, whichever is the better, in respect of their operations.

Article 24

1.   Without prejudice to the provisions of Article 97, the provisions of Article 23 shall not apply to air transport, inland waterways transport and maritime transport.

2.   However, in respect of activities, as indicated below, undertaken by shipping agencies for the provision of services to international maritime transport, including intermodal transport operations involving a sea-leg, each Party shall permit the companies of the other Party to have a commercial presence in its territory in the form of subsidiaries or branches, under conditions of establishment and operation no less favourable than those accorded to its own companies or to subsidiaries or branches of companies of any third country, whichever are the better, and this in conformity with the legislation and regulations applicable in each Party.

3.   Such activities include but are not limited to:

(a)   marketing and sales of maritime transport and related services through direct contact with customers, from quotation to invoicing, whether these services are operated or offered by the service supplier itself or by service suppliers with which the service seller has established standing business arrangements;

(b)   purchase and use, on their own account or on behalf of their customers (and the resale to their customers) of any transport and related services, including inward transport services by any mode, particularly inland waterways, road and rail, necessary for the supply of an integrated service;

(c)   preparation of documentation concerning transport documents, customs documents, or other documents related to the origin and character of the goods transported;

(d)   provision of business information by any means, including computerised information systems and electronic data interchange (subject to any non-discriminatory restrictions concerning telecommunications);

(e)   setting up of any business arrangement, including participation in the company's stock and the appointment of personnel recruited locally (or, in the case of foreign personnel, subject to the relevant provisions of this Agreement), with any locally established shipping agency;

(f)   acting on behalf of the companies, inter alia in organising the call of the vessel or taking over cargoes when required.

Article 25

For the purpose of this Agreement:

(a)   a "Community company" or an "Armenian company" respectively shall mean a company set up in accordance with the laws of a Member State or of the Republic of Armenia respectively and having its registered office or central administration, or principal place of business in the territory of the Community or the Republic of Armenia respectively. However, should the company, set up in accordance with the laws of a Member State or the Republic of Armenia respectively, have only its registered office in the territory of the Community or the Republic of Armenia respectively, the company shall be considered a Community or Armenian company respectively if its operations possess a real and continuous link with the economy of one of the Member States or the Republic of Armenia respectively;

(b)   "subsidiary" of a company shall mean a company which is effectively controlled by the first company;

(c)   "branch" of a company shall mean a place of business not having legal personality which has the appearance of permanency, such as the extension of a parent body, has a management and is materially equipped to negotiate business with third parties so that the latter, although knowing that there will if necessary be a legal link with the parent body, the head office of which is abroad, do not have to deal directly with such parent body but may transact business at the place of business constituting the extension;

(d)   "establishment" shall mean the right of Community or Armenian companies as referred to in point (a), to take up economic activities by means of the setting up of subsidiaries and branches in the Republic of Armenia or in the Community respectively;

(e)   "operation" shall mean the pursuit of economic activities;

(f) "   economic activities" shall mean activities of an industrial, commercial and professional character.

With regard to international maritime transport, including intermodal operations involving a sea-leg, nationals of the Member States or of the Republic of Armenia established outside the Community or the Republic of Armenia respectively, and shipping companies established outside the Community or the Republic of Armenia and controlled by nationals of a Member State or Armenian nationals respectively, shall also be beneficiaries of the provisions of this Chapter and Chapter III if their vessels are registered in that Member State or in the Republic of Armenia respectively in accordance with their respective legislation.

Article 26

1.   Notwithstanding any other provisions of this Agreement, a Party shall not be prevented from taking measures for prudential reasons, including for the protection of investors, depositors, policy holders or persons to whom a fiduciary duty is owed by a financial service supplier, or to ensure the integrity and stability of the financial system. Where such measures do not conform with the provisions of this Agreement, they shall not be used as a means of avoiding the obligations of a Party under this Agreement.

2.   Nothing in this Agreement shall be construed as requiring a Party to disclose information relating to the affairs and accounts of individual customers or any confidential or proprietary information in the possession of public entities.

3.   For the purpose of this Agreement, "financial services" shall mean those activities described in Annex III.

Article 27

The provisions of this Agreement shall not prejudice the application by each Party of any measure necessary to prevent the circumvention of its measures concerning third-country access to its market, through the provisions of this Agreement.

Article 28

1.   Notwithstanding the provisions of Chapter I of this Title, a Community company or an Armenian company established in the territory of the Republic of Armenia or the Community respectively shall be entitled to employ, or have employed by one of its subsidiaries or branches, in accordance with the legislation in force in the host country of establishment, in the territory of the Republic of Armenia and the Community respectively, employees who are nationals of Community Member States and the Republic of Armenia respectively, provided that such employees are key personnel as defined in paragraph 2, and that they are employed exclusively by companies, or branches. The residence and work permits of such employees shall only cover the period of such employment.

2.   Key personnel of the abovementioned companies herein referred to as "organisations" are "intra-corporate transferees" as defined in (c) in the following categories, provided that the organisation is a legal person and that the persons concerned have been employed by it or have been partners in it (other than majority shareholders), for at least the year immediately preceding such movement:

(a)   persons working in a senior position with an organisation, who primarily direct the management of the establishment, receiving general supervision or direction principally from the board of directors or stockholders of the business or their equivalent, including:

- directing the establishment or a department or subdivision of the establishment,

- supervising and controlling the work of other supervisory, professional or managerial employees,

- having the authority personally to hire and fire or recommend hiring, firing or other personnel actions;

(b)   persons working within an organisation who possess uncommon knowledge essential to the establishment's service, research equipment, techniques or management. The assessment of such knowledge may reflect, apart from knowledge specific to the establishment, a high level of qualification referring to a type of work or trade requiring specific technical knowledge, including membership of an accredited profession;

(c)   an "intra-corporate transferee" is defined as a natural person working within an organisation in the territory of a Party, and being temporarily transferred in the context of pursuit of economic activities in the territory of the other Party; the organisation concerned must have its principal place of business in the territory of a Party and the transfer be to an establishment (branch, subsidiary) of that organisation, effectively pursuing like economic activities in the territory of the other Party.

Article 29

1. The Parties shall use their best endeavours to avoid taking any measures or actions which render the conditions for the establishment and operation of each other's companies more restrictive than the situation existing on the day preceding the date of signature of this Agreement.

2. The provisions of this Article are without prejudice to those of Article 37: the situations covered by such Article 37 shall be solely governed by its provisions to the exclusion of any other.

3. Acting in the spirit of partnership and cooperation and in the light of the provisions of Article 43 the Government of the Republic of Armenia shall inform the Community of its intentions to submit new legislation or adopt new regulations which may render the conditions for the establishment or operation in the Republic of Armenia of subsidiaries and branches of Community companies more restrictive than the situation existing on the day preceding the date of signature of this Agreement. The Community may request the Republic of Armenia to communicate the drafts of such legislation or regulations and to enter into consultations about those drafts.

4. Where new legislation or regulations introduced in the Republic of Armenia would result in rendering the conditions for operation of subsidiaries and branches of Community companies established in the Republic of Armenia more restrictive than the situation existing on the day of signature of this Agreement, such respective legislation or regulations shall not apply during three years following the entry into force of the relevant act to those subsidiaries and branches already established in the Republic of Armenia at the time of entry into force of the relevant act.

CHAPTER III

CROSS-BORDER SUPPLY OF SERVICES BETWEEN THE COMMUNITY AND THE REPUBLIC OF ARMENIA

Article 30

1. The Parties undertake in accordance with the provisions of this Chapter to take the necessary steps to allow progressively the supply of services by Community or Armenian companies which are established in a Party other than that of the person for whom the services are intended taking into account the development of the service sectors in the Parties.

2. The Cooperation Council shall make recommendations for the implementation of paragraph 1.

Article 31

The Parties shall cooperate with the aim of developing a market-oriented service sector in the Republic of Armenia.

Article 32

1.   The Parties undertake to apply effectively the principle of unrestricted access to the international maritime market and traffic on a commercial basis:

(a)   the above provision does not prejudice the rights and obligations arising from the United Nations Convention on a Code of Conduct for Liner Conferences, as applicable to one or other Party to this Agreement. Non-conference lines will be free to operate in competition with a conference as long as they adhere to the principle of fair competition on a commercial basis;

(b)   the Parties affirm their commitment to a freely competitive environment as being an essential feature of the dry and liquid bulk trade.

2.   In applying the principles of paragraph 1, the Parties shall:

(a)   not apply, as from the entry into force of this Agreement, any cargo sharing provisions of bilateral agreements between any Member States of the Community and the former Soviet Union;

(b)   not introduce cargo sharing clauses into future bilateral agreements with third countries, other than in those exceptional circumstances where liner shipping companies from one or other Party to this Agreement would not otherwise have an effective opportunity to ply for trade to and from the third country concerned;

(c)   prohibit cargo sharing arrangements in future bilateral agreements concerning dry and liquid bulk trade;

(d)   abolish upon entry into force of this Agreement, all unilateral measures, administrative, technical and other obstacles which could have restrictive or discriminatory effects on the free supply of services in international maritime transport.

3.   Each party shall grant, inter alia, no less favourable treatment, for the ships operated by nationals or companies of the other Party, than that accorded to a Party's own ships, with regard to access to ports open to international trade, the use of infrastructure and auxiliary maritime services of the ports, as well as related fees and charges, customs facilities and the assignment of berths and facilities for loading and unloading.

4.   Nationals and companies of the Community providing international maritime transport services shall be free to provide international sea-river services in the inland waterways of the Republic of Armenia and vice versa.

Article 33

With a view to assuring a coordinated development of transport between the Parties, adapted to their commercial needs, the conditions of mutual market access and provision of services in transport by road, rail and inland waterways and, if applicable, in air transport may be dealt with by specific agreements where appropriate negotiated between the Parties after entry into force of this Agreement.

CHAPTER IV

GENERAL PROVISIONS

Article 34

1.   The provisions of this Title shall be applied subject to limitations justified on grounds of public policy, public security or public health.

2.   They shall not apply to activities which in the territory of either Party are connected, even occasionally, with the exercise of official authority.

Article 35

For the purpose of this Title, nothing in this Agreement shall prevent the Parties from applying their laws and regulations regarding entry and stay, work, labour conditions and establishment of natural persons and supply of services, provided that, in so doing, they do not apply them in a manner as to nullify or impair the benefits accruing to any Party under the terms of a specific provision of this Agreement. The above provision does not prejudice the application of Article 34.

Article 36

Companies which are controlled and exclusively owned by Armenian companies and Community companies jointly shall also be beneficiaries of the provisions of Chapters II, III and IV.

Article 37

Treatment granted by either Party to the other thereunder shall, as from the day one month prior to the date of entry into force of the relevant obligations of the General Agreement on Trade in Services (GATS), in respect of sectors or measures covered by the GATS, in no case be more favourable than that accorded by such first Party under the provisions of GATS and this in respect of each service sector, sub-sector and mode of supply.

Article 38

For the purposes of Chapters II, III and IV, no account shall be taken of treatment accorded by the Community, its Member States or the Republic of Armenia pursuant to commitments entered into in economic integration agreements in accordance with the principles of Article V of GATS.

Article 39

1.   The most-favoured-nation treatment granted in accordance with the provisions of this Title shall not apply to the tax advantages which the Parties are providing or will provide in the future on the basis of agreements to avoid double taxation, or other tax arrangements.

2.   Nothing in this Title shall be construed to prevent the adoption or enforcement by the Parties of any measure aimed at preventing the avoidance or evasion of taxes pursuant to the tax

provisions of agreements to avoid double taxation and other tax arrangements, or domestic fiscal legislation.

3.   Nothing in this Title shall be construed to prevent Member States or the Republic of Armenia from distinguishing, in the application of the relevant provisions of their fiscal legislation, between tax payers who are not in identical situations, in particular as regards their place of residence.

Article 40

Without prejudice to Article 28, no provision of Chapters II, III and IV shall be interpreted as giving the right to:

- nationals of the Member States or of the Republic of Armenia respectively to enter, or stay in, the territory of the Republic of Armenia or the Community respectively in any capacity whatsoever, and in particular as a shareholder or partner in a company or manager or employee thereof or supplier or recipient of services,

- Community subsidiaries or branches of Armenian companies to employ or have employed in the territory of the Community nationals of the Republic of Armenia,

- Armenian subsidiaries or branches of Community companies to employ or have employed in the territory of the Republic of Armenia nationals of the Member States,

- Armenian companies or Community subsidiaries or branches of Armenian companies to supply Armenian persons to act for and under the control of other persons by temporary employment contracts,

- Community companies or Armenian subsidiaries or branches of Community companies to supply workers who are nationals of the Member States by temporary employment contracts.

CHAPTER V

CURRENT PAYMENTS AND CAPITAL

Article 41

1.   The Parties undertake to authorise, in freely convertible currency, any current payments between residents of the Community and of the Republic of Armenia connected with the movement of goods, services or persons made in accordance with the provisions of this Agreement.

2.   With regard to transactions on the capital account of balance of payments, from entry into force of this Agreement, the free movement of capital relating to direct investments made in companies formed in accordance with the laws of the host country and investments made in accordance with the provisions of Chapter II, and the liquidation or repatriation of these investments and of any profit stemming therefrom shall be ensured.

3.   Without prejudice to paragraph 2 or to paragraph 5, as from the entry into force of this Agreement, no new foreign exchange restrictions on the movement of capital and current payments connected therewith between residents of the Community and the Republic of Armenia shall be introduced and the existing arrangements shall not become more restrictive.

4.   The Parties shall consult each other with a view to facilitating the movement of forms of capital other than those referred to in paragraph 2 above between the Community and the Republic of Armenia in order to promote the objectives of this Agreement.

5.   With reference to the provisions of this Article, until a full convertibility of the Armenian currency within the meaning of Article VIII of the Articles of Agreement of the International Monetary Fund (IMF) is introduced, the Republic of Armenia may in exceptional circumstances apply exchange restrictions connected with the granting or taking up of short and medium-term financial credits to the extent that such restrictions are imposed on the Republic of Armenia for the granting of such credits and are permitted according to the Republic of Armenia's status under the IMF. The Republic of Armenia shall apply these restrictions in a non-discriminatory manner. They shall be applied in such a manner as to cause the least possible disruption to this Agreement. The Republic of Armenia shall inform the Cooperation Council promptly of the introduction of such measures and of any changes therein.

6.   Without prejudice to paragraphs 1 and 2, where, in exceptional circumstances, movements of capital between the Community and the Republic of Armenia cause, or threaten to cause, serious difficulties for the operation of exchange rate policy or monetary policy in the Community or the Republic of Armenia, the Community and the Republic of Armenia, respectively, may take safeguard measures with regard to movements of capital between the Community and the Republic of Armenia for a period not exceeding six months if such measures are strictly necessary.

CHAPTER VI

INTELLECTUAL, INDUSTRIAL AND COMMERCIAL PROPERTY PROTECTION

Article 42

1.   Pursuant to the provisions of this Article and of Annex II, the Republic of Armenia shall continue to improve the protection of intellectual, industrial and commercial property rights in order to provide, by the end of the fifth year after the entry into force of this Agreement, for a level of protection similar to that existing in the Community, including effective means of enforcing such rights.

2.   By the end of the fifth year after entry into force of this Agreement, the Republic of Armenia shall accede to the multilateral conventions on intellectual, industrial and commercial property rights referred to in paragraph 1 of Annex II to which Member States are parties or which are de facto applied by Member States, according to the relevant provisions contained in these conventions.

TITLE V

LEGISLATIVE COOPERATION

Article 43

1.   The Parties recognise that an important condition for strengthening the economic links between the Republic of Armenia and the Community is the approximation of the Republic of Armenia's existing and future legislation to that of the Community. The Republic of Armenia shall endeavour to ensure that its legislation will be gradually made compatible with that of the Community.

2.   The approximation of laws shall extend to the following areas in particular: customs law, company law, banking law, company accounts and taxes, intellectual property, protection of workers at the workplace, financial services, rules on competition, public procurement, protection of health and life of humans, animals and plants, the environment, consumer protection, indirect taxation, technical rules and standards, nuclear laws and regulations and transport.

3.   The Community shall provide the Republic of Armenia with technical assistance for the implementation of these measures, which may include inter alia:

- the exchange of experts,
- the provision of early information especially on relevant legislation,
- organisation of seminars,
- training activities,
- aid for translation of Community legislation in the relevant sectors.

4.   The Parties agree to examine ways to apply their respective competition laws on a concerted basis in such cases where trade between them is affected.

TITLE VI

ECONOMIC COOPERATION

Article 44

1.   The Community and the Republic of Armenia shall establish economic cooperation aimed at contributing to the process of economic reform and recovery and sustainable development of the Republic of Armenia. Such cooperation shall strengthen existing economic links, to the benefit of both parties.

2.   Policies and other measures will be designed to bring about economic and social reforms and restructuring of the economic and trading systems in the Republic of Armenia and will be guided by the requirements of sustainability and harmonious social development; they will also fully incorporate environmental considerations.

3.   To this end, cooperation will concentrate, in particular, on economic and social development, human resources development, support for enterprises (including privatisation,

investment promotion and protection, small and medium-sized enterprises), mining and raw materials, science and technology, agriculture and food, energy, transport, tourism, telecommunications, financial services, combating of money laundering, trade, customs, statistical cooperation, information and communication, environmental protection and regional cooperation.

4.   Special attention shall be devoted to measures capable of fostering cooperation among the Independent States of the Transcaucasus region, and with other neighbouring states, with a view to stimulating a harmonious development of the region.

5.   Where appropriate, economic cooperation and other forms of cooperation provided for in this Agreement may be supported by technical assistance from the Community, taking into account the Community's relevant Council regulation applicable to technical assistance in the Independent States, the priorities agreed upon in the indicative programme related to Community technical assistance to the Republic of Armenia and its established coordination and implementation procedures.

Article 45
Cooperation in the field of trade in goods and services

The Parties will cooperate with a view to ensuring that the Republic of Armenia's international trade is conducted in conformity with the rules of the WTO.

Such cooperation shall include specific issues directly relevant to trade facilitation, including:

- formulation of policy on trade and trade-related questions, including payments, and clearing mechanisms,

- drafting of relevant legislation,

- continuing assistance to prepare for the Republic of Armenia's eventual accession to the WTO.

Article 46
Industrial cooperation

1. Cooperation shall aim at promoting the following in particular:

- the development of business links between economic operators of both sides,

- Community participation in the Republic of Armenia's efforts to restructure, and attract follow-up investment to, its industry,

- the improvement of management,

- the development of appropriate commercial rules and practices,

- environmental protection.

2.   The provisions of this Article shall not affect the enforcement of Community competition rules applicable to undertakings.

Article 47
Investment promotion and protection

1.   Bearing in mind the respective powers and competences of the Community and the Member States, cooperation shall aim to establish a favourable climate for private investment, both domestic and foreign, especially through better conditions for investment protection, the transfer of capital and the exchange of information on investment opportunities.

2.   The aims of cooperation shall be in particular:

- the conclusion, where appropriate, between the Member States and the Republic of Armenia of agreements for the promotion and protection of investment,

- the conclusion, where appropriate, between the Member States and the Republic of Armenia of agreements to avoid double taxation,

- the creation of favourable conditions for attracting foreign investments into the Armenian economy,

- to establish stable and adequate business law and conditions, and to exchange information on laws, regulations and administrative practices in the field of investment,

- to exchange information on investment opportunities in the form of, inter alia, trade fairs, exhibitions, trade weeks and other events.

Article 48
Public procurement

The Parties shall cooperate to develop conditions for open and competitive award of contracts for goods and services in particular through calls for tenders.

Article 50
Mining and raw materials

1.   The Parties shall aim at increasing investment and trade in mining and raw materials.

2.   The cooperation shall focus in particular on the following areas:

- exchange of information on the prospects of the mining and non-ferrous metals sectors,
- the establishment of a legal framework for cooperation,
- trade matters,
- the adoption and implementation of environmental legislation,
- training,
- safety in the mining industry.

Article 51
Cooperation in science and technology

1.   The Parties shall promote cooperation in civil scientific research and technological development (RTD) on the basis of mutual benefit and, taking into account the availability of resources, adequate access to their respective programmes and subject to appropriate levels of effective protection of intellectual, industrial and commercial property rights (IPR).

2.   Science and technology cooperation shall cover:

- the exchange of scientific and technical information,

- joint RTD activities,

- training activities and mobility programmes for scientists, researchers and technicians engaged in RTD on both sides.

Where such cooperation takes the form of activities involving education and/or training, it should be carried out in accordance with the provisions of Article 52.

The Parties, on the basis of mutual agreement, can engage in other forms of cooperation in science and technology.

In carrying out such cooperation activities, special attention shall be devoted to the redeployment of scientists, engineers, researchers and technicians which are or have been engaged in research and/or production of weapons of mass destruction.

3.   The cooperation covered by this Article shall be implemented according to specific arrangements to be negotiated and concluded in accordance with the procedures adopted by each Party, and which shall set out, inter alia, appropriate IPR provisions.

Article 54
Energy

1.   Cooperation shall take place within the principles of the market economy and the European Energy Charter and bearing in mind the Energy Charter Treaty and the Protocol on Energy Efficiency and Related Environmental Aspects, against a background of the progressive integration of the energy markets in Europe.

2.   The cooperation shall include among others the following areas:

- formulation and development of energy policy,

- improvement in management and regulation of the energy sector in line with a market economy,

- improvement of energy supply, including security of supply, in an economic and environmentally sound manner,

- promotion of energy saving and energy efficiency and implementation of the Energy Charter Protocol on Energy Efficiency and related environmental aspects,

- modernisation of energy infrastructures,

- improvement of energy technologies in supply and end use across the range of energy types,

- management and technical training in the energy sector,

- transportation and transit of energy materials and products,

- the introduction of the range of institutional, legal, fiscal and other conditions necessary to encourage increased energy trade and investment,

- development of hydro-electric and other renewable energy resources.

3.   The Parties shall exchange relevant information relating to investment projects in the energy sector, in particular concerning the construction and refurbishing of oil and gas pipelines or other means of transporting energy products. They shall cooperate with a view to implementing as efficaciously as possible the provisions of Title IV and of Article 47, in respect of investments in the energy sector.

Article 58
Financial services

Cooperation shall in particular aim at facilitating the involvement of the Republic of Armenia in universally accepted systems of mutual settlements. Technical assistance shall focus on:

- the development of banking and financial services, the development of a common market of credit resources, the involvement of the Republic of Armenia in a universally accepted system of mutual settlements,

- the development of a fiscal system and its institutions in the Republic of Armenia, exchange of experience and personnel training,

- the development of insurance services, which would, inter alia, create a favourable framework for Community companies' participation in the establishment of joint ventures in the insurance sector in the Republic of Armenia, as well as the development of export credit insurance.

This cooperation shall in particular contribute to foster the development of relations between the Republic of Armenia and the Member States in the financial services sector.

Article 62
Small and medium-sized enterprises

1.   The Parties shall aim to develop and strengthen small and medium-sized enterprises and their associations and cooperation between SMEs in the Community and the Republic of Armenia.

2.   Cooperation shall include technical assistance, in particular in the following areas:

- the development of a legislative framework for SMEs,

- the development of an appropriate infrastructure (an agency to support SMEs, communications, assistance to the creation of a fund for SMEs),

- the development of technology parks.

ANNEX II

INTELLECTUAL, INDUSTRIAL AND COMMERCIAL PROPERTY CONVENTIONS REFERRED TO IN ARTICLE 42

1.   Article 42(2) concerns the following multilateral conventions:

- Berne Convention for the Protection of Literary and Artistic Works (Paris Act, 1971),

- International Convention for the Protection of Performers, Producers of Phonograms and Broadcasting Organisations (Rome, 1961),

- Protocol relating to the Madrid Agreement concerning the International Registration of Marks (Madrid, 1989),

- Nice Agreement concerning the International Classification of Goods and Services for the purposes of the Registration of Marks (Geneva 1977, and amended in 1979),

- Budapest Treaty on the International Recognition of the Deposit of Micro-organisms for the purposes of Patent Procedures (1977, modified in 1980),

- International Convention for the Protection of New Varieties of Plants (UPOV) (Geneva Act, 1991).

2.   The Cooperation Council may recommend that Article 42(2) shall apply to other multilateral conventions. If problems in the area of intellectual, industrial and commercial property affecting trading conditions were to occur, urgent consultations will be undertaken, at the request of either party, with a view to reaching mutually satisfactory solutions.

3.   The Parties confirm the importance they attach to the obligations arising from the following multilateral conventions:

- Paris Convention for the Protection of Industrial Property (Stockholm Act, 1967, and amended in 1979),

- Madrid Agreement concerning the Interational Registration of Marks (Stockholm Act, 1967, and amended in 1979),

- Patent Cooperation Treaty (Washington, 1970, amended in 1979 and modified in 1984).

4.   From the entry into force of this Agreement, the Republic of Armenia shall grant to Community companies and nationals, in respect of the recognition and protection of intellectual, industrial and commercial property, treatment no less favourable than that granted by it to any third country under bilateral agreements.

5.   The provisions of paragraph 4 shall not apply to advantages granted by the Republic of Armenia to any third country on an effective reciprocal basis and to advantages granted by the Republic of Armenia to another country of the former USSR.

ANNEX III

FINANCIAL SERVICES REFERRED TO IN ARTICLE 26 (3)

A financial service is any service of a financial nature offered by a financial service provider of a Party. Financial services include the following activities:

A.   All insurance and insurance-related services

    1.   Direct insurance (including co-insurance):

        (i)   life,

        (ii)   non-life.

    2.   Reinsurance and retrocession.

    3.   Insurance intermediation, such as brokerage and agency.

    4.   Services auxiliary to insurance, such as consultancy, actuarial, risk assessment and claim settlement services.

B.   Banking and other financial services (excluding insurance)

    1.   Acceptance of deposits and other repayable funds from the public.

    2.   Lending of all types, including, inter alia, consumer credit, mortgage credit, factoring and financing of commercial transactions.

    3.   Financial leasing.

    4.   All payment and money transmission services, including credit charge and debit cards, travellers cheques and bankers drafts.

    5.   Guarantees and commitments.

    6.   Trading for own account or for the account of customers, whether on an exchange, in an over the counter market or otherwise, the following:

        (a)   money market instruments (cheques, bills, certificates of deposits, etc.);

(b)   foreign exchange;

(c)   derivative products including, but not limited to, futures and options;

(d)   exchange rates and interest rate instruments, including products such as swaps, forward rate agreements, etc.;

(e)   transferable securities;

(f)   other negotiable instruments and financial assets, including bullion.

7.   Participation in issues of all kinds of securities, including underwriting and placement as agent (whether publicly or privately) and provision of services related to such issues.

8.   Money brokering.

9.   Asset management, such as cash or portfolio management, all forms of collective investment management, pension fund management, custodial depository and trust services.

10.   Settlement and clearing services for financial assets, including securities, derivative products, and other negotiable instruments.

11.   Advisory intermediation and other auxiliary financial services on all the activities listed in points 1 to 10 above, including credit reference and analysis, investment and portfolio research and advice, advice on acquisitions and on corporate restructuring and strategy.

. 12.   Provision and transfer of financial information, and financial data processing and related software by providers of other financial services.

The following activities are excluded from the definition of financial services:

(a)   activities carried out by central banks or by any other public institution in pursuit of monetary and exchange rate policies;

(b)   activities conducted by central banks, government agencies or departments, or public institutions, for the account or with the guarantee of the government, except when those activities may be carried out by financial service providers in competition with such public entities;

(c)   activities forming part of a statutory system of social security or public retirement plans, except when those activities may be carried out by financial service providers in competition with public entities or private institutions.

*

PARTNERSHIP AND COOPERATION AGREEMENT BETWEEN THE EUROPEAN COMMUNITIES AND THEIR MEMBER STATES, OF THE ONE PART, AND GEORGIA, OF THE OTHER PART*
[excerpts]

The Partnership and Cooperation Agreement between the European Communities and Their Member States, of the One Part, and Georgia, of the Other Part was signed on 22 April 1996. It entered into force on 1 July 1999. The member States of the European Communities are: Austria, Belgium, Denmark, Finland, France, Germany, Greece, Ireland, Italy, Luxembourg, the Netherlands, Portugal, Spain, Sweden and the United Kingdom.

TITLE IV

PROVISIONS AFFECTING BUSINESS AND INVESTMENT

CHAPTER II

CONDITIONS AFFECTING THE ESTABLISHMENT AND OPERATION OF COMPANIES

Article 23

1.   The Community and its Member States shall grant treatment no less favourable than that accorded to any third country for the establishment of Georgian companies as defined in Article 25(d).

2.   Without prejudice to the reservations listed in Annex IV, the Community and its Member States shall grant to subsidiaries of Georgian companies established in their territories a treatment no less favourable than that granted to any Community companies, in respect of their operation.

3.   The Community and its Member States shall grant to branches of Georgian companies established in their territories treatment no less favourable than that accorded to branches of companies of any third country, in respect of their operation.

4.   Without prejudice to the reservations listed in Annex V, and subject to the conditions set out therein, Georgia shall grant for the establishment of Community companies as defined in Article 25(d) treatment no less favourable than that accorded to Georgian companies or to any third country companies, whichever is the better, and shall grant to subsidiaries and branches of

---

*   *Source*: European Communities (1999). "Partnership and Cooperation Agreement between the European Communities and Their Member States, of the One Part, and Georgia, of the Other Part", *Official Journal of the European Communities*, L 205, 04 August 1999, pp. 3 - 52; available also on the Internet (http://www.europa.eu.int). [Note added by the editor.]

Community companies established in its territory treatment no less favourable than that accorded to its own companies or branches or to any third country company or branch, whichever is the better, in respect of their operations.

Article 24

1.   Without prejudice to the provisions of Article 100, the provisions of Article 23 shall not apply to air transport, inland waterways transport and maritime transport.

2.   However, in respect of activities, as indicated below, undertaken by shipping agencies for the provision of services to international maritime transport, including intermodal transport operations involving a sea-leg, each Party shall permit the companies of the other Party to have a commercial presence in its territory in the form of subsidiaries or branches, under conditions of establishment and operation no less favourable than those accorded to its own companies or to subsidiaries or branches of companies of any third country, whichever are the better, and this in conformity with the legislation and regulations applicable in each Party.

3.   Such activities include but are not limited to:

   (a)   marketing and sales of maritime transport and related services through direct contact with customers, from quotation to invoicing, whether these services are operated or offered by the service supplier itself or by service suppliers with which the service seller has established standing business arrangements;

   (b)   purchase and use, on their own account or on behalf of their customers (and the resale to their customers) of any transport and related services, including inward transport services by any mode, particularly inland waterways, road and rail, necessary for the supply of an integrated service;

   (c)   preparation of documentation concerning transport documents, customs documents, or other documents related to the origin and character of the goods transported;

   (d)   provision of business information by any means, including computerised information systems and electronic data interchange (subject to any non-discriminatory restrictions concerning telecommunications);

   (e)   setting up of any business arrangement, including participation in the company's stock and the appointment of personnel recruited locally (or, in the case of foreign personnel, subject to the relevant provisions of this Agreement), with any locally established shipping agency;

   (f)   acting on behalf of the companies, inter alia, in organising the call of the vessel or taking over cargoes when required.

Article 25

For the purpose of this Agreement:

(a)   a "Community company" or a "Georgian company" respectively shall mean a company set up in accordance with the laws of a Member State or of Georgia respectively and having its registered office or central administration, or principal place of business in the territory of the Community or Georgia respectively. However, should the company, set up in accordance with the laws of a Member State or Georgia respectively, have only its registered office in the territory of the Community or Georgia respectively, the company shall be considered a Community or Georgian company respectively if its operations possess a real and continuous link with the economy of one of the Member States or Georgia respectively;

(b)   "subsidiary" of a company shall mean a company which is effectively controlled by the first company;

(c)   "branch" of a company shall mean a place of business not having legal personality which has the appearance of permanency, such as the extension of a parent body, has a management and is materially equipped to negotiate business with third parties so that the latter, although knowing that there will if necessary be a legal link with the parent body, the head office of which is abroad, do not have to deal directly with such parent body but may transact business at the place of business constituting the extension;

(d)   "establishment" shall mean the right of Community or Georgian companies as referred to in point (a), to take up economic activities by means of the setting up of subsidiaries and branches in Georgia or in the Community respectively;

(e)   "operation" shall mean the pursuit of economic activities;

(f)   "economic activities" shall mean activities of an industrial, commercial and professional character.

With regard to international maritime transport, including intermodal operations involving a sea-leg, nationals of the Member States or of Georgia established outside the Community or Georgia respectively, and shipping companies established outside the Community or Georgia and controlled by nationals of a Member State or Georgian nationals respectively, shall also be beneficiaries of the provisions of this Chapter and Chapter III if their vessels are registered in that Member State or in Georgia respectively in accordance with their respective legislation.

Article 26

1.   Notwithstanding any other provisions of this Agreement, a Party shall not be prevented from taking measures for prudential reasons, including for the protection of investors, depositors, policy-holders or persons to whom a fiduciary duty is owed by a financial service supplier, or to ensure the integrity and stability of the financial system. Where such measures do not conform with the provisions of this Agreement, they shall not be used as a means of avoiding the obligations of a Party under this Agreement.

2.   Nothing in this Agreement shall be construed as requiring a Party to disclose information relating to the affairs and accounts of individual customers or any confidential or proprietary information in the possession of public entities.

3.   For the purpose of this Agreement, "financial services" shall mean those activities described in Annex III.

Article 27

The provisions of this Agreement shall not prejudice the application by each Party of any measure necessary to prevent the circumvention of its measures concerning third country access to its market, through the provisions of this Agreement.

Article 28

1.   Notwithstanding the provisions of Chapter I of this Title, a Community company or a Georgian company established in the territory of Georgia or the Community respectively shall be entitled to employ, or have employed by one of its subsidiaries or branches, in accordance with the legislation in force in the host country of establishment, in the territory of Georgia and the Community respectively, employees who are nationals of Community Member States and Georgia respectively, provided that such employees are key personnel as defined in paragraph 2, and that they are employed exclusively by companies, or branches. The residence and work permits of such employees shall only cover the period of such employment.

2.   Key personnel of the abovementioned companies herein referred to as "organisations" are "intracorporate transferees" as defined in (c) in the following categories, provided that the organisation is a legal person and that the persons concerned have been employed by it or have been partners in it (other than majority shareholders), for at least the year immediately preceding such movement:

(a)   persons working in a senior position with an organisation, who primarily direct the management of the establishment, receiving general supervision or direction principally from the board of directors or stockholders of the business or their equivalent, including:

- directing the establishment or a department or subdivision of the establishment,

- supervising and controlling the work of other supervisory, professional or managerial employees,

- having the authority personally to hire and fire or recommend hiring, firing or other personnel actions;

(b)   persons working within an organisation who possess uncommon knowledge essential to the establishment's service, research equipment, techniques or management. The assessment of such knowledge may reflect, apart from knowledge specific to the establishment, a high level of qualification referring to a type of work or trade requiring specific technical knowledge, including membership of an accredited profession;

(c)   an "intracorporate transferee" is defined as a natural person working within an organisation in the territory of a Party, and being temporarily transferred in the context of pursuit of economic activities in the territory of the other Party; the organisation concerned must have its principal place of business in the territory of a Party and the transfer be to an establishment (branch, subsidiary) of that organisation, effectively pursuing like economic activities in the territory of the other Party.

Article 29

1.   The Parties shall use their best endeavours to avoid taking any measures or actions which render the conditions for the establishment and operation of each other's companies more restrictive than the situation existing on the day preceding the date of signature of this Argeement.

2.   The provisions of this Article are without prejudice to those of Article 37; the situations covered by such Article 37 shall be solely governed by its provisions to the exclusion of any other.

3.   Acting in the spirit of partnership and cooperation and in the light of the provisions of Article 43 the Government of Georgia shall inform the Community of its intentions to submit new legislation or adopt new regulations which may render the conditions for the establishment or operation in Georgia of subsidiaries and branches of Community companies more restrictive than the situation existing on the day preceding the date of signature of this Agreement. The Community may request Georgia to communicate the drafts of such legislation or regulations and to enter into consultations about those drafts.

4.   Where new legislation or regulations introduced in Georgia would result in rendering the conditions for operation of subsidiaries and branches of Community companies established in Georgia more restrictive than the situation existing on the day of signature of this Agreement, such respective legislation or regulations shall not apply during three years following the entry into force of the relevant act to those subsidiaries and branches already established in Georgia at the time of entry into force of the relevant act.

CHAPTER III

CROSS-BORDER SUPPLY OF SERVICES BETWEEN THE COMMUNITY AND GEORGIA

Article 30

1.   The Parties undertake in accordance with the provisions of this Chapter to take the necessary steps to allow progressively the supply of services by Community or Georgian companies which are established in a Party other than that of the person for whom the services are intended taking into account the development of the service sectors in the Parties.

2.   The Cooperation Council shall make recommendations for the implementation of paragraph 1.

Article 31

The Parties shall cooperate with the aim of developing a market oriented service sector in Georgia.

Article 32

1.   The Parties undertake to apply effectively the principle of unrestricted access to the international maritime market and traffic on a commercial basis:

    (a)   the above provision does not prejudice the rights and obligations arising from the United Nations Convention on a Code of Conduct for Liner Conferences, as applicable to one or other Party to this Agreement. Non-conference lines will be free to operate in competition with a conference as long as they adhere to the principle of fair competition on a commercial basis;

    (b)   the Parties affirm their commitment to a freely competitive environment as being an essential feature of the dry and liquid bulk trade.

2.   In applying the principles of paragraph 1, the Parties shall:

    (a)   not apply, as from the entry into force of this Agreement, any cargo sharing provisions of bilateral agreements between any Member States of the Community and the former Soviet Union;

    (b)   not introduce cargo-sharing clauses into future bilateral agreements with third countries, other than in those exceptional circumstances where liner shipping companies from one or other Party to this Agreement would not otherwise have an effective opportunity to ply for trade to and from the third country concerned;

    (c)   prohibit cargo sharing arrangements in future bilateral agreements concerning dry and liquid bulk trade;

    (d)   abolish on entry into force of this Agreement, all unilateral measures, administrative, technical and other obstacles which could have restrictive or discriminatory effects on the free supply of services in international maritime transport.

3.   Each party shall grant, inter alia, no less favourable treatment, for the ships operated by nationals or companies of the other Party, than that accorded to a Party's own ships, with regard to access to ports open to international trade, the use of infrastructure and auxiliary maritime services of the ports, as well as related fees and charges, customs facilities and the assignment of berths and facilities for loading and unloading.

4.   Nationals and companies of the Community providing international maritime transport services shall be free to provide international sea-river services in the inland waterways of Georgia and vice versa.

Article 33

With a view to assuring a coordinated development of transport between the Parties, adapted to their commercial needs, the conditions of mutual market access and provision of services in transport by road, rail and inland waterways and, if applicable, in air transport may be dealt with by specific agreements where appropriate negotiated between the Parties after entry into force of this Agreement.

CHAPTER IV

GENERAL PROVISIONS

Article 34

1.   The provisions of this Title shall be applied subject to limitations justified on grounds of public policy, public security or public health.

2.   They shall not apply to activities which in the territory of either Party are connected, even occasionally, with the exercise of official authority.

Article 35

For the purpose of this Title, nothing in this Agreement shall prevent the Parties from applying their laws and regulations regarding entry and stay, work, labour conditions and establishment of natural persons and supply of services, provided that, in so doing, they do not apply them in a manner as to nullify or impair the benefits accruing to any Party under the terms of a specific provision of this Agreement. The above provision does not prejudice the application of Article 34.

Article 36

Companies which are controlled and exclusively owned by Georgian companies and Community companies jointly shall also be beneficiaries of the provisions of Chapters II, III and IV.

Article 37

Treatment granted by either Party to the other thereunder shall, as from the day one month prior to the date of entry into force of the relevant obligations of the General Agreement on Trade in Services (GATS), in respect of sectors or measures covered by the GATS, in no case be more favourable than that accorded by such first Party under the provisions of GATS and this in respect of each service sector, subsector and mode of supply.

Article 38

For the purposes of Chapters II, III and IV, no account shall be taken of treatment accorded by the Community, its Member States or Georgia pursuant to commitments entered into in economic integration agreements in accordance with the principles of Article V of the GATS.

Article 39

1.   The most-favoured-nation treatment granted in accordance with the provisions of this Title shall not apply to the tax advantages which the Parties are providing or will provide in the future on the basis of agreements to avoid double taxation, or other tax arrangements.

2.   Nothing in this Title shall be construed to prevent the adoption or enforcement by the Parties of any measure aimed at preventing the avoidance or evasion of taxes pursuant to the tax provisions of agreements to avoid double taxation and other tax arrangements, or domestic fiscal legislation.

3.   Nothing in this Title shall be construed to prevent Member States or Georgia from distinguishing, in the application of the relevant provisions of their fiscal legislation, between taxpayers who are not in identical situations, in particular as regards their place of residence.

Article 40

Without prejudice to Article 28, no provision of Chapters II, III and IV shall be interpreted as giving the right to:

- nationals of the Member States or of Georgia respectively to enter, or stay in, the territory of Georgia or the Community respectively in any capacity whatsoever, and in particular as a shareholder or partner in a company or manager or employee thereof or supplier or recipient of services,

- Community subsidiaries or branches of Georgian companies to employ or have employed in the territory of the Community nationals of Georgia,

- Georgian subsidiaries or branches of Community companies to employ or have employed in the territory of Georgia nationals of the Member States,

- Georgian companies or Community subsidiaries or branches of Georgian companies to supply Georgian persons to act for and under the control of other persons by temporary employment contracts,

- Community companies or Georgian subsidiaries or branches of Community companies to supply workers who are nationals of the Member States by temporary employment contracts.

CHAPTER V

CURRENT PAYMENTS AND CAPITAL

Article 41

1.   The Parties undertake to authorise in freely convertible currency, any current payments between residents of the Community and of Georgia connected with the movement of goods, services or persons made in accordance with the provisions of this Agreement.

2.   With regard to transactions on the capital account of balance of payments, from entry into force of this Agreement, the free movement of capital relating to direct investments made in companies formed in accordance with the laws of the host country and investments made in accordance with the provisions of Chapter II, and the liquidation or repatriation of these investments and of any profit stemming therefrom shall be ensured.

3.   Without prejudice to paragraph 2 or to paragraph 5, as from the entry into force of this Agreement, no new foreign exchange restrictions on the movement of capital and current payments connected therewith between residents of the Community and Georgia shall be introduced and the existing arrangements shall not become more restrictive.

4.   The Parties shall consult each other with a view to facilitating the movement of forms of capital other than those referred to in paragraph 2 between the Community and Georgia in order to promote the objectives of this Agreement.

5.   With reference to the provisions of this Article, until a full convertibility of the Georgian currency within the meaning of Article VIII of the Articles of Agreement of the International Monetary Fund (IMF) is introduced, Georgia may in exceptional circumstances apply exchange restrictions connected with the granting or taking up of short and medium-term financial credits to the extent that such restrictions are imposed on Georgia for the granting of such credits and are permitted according to Georgia's status under the IMF. Georgia shall apply these restrictions in a non-discriminatory manner. They shall be applied in such a manner as to cause the least possible disruption to this Agreement. Georgia shall inform the Cooperation Council promptly of the introduction of such measures and of any changes therein.

6.   Without prejudice to paragraphs 1 and 2, where, in exceptional circumstances, movement of capital between the Community and Georgia cause, or threaten to cause, serious difficulties for the operation of exchange-rate policy or monetary policy in the Community or Georgia, the Community and Georgia, respectively, may take safeguard measures with regard to movements of capital between the Community and Georgia for a period not exceeding six months if such measures are strictly necessary.

CHAPTER VI

INTELLECTUAL, INDUSTRIAL AND COMMERCIAL PROPERTY PROTECTION

Article 42

1.   Pursuant to the provisions of this Article and of Annex II, Georgia shall continue to improve the protection of intellectual, industrial and commercial property rights in order to provide, by the end of the fifth year after the entry into force of this Agreement, for a level of protection similar to that existing in the Community, including effective means of enforcing such rights.

2.   By the end of the fifth year after entry into force of this Agreement, Georgia shall accede to the multilateral conventions on intellectual, industrial and commercial property rights referred to in paragraph 1 of Annex II to which Member States are parties or which are, de facto, applied by Member States, according to the relevant provisions contained in these conventions.

TITLE V

LEGISLATIVE COOPERATION

Article 43

1.   The Parties recognise that an important condition for strengthening the economic links between Georgia and the Community is the approximation of Georgia's existing and future legislation to that of the Community. Georgia shall endeavour to ensure that its legislation will be gradually made compatible with that of the Community.

2.   The approximation of laws shall extend to the following areas in particular: laws and regulations governing investments by companies, customs law, company law, banking law, company accounts and taxes, intellectual property, protection of workers at the workplace, financial services, rules on competition, public procurement, protection of health and life of humans, animals and plants, the environment, consumer protection, indirect taxation, technical rules and standards, nuclear laws and regulations and transport.

3.   The Community shall provide Georgia with technical assistance for the implementation of these measures, which may include, inter alia:

- the exchange of experts,
- the provision of early information especially on relevant legislation,
- organisation of seminars,
- training activities,
- aid for translation of Community legislation in the relevant sectors.

Article 44

1.   Further to Article 43, the Community shall provide Georgia with technical assistance regarding the formulation and implementation of legislation in the field of competition, in particular as concerns:

- agreements and associations between undertakings and concerted practices which may have the effect of preventing, restricting or distorting competition,

- abuse by undertakings of a dominant position in the market,

- State aids which have the effect of distorting competition,

- State monopolies of a commercial character,

- public undertakings and undertakings with special or exclusive rights,

- review and supervision of the application of competition laws and means of ensuring compliance with them.

2.   The Parties agree to examine ways to apply their respective competition laws on a concerted basis in such cases where trade between them is affected.

TITLE VI

ECONOMIC COOPERATION

Article 45

1.   The Community and Georgia shall establish economic cooperation aimed at contributing to the process of economic reform and recovery and sustainable development of Georgia. Such cooperation shall strengthen existing economic links, to the benefit of both parties.

2.   Policies and other measures will be designed to bring about economic and social reforms and restructuring of the economic and trading systems in Georgia and will be guided by the requirements of sustainability and harmonious social development; they will also fully incorporate environmental considerations.

3.   To this end, cooperation will concentrate, in particular, on economic and social development, human resources development, support for enterprises (including privatisation, investment and development of financial services), agriculture and food, energy, transport, tourism, environmental protection, regional cooperation and monetary policy.

4.   Special attention shall be devoted to measures capable of fostering cooperation among the Independent States of the transcaucasus region, and with other neighbouring States, with a view to stimulating a harmonious development of the region.

5.   Where appropriate, economic cooperation and other forms of cooperation provided for in this Agreement may be supported by technical assistance from the Community, taking into account the Community's relevant Council Regulation applicable to technical assistance in the Independent States, the priorities agreed on in the indicative programme related to Community technical assistance to Georgia and its established coordination and implementation procedures.

Article 46
Cooperation in the field of trade in goods and services

The Parties will cooperate with a view to ensuring that Georgia's international trade is conducted in conformity with the rules of the WTO.

Such cooperation shall include specific issues directly relevant to trade facilitation, including:

- formulation of policy on trade and trade-related questions, including payments, and clearing mechanisms,

- drafting of relevant legislation,

- assistance to prepare for Georgia's eventual accession to the WTO.

Article 47
Industrial cooperation

1.   Cooperation shall aim at promoting the following in particular:

- the development of business links between economic operators of both sides,

- Community participation in Georgia's efforts to restructure its industry,

- the improvement of management,

- the development of appropriate commercial rules and practices,

- environmental protection,

- conversion of the military-industrial complex.

2.   The provisions of this Article shall not affect the enforcement of Community competition rules applicable to undertakings.

Article 49
Investment promotion and protection

1.   Bearing in mind the respective powers and competences of the Community and the Member States, cooperation shall aim to establish a favourable climate for private investment, both domestic and foreign, especially through better conditions for investment protection, the transfer of capital and the exchange of information on investment opportunities.

2.   The aims of cooperation shall be in particular:

- the conclusion, where appropriate, between the Member States and Georgia of agreements for the promotion and protection of investment,

- the conclusion, where appropriate, between the Member States and Georgia of agreements to avoid double taxation,

- the creation of favourable conditions for attracting foreign investments into the Georgian economy,

- to establish stable and adequate business law and conditions, and to exchange information on laws, regulations and administrative practices in the field of investment,

- to exchange information on investment opportunities in the form of, inter alia, trade fairs, exhibitions, trade weeks and other events.

Article 50
Public procurement

The Parties shall cooperate to develop conditions for open and competitive award of contracts for goods and services in particular through calls for tenders.

Article 52
Mining and raw materials

1.   The Parties shall aim at increasing investment and trade in mining and raw materials.

2.   The cooperation shall focus in particular on the following areas:

- exchange of information on the prospects of the mining and non-ferrous metals sectors,
- the establishment of a legal framework for cooperation,
- trade matters,
- the adoption and implementation of environmental legislation,
- training,
- safety in the mining industry.

Article 58
Transport

The Parties shall develop and strengthen their cooperation in the field of transport.

This cooperation, shall, inter alia, aim at restructuring and modernising transport systems and networks in Georgia, and developing and ensuring, where appropriate, compatibility of transportation systems in the context of achieving a more global transport system. Particular consideration shall be given to traditional communication links among Independent States in the transcaucasus region and with other neighbouring States.

The cooperation shall include, inter alia:

- the modernising of management and operations of road transport, railways, ports and airports,

- modernisation and development of railways, waterways, roads, ports, airports and air navigation infrastructure including the modernisation of major routes of common interest and the trans-European links for the above modes, particularly those related to the Traceca project,

- promotion and development of multimodal transport,

- the promotion of joint research and development programmes,

- preparation of the legislative and institutional framework for policy development and implementation including privatisation of the transport sector.

Article 59
Postal services and telecommunications

Within their respective powers and competences the Parties shall expand and strengthen cooperation in the following areas:

- the establishment of policies and guidelines for the development of the telecommunications sector and postal services,

- development of principles of a tariff policy and marketing in telecommunications and postal services,

- carry out transfer of technology and know how, including on European technical standards and certification systems,

- encouraging the development of projects for telecommunications and postal services and attracting investment,

- enhancing efficiency and quality of the provision of telecommunications and postal services, amongst others through liberalisation of activities of subsectors,

- advanced application of telecommunications, notably in the area of electronic funds transfer,

- management of telecommunications networks and their "optimisation",

- an appropriate regulatory basis for the provision of telecommunications and postal services and for the use of the radio frequency spectrum,

- training in the field of telecommunications and postal services for operations in market conditions.

Article 60
Financial services

Cooperation shall in particular aim at facilitating the involvement of Georgia in universally accepted systems of mutual settlements. Technical assistance shall focus on:

- the development of banking and financial services, the development of a common market of credit resources, the involvement of Georgia in a universally accepted system of mutual settlements,

- the development of a fiscal system and its institutions in Georgia, exchange of experience and personnel training,

- the development of insurance services, which would, inter alia, create a favourable framework for Community companies participation in the establishment of joint ventures in the insurance sector in Georgia, as well as the development of export credit insurance.

This cooperation shall in particular contribute to foster the development of relations between Georgia and the Member States in the financial services sector.

Article 64
Small and medium-sized enterprises

1.   The Parties shall aim to develop and strengthen small and medium-sized enterprises and their associations and cooperation between SMEs in the Community and Georgia.

2.   Cooperation shall include technical assistance, in particular in the following areas:

- the development of a legislative framework for SMEs,

- the development of an appropriate infrastructure (an agency to support SMEs, communications, assistance for the creation of a fund for SMEs),

- the development of technology parks.

ANNEX II

INTELLECTUAL, INDUSTRIAL AND COMMERCIAL PROPERTY CONVENTIONS REFERRED TO IN ARTICLE 42

1.   Article 42(2) concerns the following multilateral conventions:

- International Convention for the Protection of Performers, Producers of Phonograms and Broadcasting Organisations (Rome, 1961),

- Protocol relating to the Madrid Agreement concerning the International Registration of Marks (Madrid, 1989),

- Nice Agreement concerning the International Classification of Goods and Services for the purposes of the Registration of Marks (Geneva 1977 and amended in 1979),

- Budapest Treaty on the International Recognition of the Deposit of Micro-organisms for the purposes of Patent Procedures (1977, modified in 1980),

- International Convention for the Protection of New Varieties of Plants (UPOV) (Geneva Act, 1991).

2.   The Cooperation Council may recommend that Article 42(2) shall apply to other multilateral conventions. If problems in the area of intellectual, industrial and commercial property affecting trading conditions occur, urgent consultations will be undertaken, at the request of either party, with a view to reaching mutually satisfactory solutions.

3.   The Parties confirm the importance they attach to the obligations arising from the following multilateral conventions:

- Berne Convention for the Protection of Literary and Artistic Works (Paris Act, 1971),

- Paris Convention for the Protection of Industrial Property (Stockholm Act, 1967 and amended in 1979),

- Madrid Agreement concerning the International Registration of Marks (Stockholm Act, 1967 and amended in 1979),

- Patent Cooperation Treaty (Washington, 1970, amended in 1979 and modified in 1984).

4.   From the entry into force of this Agreement, Georgia shall grant to Community companies and nationals, in respect of the recognition and protection of intellectual, industrial and commercial property, treatment no less favourable than that granted by it to any third country under bilateral agreements.

5.   The provisions of paragraph 4 shall not apply to advantages granted by Georgia to any third country on an effective reciprocal basis and to advantages granted by Georgia to another country of the former USSR.

ANNEX III

FINANCIAL SERVICES REFERRED TO IN ARTICLE 26(3)

A financial service is any service of a financial nature offered by a financial service provider of a Party. Financial services include the following activities:

A.   All insurance and insurance-related services

    1.   Direct insurance (including coinsurance)

        (i)   life

        (ii)   non-life

    2.   Reinsurance and retrocession

    3.   Insurance intermediation, such as brokerage and agency

    4.   Services auxiliary to insurance, such as consultancy, actuarial, risk assessment and claim settlement services

B.   Banking and other financial services (excluding insurance)

    1.   Acceptance of deposits and other repayable funds from the public

    2.   Lending of all types, including, inter alia, consumer credit, mortgage credit, factoring and financing of commercial transactions

    3.   Financial leasing

    4.   All payment and money transmission services, including credit charge and debit cards, travellers cheques and bankers drafts

    5.   Guarantees and commitments

    6.   Trading for own account or for the account of customers, whether on an exchange, in an over the counter market or otherwise, the following:

        (a)   money market instruments (cheques, bills, certificates of deposits, etc.)

        (b)   foreign exchange

        (c)   derivative products including, but not limited to, futures and options

        (d)   exchange rates and interest rate instruments, including products such as swaps, forward rate agreements, etc.

        (e)   transferable securities

(f)   other negotiable instruments and financial assets, including bullion

7.   Participation in issues of all kinds of securities, including underwriting and placement as agent (whether publicly or privately) and provision of services related to such issues

8.   Money brokering

9.   Asset management, such as cash or portfolio management, all forms of collective investment management, pension fund management, custodial depository and trust services

10.   Settlement and clearing services for financial assets, including securities, derivative products, and other negotiable instruments

11.   Advisory intermediation and other auxiliary financial services on all the activities listed in points 1 to 10, including credit reference and analysis, investment and portfolio research and advice, advice on acquisitions and on corporate restructuring and strategy

12.   Provision and transfer of financial information, and financial data-processing and related software by providers of other financial services

The following activities are excluded from the definition of financial services:

(a)   activities carried out by central banks or by any other public institution in pursuit of monetary and exchange-rate policies

(b)   activities conducted by central banks, government agencies or departments, or public institutions, for the account or with the guarantee of the government, except when those activities may be carried out by financial service providers in competition with such public entities

(c)   activities forming part of a statutory system of social security or public retirement plans, except when those activities may be carried out by financial service providers in competition with public entities or private institutions

*

PART THREE

PROTOTYPE INSTRUMENTS

AGREEMENT BETWEEN THE REPUBLIC OF AUSTRIA AND THE _____ FOR THE PROMOTION AND PROTECTION OF INVESTMENTS[*]

THE REPUBLIC OF AUSTRIA AND THE _____ hereinafter referred to as "Contracting Parties",

DESIRING to create favourable conditions for greater economic co-operation between the Contracting Parties,

RECOGNIZING that the promotion and protection of investments may strengthen the readiness for such investments and hereby make an important contribution to the development of economic relations,

REAFFIRMING their commitment to the observance of internationally recognized labour standards,

HAVE AGREED AS FOLLOWS:

CHAPTER ONE: GENERAL PROVISIONS

ARTICLE 1
Definitions

For the purpose of this Agreement

(1)   "investor of a Contracting Party" means:

    (a)   a natural person having the nationality of a Contracting Party in accordance with its applicable law, or

    (b)   an enterprise constituted or organised under the applicable law of a Contracting Party making or having made an investment in the other Contracting Party's territory.

(2)   "investment by an investor of a Contracting Party" means every kind of asset in the territory of one Contracting Party, owned or controlled, directly or indirectly, by an investor of the other Contracting Party, including:

    (a)   an enterprise constituted or organised under the applicable law of the first Contracting Party;

    (b)   shares, stocks and other forms of equity participation in an enterprise as referred to in subparagraph (a), and rights derived therefrom;

    (c)   bonds, debentures, loans and other forms of debt and rights derived therefrom;

---

[*]   *Source*: The Government of Austria, Ministry of Foreign Affairs. [Note added by the editor.]

(d)   any right whether conferred by law or contract, including turnkey contracts, concessions, licences, authorisations or permits to undertake an economic activity;

(e)   claims to money and claims to performance pursuant to a contract having an economic value;

(f)   intellectual property rights as defined in the multilateral agreements concluded under the auspices of the World Intellectual Property Organisation, including industrial property rights,copyright, trademarks, patents, industrial designs and technical processes, know-how, trade secrets, trade names and goodwill;

(g)   any other tangible or intangible, movable or immovable property, or any related property rights, such as leases, mortgages, liens, pledges or usufructs.

(3)   "enterprise" means a legal person or any entity constituted or organised under the applicable law of a Contracting Party, whether or not for profit, and whether private or government owned or controlled, including a corporation, trust, partnership, sole proprietorship, branch, joint venture or association

(4)   "returns" means the amounts yielded by an investment and, in particular, profits, interests, capital gains, dividends, royalties, licence fees and other fees.

(5)   „without delay" means such period as is normally required for the completion of necessary formalities for the payments of compensation or for the transfer of payments. This period shall commence for payments of compensation on the day of expropriation and for transfers of payments on the day on which the request for transfer has been submitted. It shall in no case exceed one month.

(6)   "territory" means with respect to each Contracting Party the land territory, internal waters, maritime and airspace under its sovereignty, including the exclusive economic zone and the continental shelf where the Contracting Party exercises, in conformity with international law, sovereign rights and jurisdiction.

ARTICLE 2
Promotion and Admission of Investments

(1)   Each Contracting Party shall, according to its laws and regulations, promote and admit investments by investors of the other Contracting Party.

(2)   Any alteration of the form in which assets are invested or reinvested shall not affect their character as an investment provided that such alteration is in accordance with the laws and regulations of the Contracting Party in whose territory the investment was made.

ARTICLE 3
Treatment of Investments

(1)   Each Contracting Party shall accord to investments by investors of the other Contracting Party fair and equitable treatment and full and constant protection and security.

(2)   A Contracting Party shall not impair by unreasonable or discriminatory measures the management, operation, maintenance, use, enjoyment, sale and liquidation of an investment by investors of the other Contracting Party.

(3)   Each Contracting Party shall accord to investors of the other Contracting Party and to their investments treatment no less favourable than that it accords to its own investors and their investments or to investors of any third country and their investments with respect to the management, operation, maintenance, use, enjoyment, sale and liquidation of an investment, whichever is more favourable to the investor.

(4)   No provision of this Agreement shall be construed as to oblige a Contracting Party to extend to the investors of the other Contracting Party and to their investments the present or future benefit of any treatment, preference or privilege resulting from

> (a)   any membership in a free trade area, customs union, common market, economic communityor any multilateral agreement on investment;

> (b)   any international agreement, international arrangement or domestic legislation regarding taxation.

ARTICLE 4
Transparency

(1)   Each Contracting Party shall promptly publish, or otherwise make publicly available, its laws, regulations, procedures as well as international agreements which may affect the operation of the Agreement.

(2)   Each Contracting Party shall promptly respond to specific questions and provide, upon request, information to the other Contracting Party on matters referred to in paragraph (1).

(3)   No Contracting Party shall be required to furnish or allow access to information concerning particular investors or investments the disclosure of which would impede law enforcement or would be contrary to its laws and regulations protecting confidentiality.

ARTICLE 5
Expropriation and Compensation

(1)   A Contracting Party shall not expropriate or nationalize directly or indirectly an investment of an investor of the other Contracting Party or take any measures having equivalent effect (hereinafter referred to as expropriation) except:

> (a)   or a purpose which is in the public interest,
> (b)   on a non-discriminatory basis,
> (c)   in accordance with due process of law, and
> (d)   accompanied by payment of prompt, adequate and effective compensation in accordance with paragraphs (2) and (3).

(2)   Compensation shall:

(a)   be paid without delay. In case of delay any exchange rate loss arising from this delay shall be borne by the host country.

(b)   be equivalent to the fair market value of the expropriated investment immediately before the expropriation occurred. The fair market value shall not reflect any change in value occurring because the expropriation had become publicly known earlier.

(c)   be paid and made freely transferable to the country designated by the claimants concerned and in the currency of the country of which the claimants are nationals or in any freely convertible currency accepted by the claimants.

(d)   include interest at a commercial rate established on a market basis for the currency of payment from the date of expropriation until the date of actual payment.

(3)   An investor of a Contracting Party which claims to be affected by expropriation by the other Contracting Party shall have the right to prompt review of its case, including the valuation of its investment and the payment of compensation in accordance with the provisions of this Article, by a judicial authority or another competent and independent authority of the latter Contracting Party.

ARTICLE 6
Compensation for Losses

(1)   An investor of a Contracting Party who has suffered a loss relating to its investment in the territory of the other Contracting Party due to war or to other armed conflict, state of emergency, revolution, insurrection, civil disturbance, or any other similar event, or acts of God or force majeure, in the territory of the latter Contracting Party, shall be accorded by the latter Contracting Party, as regards restitution, indemnification, compensation or any other settlement,

treatment no less favourable than that which it accords to its own investors or to investors of any third state, whichever is most favourable to the investor.

(2)   An investor of a Contracting Party who in any of the events referred to in paragraph (1) suffers loss resulting from:

(a)   requisitioning of its investment or part thereof by the forces or authorities of the other Contracting Party, or

(b)   destruction of its investment or part thereof by the forces or authorities of the other Contracting Party, which was not required by the necessity of the situation, shall in any case be accorded by the latter Contracting Party restitution or compensation which in either case shall be prompt, adequate and effective and, with respect to compensation, shall be in accordance with Article 5 (2) and (3).

ARTICLE 7
Transfers

(1)   Each Contracting Party shall guarantee that all payments relating to an investment by an investor of the other Contracting Party may be freely transferred into and out of its territory without delay. Such transfers shall include, in particular:

(a)   the initial capital and additional amounts to maintain or increase an investment;
(b)   returns;
(c)   payments made under a contract including a loan agreement;
(d)   proceeds from the sale or liquidation of all or any part of an investment;
(e)   payments of compensation under Articles 5 and 6;
(f)   payments arising out of the settlement of a dispute;
(g)   earnings and other remuneration of personnel engaged from abroad in connection with an investment.

(2)   Each Contracting Party shall further guarantee that such transfers may be made in a freely convertible currency at the market rate of exchange prevailing on the date of transferin the territory of the Contracting Party from which the transfer ismade. The bank charges shall be fair and equitable.

(3)   In the absence of a market for foreign exchange, the rate to be used shall be the most recent exchange rate for conversion of currencies into Special Drawing Rights.

(4)   Notwithstanding paragraphs (1) to (3), a Contracting Party may prevent a transfer through the equitable, non-discriminatory and good faith application of measures to protect the rights of creditors, relating to or ensuring compliance with laws and regulations on the issuing, trading and dealing in securities, futures and derivatives, reports or records of transfer, or in connection with criminal offences and orders or judgements in administrative and adjudicatory proceedings, provided that such measures and their application shall not be used as a means of avoiding the Contracting Party's commitments or obligations under this Agreement.

ARTICLE 8
Subrogation

If a Contracting Party or its designated agency makes a payment under an indemnity, guarantee or contract of insurance given in respect of an investment by an investor in the territory of the other Contracting Party, the latter Contracting Party shall recognize without prejudice to the rights of the investor under Chapter Two Part One the assignment of any right or claim of such investor to the former Contracting

Party or its designated agency and the right of the former Contracting Party or its designated agency to exercise by virtue of subrogation any such right and claim to the same extent as its predecessor in title.

ARTICLE 9
Other Obligations

(1)   Each Contracting Party shall observe any obligation it may have entered into with regard to specific investments by investors of the other Contracting Party.

(2)   If the laws of either Contracting Party or obligations under international law existing at present or established hereafter between the Contracting Parties in addition to the present Agreement contain rules, whether general or specific, entitling investments by nationals or enterprises of the other Contracting Party to a treatment more favourable than is provided for by the present Agreement, such rules shall to the extent that they are more favourable prevail over the present Agreement.

ARTICLE 10
Denial of Benefits

A Contracting Party may deny the benefits of this Agreement to an investor of the other Contracting Party and to its investments, if investors of a Non-Contracting Party own or control the first mentioned investor and that investor has no substantial business activity in the territory of the Contracting Party under whose law it is constituted or organized.

CHAPTER TWO: DISPUTE SETTLEMENT

PART ONE: Settlement of Disputes between an Investor and a Contracting Party

ARTICLE 11
Scope and Standing

This Part applies to disputes between a Contracting Party and an investor of the other Contracting Party concerning an alleged breach of an obligation of the former under this Agreement which causes loss or damage to the investor or his investment.

ARTICLE 12
Means of Settlement, Time Periods

(1)   A dispute between a Contracting Party and an investor of the other Contracting Party, shall, if possible, be settled by negotiation or consultation. If it is not so settled, the investor may choose to submit it for resolution:

    (a)   to the competent courts or administrative tribunals of the Contracting Party, party to the dispute;

    (b)   in accordance with any applicable previously agreed dispute settlement procedure; or

    (c)   in accordance with this Article to:

        (i)   the International Centre for Settlement of Investment Disputes ("the Centre"), established pursuant to the Convention of the Settlement of Investment Disputes between States and Nationals of other States, signed in Washington on 18 March 1965 ("the ICSID Convention"), if the Contracting Party of the investor and the Contracting Party, party to the dispute, are both parties to the ICSID Convention;

(ii)   the Centre under the rules governing the Additional Facility for the Administration of Proceedings by the Secretariat of the Centre, if the Contracting Party of the investor or the Contracting Party, party to the dispute, but not both, is a party to the ICSID Convention;

(iii)   a sole arbitrator or an ad hoc arbitration tribunal established under the Arbitration Rules of the United Nations Commission on International Trade Law ("UNCITRAL");

(iv)   the International Chamber of Commerce, by a sole arbitrator or an ad hoc tribunal under its rules of arbitration.

(2)   A dispute may be submitted for resolution pursuant to paragraph 1 (c) of this Article after 60 days from the date notice of intent to do so was provided to the Contracting Party, party to the dispute, but not later than five years from the date the investor first acquired or should have acquired knowledge of the events which gave rise to the dispute.

ARTICLE 13
Contracting Party Consent

(1)   Each Contracting Party hereby gives its unconditional consent to the submission of a dispute to international arbitration in accordance with this Part. However, a dispute may not be submitted to international arbitration if a local court in either Contracting Party has rendered its decision on the dispute.

(2)   The consent referred to in paragraph (1) implies the renunciation of the requirement that the internal administrative or juridical remedies should be exhausted.

ARTICLE 14
Place of Arbitration

Any arbitration under this Part shall, at the request of any party to the dispute, be held in a state that is party to the United Nations Convention on the Recognition and Enforcement of Foreign Arbitral Awards, signed in New York on 10 June 1958 (New York Convention). Claims submitted to arbitration under this Part shall be considered to arise out of a commercial relationship or transaction for purposes of Article 1 of the New York Convention.

ARTICLE 15
Indemnification

A Contracting Party shall not assert as a defence, counter-claim, right of set-off or for any other reason, that indemnification or other compensation for all or part of the alleged damages has been received or will be received pursuant to an indemnity, guarantee or insurance contract.

ARTICLE 16
Applicable Law

(1)   A tribunal established under this Part shall decide the dispute in accordance with this Agreement and applicable rules and principles of international law.

(2)   Issues in dispute under Article 9 shall be decided, absent other agreement, in accordance with the law of the Contracting Party, party to the dispute, the law governing the authorization or agreement and such rules of international law as may be applicable.

ARTICLE 17
Awards and Enforcement

(1)   Arbitration awards, which may include an award of interest, shall be final and binding upon the parties to the dispute and may provide the following forms of relief:

    (a)   a declaration that the Contracting Party has failed to comply with its obligations under this Agreement;

    (b)   pecuniary compensation, which shall include interest from the time the loss or damage was incurred until time of payment;

    (c)   restitution in kind in appropriate cases, provided that the Contracting Party may pay pecuniary compensation in lieu thereof where restitution is not practicable; and

    (d)   with the agreement of the parties to the dispute, any other form of relief.

(2)   Each Contracting Party shall make provision for the effective enforcement of awards made pursuant to this Article and shall carry out without delay any such award issued in a proceeding to which it is party.

PART TWO: Settlement of Disputes between the Contracting Parties

ARTICLE 18
Scope, Consultations, Mediation and Conciliation

Disputes between the Contracting Parties concerning the interpretation or application of this Agreement shall, as far as possible, be settled amicably or through consultations, mediation or conciliation.

ARTICLE 19
Initiation of Proceedings

(1)   At the request of either Contracting Party a dispute concerning the interpretation or application of this Agreement may be submitted to an arbitral tribunal for decision not earlier than 60 days after such request has been notified to the other Contracting Party.

(2)   A Contracting Party may not initiate proceedings under this Part for a dispute regarding the infringement of rights of an investor which that investor has submitted to arbitration under Part One of Chapter Two of this Agreement, unless the other Contracting Party has failed to abide by and comply with the award rendered in that dispute or those proceedings have terminated without resolution by an arbitral tribunal of the investor's claim.

ARTICLE 20
Formation of the Tribunal

(1)   The arbitral tribunal shall be constituted ad hoc as follows:

Each Contracting Party shall appoint one member and these two members shall agree upon a national of a third state as their chairman. Such members shall be appointed within two (2) months from the date one Contracting Party has informed the other Contracting Party of its intention to submit the dispute to an arbitral tribunal, the chairman of which shall be appointed within two (2) further months.

(2)   If the periods specified in paragraph (1) of this Article are not observed, either Contracting Party may, in the absence of any relevant arrangement, invite the President of the International Court of Justice to make the necessary appointments. If the President of the International Court of Justice is a national of either of the Contracting Parties or if he/she is otherwise prevented from discharging the said function, the Vice-President or in case of his/her inability the member of the International Court of Justice next in seniority should be invited under the same conditions to make the necessary appointments.

(3)   Members of an arbitral tribunal shall be independent and impartial.

ARTICLE 21
Applicable Law, Default Rules

(1)   The arbitral tribunal will decide disputes in accordance with this Agreement and the applicable rules and principles of international law.

(2)   Unless the parties to the dispute decide otherwise, the Permanent Court of Arbitration Optional Rules for Arbitrating Disputes shall apply to matters not governed by other provisions of this Part.

ARTICLE 22
Awards

(1)   The tribunal, in its award, shall set out its findings of law and fact, together with the reasons therefore, and may, at the request of a Contracting Party, award the following forms of relief:

    (a)   a declaration that an action of a Contracting Party is in contravention of its obligations under this Agreement;

    (b)   a recommendation that a Contracting Party brings its actions into conformity with its obligations under this Agreement;

    (c)   pecuniary compensation for any loss or damage to the requesting Contracting Party's investor or its investment; or

    (d)   any other form of relief to which the Contracting Party against whom the award is made consents, including restitution in kind to an investor.

(2)   The arbitration award shall be final and binding upon the parties to the dispute.

ARTICLE 23
Costs

Each Contracting Party shall pay the costs of its representation in the proceedings. The costs of the tribunal shall be paid for equally by the Contracting Parties unless the tribunal directs that they be shared differently.

ARTICLE 24
Enforcement

Pecuniary awards which have not been complied with within one year from the date of the award may be enforced in the courts of either Contracting Party with jurisdiction over assets of the defaulting Contracting Party.

CHAPTER THREE: FINAL PROVISIONS

ARTICLE 25
Application of the Agreement

(1)   This Agreement shall apply to investments made in the territory of either Contracting Party in accordance with its legislation by investors of the other Contracting Party prior as well as after the entry into force of this Agreement.

(2)   This Agreement shall not apply to claims which have been settled or procedures which have been initiated prior to its entry into force.

ARTICLE 26
Consultations

Each Contracting Party may propose to the other Contracting Party consultations on any matter relating to this Agreement. These consultations shall be held at a place and at a time agreed upon through diplomatic channels.

ARTICLE 27
Entry into Force and Duration

(1)   This Agreement is subject to ratification and shall enter into force on the first day of the third month that follows the month during which the instruments of ratification have been exchanged.

(2)   This Agreement shall remain in force for a period of ten years; it shall be extended thereafter for an indefinite period and may be denounced in writing through diplomatic channels by either Contracting Party giving twelve months' notice.

(3)   In respect of investments made prior to the date of termination of the present Agreement the provisions of Articles 1 to 25 of the present Agreement shall continue to be effective for a further period of ten years from the date of termination of the present Agreement.

DONE in duplicate at _____ , on _____ , in the German, _____ and English languages, all texts being equally authentic. In case of difference of interpretation the English text shall prevail.

For the Republic of Austria: For the Government of ……………………..

*

AGREEMENT BETWEEN THE BELGO-LUXEMBURG ECONOMIC UNION, ON THE ONE HAND, AND _____, ON THE OTHER HAND, ON THE RECIPROCAL PROMOTION AND PROTECTION OF INVESTMENTS[*]

The Government of the Kingdom of Belgium, acting both in its own name and in the name of the Government of the Grand-Duchy of Luxemburg, by virtue of existing agreements, the Walloon Government, the Flemish Government, and the Government of the Region of Brussels-Capital, on the one hand, and _____, on the other hand (hereinafter referred to as "the Contracting Parties"),

desiring to strengthen their economic cooperation by creating favourable conditions for investments by investors of one Contracting Party in the territory of the other Contracting Party,

have agreed as follows:

ARTICLE 1
DEFINITIONS

For the purpose of this Agreement,

1.   The term "investors" shall mean:

   a)   the "nationals", i.e. any natural person who, according to the legislation of the Kingdom of Belgium, of the Grand-Duchy of Luxemburg or of _____, is considered as a citizen of the Kingdom of Belgium, of the Grand-Duchy of Luxemburg or of _____ respectively;

   b)   the "companies", i.e. any legal person constituted in accordance with the legislation of the Kingdom of Belgium, of the Grand-Duchy of Luxemburg or of _____ and having its registered office in the territory of the Kingdom of Belgium, of the Grand-Duchy of Luxemburg or of _____ respectively.

2.   The term "investments" shall mean any kind of assets and any direct or indirect contribution in cash, in kind or in services, invested or reinvested in any sector of economic activity.

The following shall more particularly, though not exclusively, be considered as investments for the purpose of this Agreement:

   a)   movable and immovable property as well as any other rights in rem, such as mortgages, liens, pledges, usufruct and similar rights;

   b)   shares, corporate rights and any other kind of shareholdings, including minority or indirect ones, in companies constituted in the territory of one Contracting Party;

---

[*]   *Source*: The Government of Belgium and Luxemburg, Ministry of Foreign Affairs. [Note added by the editor.]

c) bonds, claims to money and to any performance having an economic value;

d) copyrights, industrial property rights, technical processes, trade names and goodwill;

e) concessions granted under public law or under contract, including concessions to explore, develop, extract or exploit natural resources.

Changes in the legal form in which assets and capital have been invested or reinvested shall not affect their designation as "investments" for the purpose of this Agreement.

3. The term "returns" shall mean the proceeds of an investment and shall include in particular, though not exclusively, profits, interests, capital gains, dividends, royalties and fees.

4. The term "territory" shall apply to the territory of the Kingdom of Belgium, to the territory of the Grand-Duchy of Luxemburg and to the territory of _____, as well as to the maritime areas, i.e. the marine and underwater areas which extend beyond the territorial waters of the States concerned and upon which the latter exercise, in accordance with international law, their sovereign rights and their jurisdiction for the purpose of exploring, exploiting and preserving natural resources.

ARTICLE 2
PROMOTION OF INVESTMENTS

1. Each Contracting Party shall promote investments in its territory by investors of the other Contracting Party and shall accept such investments in accordance with its legislation.

2. In particular, each Contracting Party shall authorise the conclusion and the fulfilment of license contracts and commercial, administrative or technical assistance agreements, as far as these activities are in connection with such investments.

ARTICLE 3
PROTECTION OF INVESTMENTS

1. All investments, whether direct or indirect, made by investors of one Contracting Party shall enjoy fair and equitable treatment in the territory of the other Contracting Party.

2. Except for measures required to maintain public order, such investments shall enjoy continuous protection and security, i.e. excluding any unjustified or discriminatory measure which could hinder, either in law or in practice, the management, maintenance, use, possession or liquidation thereof.

ARTICLE 4
NATIONAL TREATMENT AND MOST FAVOURED NATION

1. In all matters relating to the treatment of investments the investors of each Contracting Party shall enjoy national treatment and most-favoured-nation treatment in the territory of the other Party.

2.   With respect to the operation, management, maintenance, use, enjoyment and sale or other disposal of investments, each Contracting Party shall accord, in its territory, to investors of the other Contracting Party, treatment no less favourable than that granted to its own investors or to investors of any other State if the latter is more favourable.

3.   This treatment shall not include the privileges granted by one Contracting Party to investors of a third State by virtue of its participation or association in a free trade zone, customs union, common market or any other form of regional economic organisation.

4.   The provisions of this article do not apply to tax matters.

ARTICLE 5
DEPRIVATION AND LIMITATION OF OWNERSHIP

1.   Each Contracting Party undertakes not to adopt any measure of expropriation or nationalisation or any other measure having the effect of directly or indirectly dispossessing the investors of the other Contracting Party of their investments in its territory.

2.   If reasons of public purpose, security or national interest require a derogation from the provisions of paragraph 1, the following conditions shall be complied with:

   a)   the measures shall be taken under due process of law;

   b)   the measures shall be neither discriminatory, nor contrary to any specific commitments;

   c)   the measures shall be accompanied by provisions for the payment of an adequate and effective compensation.

3.   Such compensation shall amount to the actual value of the investments on the day before the measures were taken or became public.

Such compensation shall be paid in the currency of the State of which the investor is a national or in any other convertible currency. It shall be paid without delay and shall be freely transferable. It shall bear interest at the normal commercial rate from the date of the determination of its amount until the date of its payment.

4.   Investors of one Contracting Party whose investments suffer losses owing to war or other armed conflict, revolution, a state of national emergency or revolt in the territory of the other Contracting Party shall be granted by the latter Contracting Party a treatment, as regards restitution, indemnification, compensation or other settlement, at least equal to that which the latter Contracting Party grants to the investors of the most favoured nation.

5.   In respect of matters dealt with in this Article, each Contracting Party shall grant to the investors of the other Contracting Party a treatment which shall at least be equal to that granted in its territory to the investors of the most favoured nation. This treatment shall in no case be less favourable than that recognised under international law.

ARTICLE 6
TRANSFERS

1.   Each Contracting Party shall guarantee to investors of the other Contracting Party the free transfer of all payments relating to an investment, including more particularly:

   a)   amounts necessary for establishing, maintaining or expanding the investment;

   b)   amounts necessary for payments under a contract, including amounts necessary for repayment of loans, royalties and other payments resulting from licences, franchises, concessions and other similar rights, as well as salaries of expatriate personnel;

   c)   returns from investments;

   d)   proceeds from the total or partial liquidation of investments, including capital gains or increases in the invested capital;

   e)   compensation paid pursuant to Article 5.

2.   The nationals of each Contracting Party who have been authorised to work in the territory of the other Contracting Party in connection with an investment shall also be permitted to transfer an appropriate portion of their earnings to their country of origin.

3.   Transfers shall be made in freely convertible currency at the rate applicable on the day transfers are made to spottransactions in the currency used.

4.   Each Contracting Party shall issue the authorisations required to ensure that the transfers can be made without undue delay, with no expenses other than the usual banking costs.

5.   The guarantees referred to in this Article shall at least be equal to those granted to the investors of the most favoured nation.

ARTICLE 7
SUBROGATION

1.   If one Contracting Party or any public institution of this Party pays compensation to its own investors pursuant to a guarantee providing coverage for an investment, the other Contracting Party shall recognise that the former Contracting Party or the public institution concerned is subrogated into the rights of the investors.

2.   As far as the transferred rights are concerned, the other Contracting Party shall be entitled to invoke against the insurer who is subrogated into the rights of the indemnified investors the obligations of the latter under law or contract.

ARTICLE 8
APPLICABLE REGULATIONS

If an issue relating to investments is covered both by this Agreement and by the national legislation of one Contracting Party or by international conventions, existing or to be subscribed to by the Parties in the future, the investors of the other Contracting Party shall be entitled to avail themselves of the provisions that are the most favourable to them.

ARTICLE 9
SPECIFIC COMMITMENTS

1.   Investments made pursuant to a specific agreement concluded between one Contracting Party and investors of the other Party shall be covered by the provisions of this Agreement and by those of the specific agreement.

2.   Each Contracting Party undertakes to ensure at all times that the commitments it has entered into vis-à-vis investors of the other Contracting Party shall be observed.

ARTICLE 10
SETTLEMENT OF INVESTMENT DISPUTES

1.   Any investment dispute between an investor of one Contracting Party and the other Contracting Party shall be notified in writing by the first party to take action. The notification shall be accompanied by a sufficiently detailed memorandum.

As far as possible, the Parties shall endeavour to settle the dispute through negotiations, if necessary by seeking expert advice from a third party, or by conciliation between the Contracting Parties through diplomatic channels.

2.   In the absence of an amicable settlement by direct agreement between the parties to the dispute or by conciliation through diplomatic channels within six months from the notification, the dispute shall be submitted, at the option of the investor, either to the competent jurisdiction of the State where the investment was made, or international arbitration.

To this end, each Contracting Party agrees in advance and irrevocably to the settlement of any dispute by this type of arbitration. Such consent implies that both Parties waive the right to demand that all domestic administrative or judiciary remedies be exhausted.

3.   In case of international arbitration, the dispute shall be submitted for settlement to arbitration to one of the hereinafter mentioned organisations, at the option of the investor:

> - an ad hoc arbitral tribunal set up according to the arbitration rules laid down by the United Nations Commission on International Trade Law (U.N.C.I.T.R.A.L.); or

> - the International Centre for the Settlement of Investment Disputes (I.C.S.I.D.), set up by the Convention on the Settlement of Investment Disputes between States and Nationals of other States, opened for signature at Washington on March 18, 1965, when each State party to this Agreement has become a party to the said Convention. As long as this requirement is not met, each Contracting Party agrees that the dispute shall be submitted to arbitration pursuant to the Rules of the Additional Facility of the I.C.S.I.D.; or

> - the Arbitral Court of the International Chamber of Commerce in Paris;or

> - the Arbitration Institute of the Chamber of Commerce in Stockholm.

If the arbitration procedure has been introduced upon the initiative of a Contracting Party, this Party shall request the investor involved in writing to designate the arbitration organisation to which the dispute shall be referred.

4.   At any stage of the arbitration proceedings or of the execution of an arbitral award, none of the Contracting Parties involved in a dispute shall be entitled to raise as an objection the fact that the investor who is the opposing party in the dispute has received compensation totally or partly covering his losses pursuant to an insurance policy or to the guarantee provided for in Article 7 of this Agreement.

5.   The arbitral tribunal shall decide on the basis of the national law, including the rules relating to conflicts of law, of the Contracting Party involved in the dispute in whose territory the investment has been made, as well as on the basis of the provisions of this Agreement, of the terms of the specific agreement which may have been entered into regarding the investment, and of the principles of international law.

6.   The arbitral award shall be final and binding on the parties to the dispute. Each Contracting Party undertakes to execute the award in accordance with its national legislation.

ARTICLE 11
DISPUTES BETWEEN THE CONTRACTING PARTIES RELATING TO THE INTERPRETATION OR APPLICATION OF THIS AGREEMENT

1.   Any dispute relating to the interpretation or application of this Agreement shall be settled as far as possible through diplomatic channels.

2.   In the absence of a settlement through diplomatic channels, the dispute shall be submitted to a joint commission consisting of representatives of the two Parties; this commission shall convene without undue delay at the request of the first party to take action.

3.   If the joint commission cannot settle the dispute, the latter shall be submitted, at the request of either Contracting Party, to an arbitration court set up as follows for each individual case:

Each Contracting Party shall appoint one arbitrator within a period of two months from the date on which either Contracting Party has informed the other Party of its intention to submit the dispute to arbitration. Within a period of two months following their appointment, these two arbitrators shall appoint by mutual agreement a national of a third State as chairman of the arbitration court.

If these time limits have not been complied with, either Contracting Party shall request the President of the International Court of Justice to make the necessary appointment(s).

If the President of the International Court of Justice is a national of either Contracting Party or of a State with which one of the Contracting Parties has no diplomatic relations or if, for any other reason, he cannot exercise this function, the Vice-President of the International Court of Justice shall be requested to make the appointment(s).

4.   The court thus constituted shall determine its own rules of procedure. Its decisions shall be taken by a majority of votes and shall be final and binding on the Contracting Parties.

5.   Each Contracting Party shall bear the costs resulting from the appointment of its arbitrator. The expenses in connection with the appointment of the third arbitrator and the administrative cost of the court shall be borne equally by the Contracting Parties.

ARTICLE 12
PREVIOUS INVESTMENTS.

This Agreement shall also apply to investments made before its entry into force by investors of one Contracting Party in the territory of the other Contracting Party in accordance with the latter's laws and regulations.

ARTICLE 13
ENTRY INTO FORCE AND DURATION.

1.   This Agreement shall enter into force one month after the date of exchange of the instruments of ratification by the Contracting Parties. The Agreement shall remain in force for a period of ten years.

Unless notice of termination is given by either Contracting Party at least six months before the expiry of its period of validity, this Agreement shall be tacitly extended each time for a further period of ten years, it being understood that each Contracting Party reserves the right to terminate the Agreement by notification given at least six months before the date of expiry of the current period of validity.

2.   Investments made prior to the date of termination of this Agreement shall be covered by this Agreement for a period of ten years from the date of termination.

IN WITNESS WHEREOF, the undersigned representatives, duly authorised thereto by their respective Governments, have signed this Agreement.

DONE at _____, on _____, in two original copies, each in the French, Dutch and _____ languages, all texts being equally authentic. The text in the _____ language shall prevail in case of difference of interpretation.

FOR THE BELGO-LUXEMBURG   FOR THE GOVERNMENT OF
ECONOMIC UNION:_____   _____

For the Government of the Kingdom of Belgium acting both in its own name and in the name of the Government of the Grand-Duchy of Luxemburg:

For the Walloon Government:
For the Flemish Government:
For the Government of the Region of Brussels-Capital:

*

Standard Draft, August 2000

AGREEMENT BETWEEN THE GOVERNMENT OF THE KINGDOM OF DENMARK AND THE GOVERNMENT OF _____CONCERNING THE PROMOTION AND RECIPROCAL PROTECTION OF INVESTMENTS[*]

Preamble

The Government of the Kingdom of Denmark and the Government of _____hereinafter referred to as the Contracting Parties,

DESIRING to create favourable conditions for investments in both States and to intensify the co-operation between private enterprises in both States with a view to stimulating the productive use of resources,

RECOGNIZING that a fair and equitable treatment of investments on a reciprocal basis will serve this aim,

HAVE AGREED as follows:

Article 1
Definitions

For the purpose of this Agreement,

1.   The term "investment" means every kind of asset and shall include in particular, but not exclusively:

    a)   tangible and intangible, movable and immovable property, as well as any other rights such as leases, mortgages, liens, pledges, privileges, guarantees and any other similar rights,

    b)   a company or business enterprise, or shares, stock or other forms of participation in a company or business enterprise and bonds and debt of a company or business enterprise,

    c)   returns reinvested, claims to money and claims to performance pursuant to contracts having an economic value,

    d)   industrial and intellectual property rights, including copyrights, patents, trade names, technology, trademarks, goodwill, know-how and any other similar rights,

    e)   concessions or other rights conferred by law or under contract, including concessions to search for, extract or exploit natural resources.

---

[*]   *Source*: The Government of Denmark, Ministry of Foreign Affairs. [Note added by the editor.]

2.   A change in the form in which assets are invested, does not affect their character as investments.

3.   The term "returns" means the amounts yielded by an investment and includes in particular, though not exclusively, profit, interest, capital gains, dividends, royalties or fees.

4.   Returns, and in case of reinvestment amounts yielded from the reinvestment, shall be given the same protection as the investment in accordance with the provisions of this Agreement.

5.   The term "investor" means with respect to each Contracting Party:

a)   Natural persons having the citizenship or nationality of, or who are permanently residing in each Contracting Party in accordance with its laws.

b)   Any entity established in accordance with, and recognised as a legal person by the law of that Contracting Party, such as companies, firms, associations, development finance institutions, foundations or similar entities irrespective of whether their liabilities are limited and whether or not their activities are directed at profit.

6.   The term "territory" means with respect to each Contracting Party the territory under its sovereignty as well as maritime zones and continental shelf over which the Contracting Party exercises sovereign rights or jurisdiction in accordance with international law.

Article 2
Promotion and Protection of Investments

1.   Each Contracting Party shall admit investments by investors of the other Contracting Party in accordance with its legislation and administrative practice and encourage such investments, including facilitating the establishment of representative offices.

2.   Investments of investors of each Contracting Party shall at all times enjoy full protection and security in the territory of the other Contracting Party. Neither Contracting Party shall in any way impair by unreasonable or discriminatory measures the management, maintenance, use, enjoyment or disposal of investments in its territory of investors of the other Contracting Party.

3.   Each Contracting Party shall observe any obligation it may have entered into with regard to investments of investors of the other Contracting Party.

Article 3
Treatment of Investments

1.   Each Contracting Party shall in its territory accord to investments made by investors of the other Contracting Party fair and equitable treatment which in no case shall be less favourable than that accorded to its own investors or to investors of any third state, whichever is the more favourable from the point of view of the investor.

2.   Each Contracting Party shall in its territory accord investors of the other Contracting Party, as regards their management, maintenance, use, enjoyment or disposal of their investment, fair and equitable treatment which in no case shall be less favourable than that accorded to its

own investors or to investors of any third State, whichever of these standards is the more favourable from the point of view of the investor.

Article 4
Exceptions

The provisions of this Agreement relative to the granting of treatment not less favourable than that accorded to the investors of each Contracting Party or of any third State shall not be construed so as to oblige one Contracting Party to extend to the investors of the other Contracting Party the benefit of any treatment, preference or privilege resulting from:

a) membership of any existing or future Regional Economic Integration Organisation or customs union of which one of the Contracting Parties is or may become a party, or

b) any international agreement or arrangement relating wholly or mainly to taxation or any domestic legislation relating wholly or mainly to taxation.

Article 5
Expropriation and Compensation

1. Investments of investors of each Contracting Party shall not be nationalised, expropriated or subjected to measures having effect equivalent to nationalisation or expropriation (hereinafter referred to as "expropriation") in the territory of the other Contracting Party except for expropriations made in the public interest, on a basis of non-discrimination, carried out under due process of law, and against prompt, adequate and effective compensation.

2. Such compensation shall amount to the fair market value of the investment expropriated immediately before the expropriation or impending expropriation became known in such a way as to affect the value of the investment (hereinafter referred to as the "valuation date").

3. Such fair market value shall be calculated in a freely convertible currency on the basis of the market rate of exchange existing for that currency on the valuation date. Compensation shall be paid promptly and include interest at a commercial rate established on a market basis from the date of expropriation until the date of payment.

4. The investor affected shall have a right to prompt review under the law of the Contracting Party making the expropriation, by a judicial or other competent and independent authority of that Contracting Party, of its case, of the valuation of its investment, and of the payment of compensation, in accordance with the principles set out in paragraph 1 of this Article.

5. When a Contracting Party expropriates the assets of a company or an enterprise in its territory, which is incorporated or constituted under its law, and in which investors of the other Contracting Party have an investment, including through shareholding, the provisions of this Article shall apply to ensure prompt, adequate and effective compensation for those investors for any impairment or diminishment of the fair market value of such investment resulting from the expropriation.

Article 6
Compensation for Losses

1   Investors of one Contracting Party whose investments in the territory of the other Contracting Party suffer losses owing to war or other armed conflict, revolution, a state of national emergency, revolt, insurrection, or riot in the territory of the latter Contracting Party, shall be accorded by the latter Contracting Party treatment, as regards restitution, indemnification, compensation or other settlement, no less favourable than that which the latter Contracting Party accords to its own investors or to investors of any third State, whichever of these standards is the more favourable from the point of view of the investor.

2.   Without prejudice to paragraph 1 of this Article, an investor of a Contracting Party who, in any of the situations referred to in that paragraph, suffers a loss in the area of another Contracting Party resulting from..

   a)   requisitioning of its investment or part thereof by the latter's forces or authorities, or

   b)   destruction of its investment or part thereof by the latter's forces or authorities, which was not required by the necessity of the situation, shall be accorded restitution or compensation which in either case shall be prompt, adequate and effective.

Article 7
Transfer of Capital and Returns

1.   Each Contracting Party shall with respect to investments in its territory by investors of the other Contracting Party allow the free transfer into and out of its territory of:

   a)   the initial capital and any additional capital for the maintenance and development of an investment;

   b)   the invested capital or the proceeds from the sale or liquidation of all or any part of an investment;

   c)   interest, dividends, profits and other returns realised;

   d)   payments made for the reimbursement of the credits for investments, and interest due;

   e)   payments derived from rights enumerated in Article 1, paragraph 1, (d), of this Agreement;

   f)   unspent earnings and other remuneration of personnel engaged from abroad in connection with an investment;

   g)   compensation, restitution, indemnification or other settlement pursuant to Articles 5 and 6.

2.   Transfers of payments under paragraph 1 of this Article shall be effected without delay and in a freely convertible currency.

3.   Transfers shall be made at the market rate of exchange existing on the date of transfer with respect to spot transactions in the currency to be transferred. In the absence of a market for foreign exchange, the rate to be used will be the most recent exchange rate applied to inward investments.

Article 8
Subrogation

If one Contracting Party or its designated agency makes a payment to its own investors under a guarantee it has accorded in respect of an investment in the territory of the other Contracting Party, the latter Contracting Party shall recognise:

   a)   the assignment, whether under the law or pursuant to a legal transaction, of any right or claim by the investor to the former Contracting Party or to its designated agency and

   b)   that the former Contracting Party or its designated agency is entitled by virtue of subrogation to exercise the rights and enforce the claims of that investor.

Article 9
Settlement of disputes between a Contracting Party
and an investor of the other Contracting Party

1.   Any dispute concerning an investment between an investor of one Contracting Party and the other Contracting Party shall, if possible, be settled amicably.

2.   If any such dispute cannot be settled within six months following the date on which the dispute has been raised by the investor through written notification to the Contracting Party, each Contracting Party hereby consents to the submission of the dispute, at the investor's choice, for resolution by international arbitration to one of the following fora:

   a)   The International Centre for Settlement of Investment Disputes (ICSID) for settlement by arbitration under the Washington Convention of 18 March 1965 on the Settlement of Investment Disputes between States and Nationals of Other States provided both Contracting Parties are parties to the said Convention; or

   b)   the Additional Facility of the Centre, if the Centre is not available under the Convention; or

   c)   an ad hoc tribunal set up under Arbitration Rules of the United Nations Commission on International Trade Law (UNCITRAL). The appointing authority under the said rules shall be the Secretary General of ICSID; or

   d)   by arbitration In accordance with the Rules of Arbitration of the International Chamber of Commerce (ICC).

3.   For the purpose of this Article and Article 25(2)(b) of the said Washington Convention, any legal person which is constituted in accordance with the legislation of one Contracting Party and which, before a dispute arises, was controlled by an investor of the other Contracting Party, shall be treated as a national of the other Contracting Party.

4.   Any arbitration under paragraph 2 b) - d) of this Article shall, at the request of either party to the dispute, be held in a state that is a party to the United Nations Convention on the Recognition and Enforcement of Foreign Arbitral Awards, done at New York, June 10, 1958 (the New York Convention).

5.   The consent given by each Contracting Party in paragraph (2) and the submission of the dispute by an investor under the said paragraph shall constitute the written consent and written agreement of the parties to the dispute to its submission for settlement for the purposes of, Chapter 11 of the Washington Convention (Jurisdiction of the Centre) and for the purpose of the Additional Facility Rules, Article 1 of the UNCITRAL Arbitration Rules, the Rules of Arbitration of the ICC and Article 11 of the New York Convention.

6.   In any proceeding involving an investment dispute, a Contracting Party shall not assert, as a defence, counterclaim or for any other reason, that indemnification or other compensation for all or part of the alleged damages has been received pursuant to an insurance or guarantee contract.

7.   Any arbitral award rendered pursuant to this Article shall be final and binding on the parties to the dispute. Each Contracting Party shall carry out without delay the provisions of any such award and provide in its territory for the enforcement of such award.

Article 10
Settlement of disputes between
the Contracting Parties

1 .   Disputes between the Contracting Parties concerning the interpretation or application of this Agreement shall be settled as far as possible by negotiations.

2.   If a dispute according to paragraph 1 of this Article cannot be settled within six (6) months, it shall, upon the request of either Contracting Party, be submitted to an arbitral tribunal.

3.   Such arbitral tribunal shall be constituted on an ad hoc basis as follows: each Contracting Party shall appoint one arbitrator and these two arbitrators shall agree upon a national of a third State as their chairman to be appointed by the two Contracting Parties. Such arbitrators shall be appointed within two (2) months from the; the date one Contracting Party has informed the other Contracting Party, of its intention to submit the dispute to an arbitral tribunal and the chairman shall be appointed within two (2) months following the appointment of the two arbitrators.

4.   If the periods specified in paragraph 3 of this Article are not observed, either Contracting Party may, in the absence of any other relevant arrangement, invite the President of the International Court of Justice to make the necessary appointments. If the President of the International Court of Justice is a national of either of the Contracting Parties or if he is otherwise prevented from discharging the said function, the Vice- President or in case of his inability the member of the International Court of Justice next in seniority should be invited under the same conditions to make the necessary appointments.

5.   The tribunal shall establish its own rules of procedure.

6.   The arbitral tribunal shall reach its decision on the basis of the present Agreement and applicable rules of international law. It shall reach its decision by a majority of votes; the decision shall be final and binding.

7.   Each Contracting Party shall bear the costs of its own member and of its legal representation in the arbitration proceedings. The costs of the chairman and the remaining costs shall be borne in equal parts by both Contracting Parties. The tribunal may, however, in its award determine another distribution of costs.

Article 11
Consultations

Each Contracting Party may propose to the other Party to consult on any matter affecting the application of this Agreement. These consultations shall be held on the proposal of one of the Contracting Parties at a place and at a time agreed upon through diplomatic channels.

Article 12
Applicability of this Agreement

The provisions of this Agreement shall apply to all investments made by investors of one Contracting Party in the territory of the other Contracting Party prior to or after the entry into force of the Agreement. It shall, however, not be applicable to divergences or disputes which have arisen prior to its entry into force.

Article 13
Amendments

At the time of entry into force of this Agreement or at any time thereafter the provisions of this Agreement may be amended in such manner as may be agreed between the Contracting Parties. Such amendments shall enter into force when the Contracting Parties have notified each other that the constitutional requirements for the entry into force have been fulfilled.

Article 14
Territorial Extension

This Agreement shall not apply to the Faroe Islands and Greenland.

The provisions of this Agreement may be extended to the Faroe Islands and Greenland as may be agreed between the Contracting Parties in an Exchange of Notes.

Article 15
Entry into Force

The Contracting Parties shall notify each other when the constitutional requirements for the entry into force of this Agreement have been fulfilled. The Agreement shall enter into force thirty days after the date of that last notification.

Article 16
Duration and Termination

1.   This Agreement shall remain in force for a period of ten years. It shall remain in force thereafter until either Contracting Party notifies in writing the other Contracting Party of its intention to terminate this Agreement. The notice of termination shall become effective one year after the date of notification.

2.   In respect of investments made prior to the date when the notice of termination of this Agreement becomes effective, the provisions of Articles 1 to 12 shall remain in force for a further period of ten years from that date.

In witness whereof the undersigned, duly authorised thereto by their respective Governments, have signed this Agreement.

Done in duplicate at _____ on _____ 20 in the Danish and English languages, all texts being equally authentic.

In the case of divergence of interpretation, the English text shall prevail.

For the Government of _____.

For the Government of the Kingdom of Denmark

*

Draft Model 2001

AGREEMENT BETWEEN THE GOVERNMENT OF THE REPUBLIC OF FINLAND AND THE GOVERNMENT OF _____ ON THE PROMOTION AND PROTECTION OF INVESTMENTS[*]

The Government of the Republic of Finland and the Government of _____, hereinafter referred to as the "Contracting Parties",

RECOGNISING the need to protect investments of the investors of one Contracting Party in the territory of the other Contracting Party on a non-discriminatory basis;

DESIRING to promote greater economic co-operation between them, with respect to investments by nationals and companies of one Contracting Party in the territory of the other Contracting Party;

RECOGNISING that agreement on the treatment to be accorded such investments will stimulate the flow of private capital and the economic development of the Contracting Parties;

AGREEING that a stable framework for investment will contribute to maximising the effective utilisation of economic resources and improve living standards;

RECOGNISING that the development of economic and business ties can promote respect for internationally recognised labour rights;

AGREEING that these objectives can be achieved without relaxing health, safety and environmental measures of general application; and

HAVING RESOLVED to conclude an Agreement concerning the promotion and protection of investments;

HAVE AGREED as follows:

ARTICLE 1
DEFINITIONS

For the purpose of this Agreement:

1.   The term "investment" means every kind of asset established or acquired by an investor of one Contracting Party in the territory of the other Contracting Party in accordance with the laws and regulations of the latter Contracting Party, including in particular, though not exclusively:

---

[*]   *Source*: The Government of Finland, Ministry of Foregn Affairs. [Note added by the editor.]

(a)   movable and immovable property or any property rights such as mortgages, liens, pledges, leases, usufruct and similar rights;

(b)   shares in and stocks and debentures of a company or any other forms of participation in a company;

(c)   claims to money or rights to a performance having an economic value;

(d)   intellectual property rights, such as patents, copyrights, trade marks, industrial designs, business names, geographical indications as well as technical processes, know-how and goodwill; and

(e)   concessions conferred by law, by an administrative act or under a contract by a competent authority, including concessions to search for, develop, extract or exploit natural resources.

Investments made in the territory of one Contracting Party by any legal entity of that same Contracting Party, but actually owned or controlled, directly or indirectly, by investors of the other Contracting Party, shall likewise be considered as investments of investors of the latter Contracting Party if they have been made in accordance with the laws and regulations of the former Contracting Party.

Any change in the form in which assets are invested or reinvested does not affect their character as investments.

2.   The term "returns" means the amounts yielded by investments and shall in particular, though not exclusively, include profits, dividends, interest, royalties, capital gains or any payments in kind related to an investment.

Reinvested returns shall enjoy the same treatment as the original investment.

3.   The term "investor" means, for either Contracting Party, the following subjects who invest in the territory of the other Contracting Party in accordance with the laws of the latter Contracting Party and the provisions of this Agreement:

(a)   any natural person who is a national of either Contracting Party in accordance with its laws; or

(b)   any legal entity such as company, corporation, firm, partnership, business association, institution or organisation, incorporated or constituted in accordance with the laws and regulations of the Contracting Party and having its registered office within the jurisdiction of that Contracting Party, whether or not for profit and whether its liabilities are limited or not.

4.   The term "territory" means the land territory, internal waters and territorial sea of theContracting Partyand the airspace above them, as well as the maritime zones beyond the territorial sea, including the seabed and subsoil, over which that Contracting Party exercises sovereign rights or jurisdiction in accordance with its national laws in force and international law, for the purpose of exploration and exploitation of the natural resources of such areas.

ARTICLE 2
PROMOTION AND PROTECTION OF INVESTMENTS

1.   Each Contracting Party shall promote in its territory investments by investors of the other Contracting Party and shall, in accordance with its laws and regulations, admit such investments.

2.   Each Contracting Party shall in its territory accord to investments and returns of investments of investors of the other Contracting Party fair and equitable treatment and full and constant protection and security.

3.   Neither Contracting Party shall in its territory impair by unreasonable or arbitrary measures the acquisition, expansion, operation, management, maintenance, use, enjoyment and sale or other disposal of investments of investors of the other Contracting Party.

ARTICLE 3
TREATMENT OF INVESTMENTS

1.   Each Contracting Party shall accord to investors of the other Contracting Party and to their investments, a treatment no less favourable than the treatment it accords to its own investors and their investments with respect to the acquisition, expansion, operation, management, maintenance, use, enjoyment and sale or other disposal of investments.

2.   Each Contracting Party shall accord to investors of the other Contracting Party and to their investments, a treatment no less favourable than the treatment it accords to investors of the most favoured nation and to their investments with respect to the establishment, acquisition, expansion, operation, management, maintenance, use, enjoyment, and sale or other disposal of investments.

3.   Each Contracting Party shall accord to investors of the other Contracting Party and to their investments the better of the treatments required by paragraph 1 and paragraph 2 of this Article, whichever is the more favourable to the investors or investments.

4.   Neither Contracting Party shall in its territory impose mandatory measures on investments by investors of the other Contracting Party, concerning purchase of materials, means of production, operation, transport, marketing of its products or similar orders having unreasonable or discriminatory effects.

ARTICLE 4
EXCEPTIONS

The provisions of this Agreement shall not be construed so as to oblige one Contracting Party to extend to the investors and investments by investors of the other Contracting Party the benefit of any treatment, preference or privilege by virtue of any existing or future:

   a)   free trade area, customs union, common market, economic and monetary union or other similar regional economic integration agreement, including regional labour market agreements, to which one of the Contracting Parties is or may become a party, or

b)   agreement for the avoidance of double taxation or other international agreement relating wholly or mainly to taxation, or

c)   multilateral agreement relating wholly or mainly to investments.

ARTICLE 5
EXPROPRIATION

1.   Investments by investors of a Contracting Party in the territory of the other Contracting Party shall not be expropriated, nationalised or subjected to any other measures, direct or indirect, having an effect equivalent to expropriation or nationalisation (hereinafter referred to as "expropriation"), except for a purpose which is in the public interest, on a non-discriminatory basis, in accordance with due process of law, and against prompt, adequate and effective compensation.

2.   Such compensation shall amount to the value of the expropriated investment at the time immediately before the expropriation or before the impending expropriation became public knowledge, whichever is the earlier. The value shall be determined in accordance with generally accepted principles of valuation, taking into account, inter alia, the capital invested, replacement value, appreciation, current returns, the projected flow of future returns, goodwill and other relevant factors.

3.   Compensation shall be fully realisable and shall be paid without any restriction or delay. It shall include interest at a commercial rate established on a market basis for the currency of payment from the date of dispossession of the expropriated property until the date of actual payment.

4.   The Contracting Parties affirm that when a Contracting Party expropriates the assets or a part thereof of a company which has been incorporated or constituted in accordance with the law in force in its territory, and in which investors of the other Contracting Party own shares, or when the object of expropriation is a joint-venture constituted in the territory of a Contracting Party, the host Contracting Party shall ensure that that the articles of association and possible other relevant documents of the companies or joint-ventures concerned, as they exist at the time of expropriation, are fully honoured.

5.   The investor whose investments are expropriated shall have the right to prompt review of its case and of valuation of its investments in accordance with the principles set out in this Article, by a judicial or other competent authority of that Contracting Party.

ARTICLE 6
COMPENSATION FOR LOSSES

1.   Investors of one Contracting Party whose investments in the territory of the other Contracting Party suffer losses owing to war or other armed conflict, a state of national emergency, revolt, insurrection or riot in the territory of the latter Contracting Party, shall be accorded by the latter Contracting Party, as regards restitution, indemnification, compensation or other settlement, a treatment no less favourable than the one accorded by the latter Contracting Party to its own investors or investors of the most favoured nation, whichever, according to the investor, is the more favourable.

2.   Without prejudice to paragraph 1 of this Article, investors of one Contracting Party who, in any of the situations referred to in that paragraph, suffer losses in the territory of the other Contracting Party resulting from:

   (a)   requisitioning of its investment or a part thereof by the latter's armed forces or authorities, or

   (b)   destruction of its investment or a part thereof by the latter's armed forces or authorities, which was not required by the necessity of the situation,

shall be accorded by the latter Contracting Party restitution or compensationwhich in either case shall be prompt, adequate and effective and with respect to any resulting compensation, shall be fully realisable, shall be paid without delay, and shall include interest at a commercial rate established on a market basis for the currency of payment from the date of requisitioning or destruction until the date of actual payment.

3.   Investors whose investments suffer losses in accordance with this Article, shall have the right to prompt review of its case and of valuation of its investments in accordance with the principles set out in this Article, by a judicial or other competent authority of that Contracting Party.

ARTICLE 7
FREE TRANSFER

1.   Each Contracting Party shall ensure to investors of the other Contracting Party the free transfer, into and out of its territory, of their investments and transfer payments related to investments. Such payments shall include in particular, though not exclusively:

   (a)   principal and additional amounts to maintain, develop or increase the investment;

   (b)   returns;

   (c)   proceeds obtained from the total or partial sale or disposal of an investment, including the sale of shares;

   (d)   amounts required for the payment of expenses which arise from the operation of the investment,such as loans repayments, payment of royalties, management fees, licence fees or other similar expenses;

   (e)   compensation payable pursuant to Articles 5 and 6;

   (f)   payments arising from the settlement of a dispute;

   (g)   earnings and other remuneration of personnel engaged from abroad and working in connection with an investment.

2.   Each Contracting Party shall further ensure that the transfers referred to in paragraph 1 of this Article shall be made without any restriction in a freely convertible currency and at the prevailing market rate of exchange applicable on the date of transfer to the currency to be transferred and shall be immediately transferable.

3.   In the absence of a market for foreign exchange, the rate to be used shall be the most recent exchange rate for the conversions of currencies into Special Drawing Rights.

4.   In case of a delay in transfer caused by the host Contracting Party, the transfer shall also include interest at a commercial rate established on a market basis for the currency in question from the date on which the transfer was requested until the date of actual transfer and shall be borne by that Contracting Party.

ARTICLE 8
SUBROGATION

If a Contracting Party or its designated agency makes a payment under an indemnity, guarantee or contract of insurance given in respect of an investment of an investor in the territory of the other Contracting Party, the latter Contracting Party shall recognise the assignment of any right or claim of such an investor to the former Contracting Party or its designated agency, and the right of the former Contracting Party or its designated agency to exercise by virtue of subrogation any such right and claim to the same extent as its predecessor in title.

ARTICLE 9
DISPUTES BETWEEN AN INVESTOR AND A CONTRACTING PARTY

1.   Any dispute arising directly from an investment between one Contracting Party and an investor of the other Contracting Party should be settled amicably between the two parties concerned.

2.   If the dispute has not been settled within three (3) months from the date on which it was raised in writing, the dispute may, at the choice of the investor, be submitted:

   (a)   to the competent courts of the Contracting Party in whose territory the investment is made; or

   (b)   to arbitration by the International Centre for Settlement of Investment Disputes (ICSID), established pursuant to the Convention on the Settlement of Investment Disputes between States and Nationals of other States, opened for signature at Washington on 18 March 1965 (hereinafter referred to as the "Centre"), if the Centre is available; or

   (c)   to arbitration by the Additional Facility of the Centre, if only one of the Contracting Parties is a signatory to the Convention referred to in subparagraph (b) of this paragraph; or

   (d)   to any ad hoc arbitration tribunal which unless otherwise agreed on by the parties to the dispute, is to be established under the Arbitration Rules of the United Nations Commission on International Trade Law (UNCITRAL).

3.   An investor who has submitted the dispute to a national court may nevertheless have recourse to one of the arbitral tribunals mentioned in paragraphs 2 (b) to (d) of this Article if, before a judgement has been delivered on the subject matter by a national court, the investor declares not to pursue the case any longer through national proceedings and withdraws the case.

4.   Neither of the Contracting Parties, which is a party to a dispute, can raise an objection, at any phase of the arbitration procedure or of the execution of an arbitral award, on account of the fact that the investor, which is the other party to the dispute, has received an indemnification covering a part or the whole of its losses by virtue of an insurance.

5.   The award shall be final and binding on the parties to the dispute and shall be enforced in accordance with national law.

ARTICLE 10
DISPUTES BETWEEN THE CONTRACTING PARTIES

1.   Disputes between the Contracting Parties concerning the interpretation and application of this Agreement shall, as far as possible, be settled through diplomatic channels.

2.   If the dispute cannot thus be settled within six (6) months following the date on which such negotiations were requested by either Contracting Party, it shall at the request of either Contracting Party be submitted to an Arbitral Tribunal.

3.   Such an Arbitral Tribunal shall be constituted for each individual case in the following way. Within two (2) months of the receipt of the request for arbitration, each Contracting Party shall appoint one member of the Tribunal. Those two members shall then select a national of a third State who on approval by the two Contracting Parties shall be appointed Chairman of the Tribunal. The Chairman shall be appointed within four (4) months from the date of appointment of the other two members.

4.   If the necessary appointments have not been made within the periods specified in paragraph 3 of this Article, either Contracting Party may, in the absence of any other agreement, invite the President of the International Court of Justice to make the necessary appointments. If the President is a national of either Contracting Party or is otherwise prevented from discharging the said function, the Member of the International Court of Justice next in seniority who is not a national of either Contracting Party or is not otherwise prevented from discharging the said function, shall be invited to make the necessary appointments.

5.   The Arbitral Tribunal shall reach its decision by a majority of votes. The decisions of the Tribunal shall be final and binding on both Contracting Parties. Each Contracting Party shall bear the costs of the member appointed by that Contracting Party and of its representation in the arbitral proceedings. Both Contracting Parties shall assume an equal share of the costs of the Chairman, as well as any other costs. The Tribunal may make a different decision regarding the sharing of the costs. In all other respects, the Arbitral Tribunal shall determine its own rules of procedure.

6.   Issues subject to dispute referred to in paragraph 1 of this Article shall be decided in accordance with the provisions of this Agreement and the generally recognised principles of international law.

ARTICLE 11
PERMITS

1.   Each Contracting Party shall, subject to its laws and regulations, treat favourably the applications relating to investments and grant expeditiously the necessary permits required in its territory in connection with investments by investors of the other Contracting Party.

2.   Each Contracting Party shall, subject to its laws and regulations, grant temporary entry and stay and provide any necessary confirming documentation to natural persons who are employed from abroad as executives, managers, specialists or technical personnel in connection with an investment by an investor of the other Contracting Party, and who are essential for the enterprise as long as these persons continue to meet the requirements of this paragraph, as well as grant temporary entry and stay to members of their families (spouse and minor children) for the same period as to the persons employed.

ARTICLE 12
APPLICATION OF OTHER RULES

1.   If the provisions of law of either Contracting Party or obligations under international law, existing at present or established hereafter between the Contracting Parties in addition to this Agreement, contain a regulation, whether general or specific, entitling investments made by investors of the other Contracting Party to a treatment more favourable than is provided by this Agreement, such provisions shall, to the extent that they are more favourable to the investor, prevail over this Agreement.

2.   Each ContractingParty shall observe any other obligation itmay have with regard to a specific investment ofan investor of the other Contracting Party.

ARTICLE 13
APPLICATION OF THE AGREEMENT

This Agreement shall apply to all investments made by investors of either Contracting Party in the territory of the other Contracting Party, whether made before or after the entry into force of this Agreement, but shall not apply to any dispute concerning an investment which arose or any claim which was settled before its entry into force.

ARTICLE 14
GENERAL EXCEPTIONS

1.   Nothing in this Agreement shall be construed as preventing a Contracting Party from taking any action necessary for the protection of its essential security interests in time of war or armed conflict, or other emergency in international relations.

2.   Provided that such measures are not applied in a manner which would constitute a means of arbitrary or unjustifiable discrimination by a Contracting Party, or a disguised investment restriction, nothing in this Agreement shall be construed as preventing the Contracting Parties from taking any measure necessary for the maintenance of public order.

3.   The provisions of this Article shall not apply to Article 5, Article 6 or paragraph 1.(e) of Article 7 of this Agreement.

ARTICLE 15
TRANSPARENCY

1.   Each Contracting Party shall promptly publish, or otherwise make publicly available, its laws, regulations, procedures and administrative rulings and judicial decisions of general application as well as international agreements which may affect the investments of investors of the other Contracting Party in the territory of the former Contracting Party.

2.   Nothing in this Agreement shall require a Contracting Party to furnish or allow access to any confidential or proprietary information, including information concerning particular investors or investments, the disclosure of which would impede law enforcement or be contrary to its laws protecting confidentiality or prejudice legitimate commercial interests of particular investors.

ARTICLE 16
CONSULTATIONS

The Contracting Parties shall, at the request of either Contracting Party, hold consultations for the purpose of reviewing the implementation of this Agreement and studying any issue that may arise from this Agreement. Such consultations shall be held between the competent authorities of the Contracting Parties in a place and at a time agreed on through appropriate channels.

ARTICLE 17
ENTRY INTO FORCE, DURATION AND TERMINATION

1.   The Contracting Parties shall notify each other when their constitutional requirements for the entry into force of this Agreement have been fulfilled. The Agreement shall enter into force on the thirtieth day following the date of receipt of the last notification.

2.   This Agreement shall remain in force for a period of twenty (20) years and shall thereafter remain in force on the same terms until either Contracting Party notifies the other in writing of its intention to terminate the Agreement in twelve (12) months.

3.   In respect of investments made prior to the date of termination of this Agreement, the provisions of Articles 1 to 16 shall remain in force for a further period of twenty (20) years from the date of termination of this Agreement.

IN WITNESS WHEREOF, the undersigned representatives, being duly authorised thereto, have signed the present Agreement.

Done in duplicate at...............................on........................200... in the Finnish, _____ and English languages, all texts being equally authentic. In case of divergence, the English text shall prevail.

For the Government of   For the Government of
the Republic of Finland   the _____

*

TREATY BETWEEN THE FEDERAL REPUBLIC OF GERMANY AND _____ CONCERNING THE ENCOURAGEMENT AND RECIPROCAL PROTECTION OF INVESTMENTS[*]

Desiring to intensify economic co-operation between both States,

Intending to create favourable conditions for investments by investors of either State in the territory of the other State,

Recognizing that the encouragement and contractual protection of such investments are apt to stimulate private business initiative and to increase the prosperity of both nations -

Have agreed as follows.

Article 1

For the purposes of this Treaty

1.   The term "investments" comprises every kind of asset, in particular:

    (a)   movable and immovable property as well as any other rights in rein, such as mortgages, liens and, pledges.

    (b)   shares of companies and other kinds of interest in companies;

    (c)   claims to money which has been used to create an economic value or claims to any performance having an economic value,

    (d)   intellectual property rights, in particular copyrights, patents, utility-model patents, industrial designs, trade-marks, trade-names, trade and business secrets, technical processes, know-how, and good will;

    (e)   business concessions under public law, including concessions to search for, extract and exploit natural resources;

any alteration of the form in which assets are invested shall not affect their classification as investment,

2.   The term "returns" means the amounts yielded by an investment for a definite period, such as profit, dividends, interest, royalties or fees',

3.   The term "Investor" means

    (a)   in respect of the Federal Republic of Germany,

---

[*]   *Source*: The Government of Germany, Federal Ministry of Economics and Technology. [Note added by the editor.]

(i)	Germans within the meaning of the Basic Law of the Federal Republic of Germany,
(ii)	any juridical person as well as any commercial or other company or association with or without legal personality having its seat in the territory of the Federal Republic of Germany, irrespective of whether or not its activities are directed at profit,

(b)   in respect of _____.

(i)   _____.

(ii)   _____.

Article 2

(1)   Each Contracting State shall in its territory promote as far as possible investments by investors of the other Contracting State and admit such investments in accordance with its legislation.

(2)   Each Contracting State shall in its territory in any case accord investments by investors of the other Contracting State fair and equitable treatment as well as full protection under the Treaty.

(3)   Neither Contracting State shall in any way impair by arbitrary or discriminatory measures the management, maintenance, use, enjoyment or disposal of investments in its territory of investors of the other Contracting State.

Article 3

(1)   Neither Contracting State shall subject investments in its territory owned or controlled by investors of the other Contracting State to treatment less favourable than it accords to investments of its own investors or to investments of investors of any third State.

(2)   Neither Contracting State shall subject investors of the other Contracting State, as regards their activity in connection with investments in its territory, to treatment less favourable than it accords to its own investors or to investors of any third State.

(3)   Such treatment shall not relate to privileges which either Contracting State accords to investors of third States on account of its membership of, or association with, a customs or economic union, a common market or a free trade area,

(4)   The treatment granted under this Article shall not relate to advantages which either Contracting State accords to investors of third States by virtue of a double taxation agreement or other agreements regarding matters of taxation.

Article 4

(1)   Investments by investors of either Contracting State shall enjoy full protection and security in the territory of the other Contracting State.

(2)   Investments by investors of either Contracting State shall not directly or indirectly be expropriated, nationalized or subjected to any other measure the effects of which would be tantamount to expropriation or nationalization in the territory of the other Contracting State except for the public benefit and against compensation. Such compensation shall be equivalent to the value of the expropriated investment immediately before the date on which the actual or threatened expropriation, nationalization or comparable measure has become publicly known. The compensation shall be paid without delay and shall carry the usual bank interest until the time of payment; it shall be effectively realizable and freely transferable, Provision shall have been made in an appropriate manner at or prior to the time of expropriation, nationalization or comparable measure for the determination and payment of such compensation. The legality of any such expropriation, nationalization or comparable measure and the amount of compensation shall be subject to review by due process of law.

(3)   Investors of either Contracting State whose investments suffer losses in the territory of the other Contracting State owing to war or other armed conflict, revolution, a state of national emergency, or revolt, shall be accorded treatment no less favourable by such other Contracting State than that which the latter Contracting State accords to its own investors as regards restitution, indemnification, compensation or other valuable consideration. Such payments shall be freely transferable,

(4)   Investors of either Contracting State shall enjoy most-favoured-nation treatment in the territory of the other Contracting State in respect of the matters provided for in this Article,

Article 5

Each Contracting State shall guarantee to investors of the other Contracting State the free transfer of payments in connection with an investment, in particular:

(a)   the principal and additional amounts to maintain or increase the investment;

(b)   the returns,

(c)   the repayment of loans,

(d)   the proceeds from the liquidation or the sale of the whole or any part of the investment;

(e)   the compensation provided for in Article 4.

Article 6

If either Contracting State makes a payment to any of its investors under a guarantee it has assumed in respect of an investment in the territory of the other Contracting State, the latter Contracting State shall, without prejudice to the rights of the former Contracting State under

Article 10, recognize the assignment, whether under a law or pursuant to a legal transaction, of any right or claim of such investor to the former Contracting State, The latter Contracting State shall also recognize the subrogation of the former Contracting State to any such right or claim (assigned claims) which that Contracting State shall be entitled to assert to the same extent as its predeces-sor in title. As regards the transfer of payments made by virtue of such assigned claims, Article 4 (2) and (3) as well as Article 5 shall apply mutatis mutandis.

Article 7

(1)   Transfers under Article 4 (2) or (3), under Article 5 or Article 6 shall be made without delay at the market rate of exchange applicable on the day of the transfer,

(2)   Should there be no foreign exchange market the cross rate obtained from those rates which would be applied by the International Monetary Fund on the date of payment for conversions of the currencies concerned into Special Drawing Rights shall apply.

Article 8

(1)   If the legislation of either Contracting State or obligations under international law existing at present or established hereafter between the Contracting States in addition to this Treaty contain a regulation, whether general or specific, entitling investments by investors of the other Contracting State to a treatment more favourable than is provided for by this Treaty, such regulation shall to the extent that it is more favourable prevail over this Treaty.

(2)   Each Contracting State shall observe any other obligation it has assumed with regard to investments in its territory by investors of the other Contracting State.

Article 9

This Treaty shall also apply to investments made prior to its entry into force by investors of either Contracting State in the territory of the other Contracting State consistent with the latter's legislation.

Article 10

(1)   Divergencies between the Contracting States concerning the interpretation or application of this Treaty should as far as possible be settled by the governments of the two Contracting States,

(2)   If a divergency cannot thus be settled, it shall upon the request of either Contracting State be submitted to an arbitration tribunal.

(3)   Such arbitration tribunal shall be constituted ad hoc as follows: each Contracting State shall appoint one member, and these two members shall agree upon a national of a third State as their chairman to be appointed by the governments of the two Contracting States. Such members shall be appointed within two months, and such chairman within three months from the date on which either Contracting State has informed the other Contracting State that it intends to submit the dispute to an arbitration tribunal.

(4)   If the periods specified in paragraph 3 above have not been observed, either Contracting State may, in the absence of any other arrangement, invite the President of the International Court of Justice to make the necessary appointments. If the President is a national of either Contracting State or if he is otherwise prevented from discharging the said function, the Vice-President should make the necessary appointments, If the Vice-President is a national of either Contracting State or if he, too, is prevented from discharging the said function, the member of the Court next in seniority who is not a national of either Contracting State should make the necessary appointments,

(5)   The arbitration tribunal shall reach its decisions by a majority of votes. Such decisions shall be binding. Each Contracting State shall bear the cost of its own member and of its representatives in the arbitration proceedings, the cost of the chairman and the remaining costs shall be borne in equal parts by the Contracting States. The arbitration tribunal may make a different regulation concerning costs. In all other respects, the arbitration tribunal shall determine its own procedure.

Model I (Membership of both
Contracting States in ICSID)

Article 11

(1)   Divergencies concerning investments between a Contracting State and an investor of the other Contracting State should as far as possible be settled amicably between the parties in dispute,

(2)   If the divergency cannot be settled within six months of the date when it has been raised by one of the parties in dispute, it shall, at the request of the investor of the other Contracting State, be submitted for arbitration. Unless the parties in dispute agree otherwise, the divergency shall be submitted for arbitration under the Convention of 18 March 1965 on the Settlement of Investment Disputes between States and Nationals of Other States.

(3)   The award shall be binding and shall not be subject to any appeal or remedy other than those provided for in the said Convention. The award shall be enforced in accordance with domestic law,

(4)   During arbitration proceedings or the enforcement of an award, the Contracting, State involved in the dispute shall not raise the objection that the investor of the other Contracting State has received compensation under an insurance contract in respect of all or part of the damage,

Model II (Membership of only
one Contracting State in ICSID)

Article 11

(1)   Divergencies concerning investments between a Contracting State and an investor of the other Contracting State shall as far as possible be settled amicably between the parties in dispute.

(2)   If the divergency cannot be settled within six months of the date when it has been raised by one of the parties in dispute, it shall, at the request of the investor of the other Contracting State, be submitted for arbitration. Unless the parties in dispute have agreed otherwise, the

provisions of Article 10 (3) to (5) shall be applied mutatis mutandis, on condition that the appointment of the members of the arbitration tribunal in accordance with Article 10 (3) is effected by the parties in dispute and that, insofar as the periods specified in Article 10 (3) are not observed, either party in dispute may, in the absence of other arrangements, invite the President of the Court of International Arbitration of the International Chamber of Commerce in Paris to make the required appointments. The award shall be enforced in accordance with domestic law.

(3)   During arbitration proceedings or the enforcement of an award, the Contracting State involved in the dispute shall not raise the objection that the investor of the other Contracting State has received compensation under an insurance contract in respect of all or part of the damage.

(4)   In the event of both Contracting States having become Contracting States of the Convention of 18 March 1965 on the Settlement of Investment Disputes between States and Nationals of Other States, divergencies under this Article between the parties in dispute shall be submitted for arbitration under the aforementioned Convention, unless the parties in dispute agree otherwise, each Contracting State herewith declares its acceptance of such a procedure.

Article 12

This Treaty shall be in force irrespective of whether or not diplomatic or consular relations exist between the Contracting States,

Article 13

The attached Protocol shall form an integral part of this Treaty.

Article 14

(1)   This Treaty shall be subject to ratification; the instruments of ratification shall be exchanged as soon as possible.

(2)   This Treaty shall enter into force one month after the date of exchange of the instruments of ratification. It shall remain in force for a period of ten years and shall be extended thereafter for an unlimited period unless denounced in writing by either Contracting State twelve months before its expiration. After the expiry of the period of ten years this Treaty may be denounced at any time by either Contracting State giving twelve months notice.

(3)   In respect of investments made prior to the date of termination of this Treaty, the provisions of the preceding Articles shall continue to be effective for a further period of twenty years from the date of termination of this Treaty.

Done at _____ on _____ in duplicate in the German and _____ languages, both texts being equally Authentic.

For the _____.

For Federal Republic of Germany _____.

PROTOCOL

TO THE TREATY BETWEEN THE FEDERAL REPUBLIC OF GERMANY AND _____ CONCERNING THE ENCOURAGEMENT AND RECIPROCAL PROTECTION OF INVESTMENTS

On signing the Treaty between the Federal Republic of Germany and _____ con cerning the Encouragement and Reciprocal Protection of Investments, the plenipotentiaries, being duly authorized, have, in addition, agreed on the following provisions, which shall be regarded as an integral part of the said Treaty:

1.   **Ad Article 1**

   (a)   Returns from the investment and, in the event of their re-investment, the returns there-from shall enjoy the same protection as the investment.

   (b)   Without prejudice to any other method of determining nationality, in particular any person in possession of a national passport issued by the competent authorities of the Con-tracting State concerned shall be deemed to be a national of that Contracting State.

2.   **Ad Article 2**

The Treaty shall also apply to the areas of the exclusive economic zone and the continental shelf insofar as international law permits the Contracting State concerned to exercise sovereign rights or jurisdiction in these areas.

3.   **Ad Article 3**

   (a)   The following shall more particularly, though not exclusively, be deemed "activity" within the meaning of Article 3 (2): the management, maintenance, use, enjoyment and disposal of an investment. The following shall, in particular, be deemed "treatment less favourable within the meaning of Article 3; unequal treatment in the case of restrictions on the purchase of raw or auxiliary materials, of energy or fuel or of means of production or operation of any kind, unequal treatment in the case of impeding the marketing of products inside or outside the country, as well as any other measures having similar effects, Measures that have to be taken for reasons of public security and order, public health or morality shall not be deemed "treatment less favourable" within the meaning of Article 3.

   (b)   The provisions of Article 3 do not oblige a Contracting State to extend to investors resident in the territory of the other Contracting State tax privileges, tax exemptions and tax reductions which according to its tax laws are granted only to investors resident in its territory.

   (c)   The Contracting States shall within the framework of their national legislation give sympathetic consideration to applications for the entry and sojourn of persons of either Contracting State who wish to enter the territory of the other Contracting State in connection with an investment; the same shall apply to employed persons of either Contracting State who in connection with an investment wish to enter the territory of the other Contracting State and sojourn there to take up employment, Applications for work permits shall also be given sympathetic consideration.

4.   Ad Article 7

A transfer shall be deemed to have been made "without delay" within the meaning of Article 7 (1) if effected within such period as is normally required for the completion of transfer formalities. The said period shall commence on the day on which the relevant request has been submitted and may on no account exceed two months.

5.   Whenever goods or persons connected with an investment are to be transported, each Contracting State shall neither exclude nor hinder transport enterprises of the other Contracting State and shall issue permits as required to carry out such transport. This shall include the transport of

    (a)   goods directly intended for an investment within the meaning of the Treaty or acquired in the territory of either Contracting State or of any third State by or on behalf of an enter prise in which assets within the meaning of the Treaty are invested;

*

SELECTED UNCTAD PUBLICATIONS ON TRANSNATIONAL CORPORATIONS AND FOREIGN DIRECT INVESTMENT

(For more information, please visit www.unctad.org/ en/pub on the web.)

A. Serial publications

World Investment Report Series
http://www.unctad.org/wir

World Investment Report 2001: Promoting Linkages. 356 p. Sales No. E.01.II.D.12 $ 45.

World Investment Report 2001: Promoting Linkages: An Overview. Free of Charge
[1]Available in six UN official languages and also from the web page in electronic format.

Ten Years of World Investment Reports: The Challenges Ahead. Proceedings of an UNCTAD special event on future challenges in the area of FDI.October 2000. UNCTAD/ITE/Misc.45. Free of charge also available from the web page.

World Investment Report 2000: Cross-border Mergers and Acquisitions and Development. 368 p. Sales No. E.00.II.D.20. $45.

World Investment Report 2000: Cross-border Mergers and Acquisitions and Development. An Overview. 75 p. Free-of-charge.

World Investment Report 1999: Foreign Direct Investment and the Challenge of Development. 536 p. Sales No. E.99.II.D.3. $45.

World Investment Report 1999: Foreign Direct Investment and Challenge of Development. An Overview. 75 p. Free-of-charge.

World Investment Report 1998: Trends and Determinants. 430 p. Sales No. E.98.II.D.5. $45.

World Investment Report 1998: Trends and Determinants. An Overview. 67 p. Free-of-charge.

World Investment Report 1997: Transnational Corporations, Market Structure and Competition Policy. 420 p. Sales No. E.97.II.D.10. $45.

World Investment Report 1997: Transnational Corporations, Market Structure and Competition Policy. An Overview. 70 p. Free-of-charge.

World Investment Report 1996: Investment, Trade and International Policy Arrangements. 332 p. Sales No. E.96.II.A.14. $45.

World Investment Report 1996: Investment, Trade and International Policy Arrangements. An Overview. 51 p. Free-of-charge.

---

[1] All overviews are free of charge and are available also in electronic format on the web page of the World Investment Report http://www.unctad.org/wir

World Investment Report 1995: Transnational Corporations and Competitiveness.
491 p. Sales No. E.95.II.A.9. $45.

World Investment Report 1995: Transnational Corporations and Competitiveness. An Overview. 51 p. Free-of-charge..

World Investment Report 1994: Transnational Corporations, Employment and the Workplace. 482 p. Sales No. E.94.II.A.14. $45.

World Investment Report 1994: Transnational Corporations, Employment and the Workplace. An Executive Summary. 34 p.

World Investment Report 1993: Transnational Corporations and Integrated International Production. 290 p. Sales No. E.93.II.A.14. $45.

World Investment Report 1993: Transnational Corporations and Integrated International Production. An Executive Summary. 31 p. ST/CTC/159. Free-of-charge.

World Investment Report 1992: Transnational Corporations as Engines of Growth. 356 p. Sales No. E.92.II.A.19. $45.

World Investment Report 1992: Transnational Corporations as Engines of Growth: An Executive Summary. 30 p. Sales No. E.92.II.A.24.

World Investment Report 1991: The Triad in Foreign Direct Investment. 108 p. Sales No.E.91.II.A.12. $25. Full version at http://www.unctad.org/wir/contents/wir91content.en.htm.

<u>World Investment Directory Series</u>:

World Investment Directory. Vol. VII (Parts I and II): Asia and the Pacific. 646 p. Sales No. E.00.II.D.11.

World Investment Directory. Vol. VI: West Asia. 192 p. Sales No. E.97.II.A.2. $35.

World Investment Directory. Vol. V: Africa. 508 p. Sales No. E.97.II.A.1. $75.

World Investment Directory. Vol. IV: Latin America and the Caribbean. 478 p. Sales No. E.94.II.A.10. $65.

World Investment Directory 1992. Vol. III: Developed Countries. 532 p. Sales No. E.93.II.A.9. $75.

World Investment Directory 1992. Vol. II: Central and Eastern Europe. 432 p. Sales No. E.93.II.A.1. $65. (Joint publication with the United Nations Economic Commission for Europe.)

World Investment Directory 1992. Vol. I: Asia and the Pacific. 356 p. Sales No. E.92.II.A.11. $65.

<u>Investment Policy Review Series:</u>
http://www.unctad.org/en/pub/investpolicy.en.htm

Investment and Innovation Policy Review of Ethiopia. 115 pages.
UNCTAD/ITE/IPC/Misc.4. New York and Geneva 2002

Investment Policy Review of Ecuador. 117 pages. UNCTAD/ITE/IPC/Misc.2. Sales No.
E.01.II D.31 $ 22. New York and Geneva 2001

Investment Policy Review of Mauritius. 84 p. Sales No. E.01.II.D.11. $22. New York and
Geneva 2001

Investment Policy Review of Peru. 108 p. Sales No. E.00.II.D. 7. $22. New York and Geneva
2000 (Also available in Spanish-Tambien disponible en español)

Investment Policy Review of Uganda. 75 p. Sales No. E.99.II.D.24. $15. New York and
Geneva 1999

Investment Policy Review of Egypt. 113 p. Sales No. E.99.II.D.20. $19. New York and Geneva
1999

Investment Policy Review of Uzbekistan. 64 p. UNCTAD/ITE/IIP/Misc. 13. New York and
Geneva

<u>International Investment Instruments: Compendia</u>

International Investment Instruments: A Compendium Vol. VI 568 p. Sales No.
E.01.II.D.34

International Investment Instruments: A Compendium, Vol. IV, 319 p. Sales No.
E.00.II.D.13. $55, **Vol. V**, 505 p. Sales No. E.00.II.D.14. $55.

International Investment Instruments: A Compendium. Vol. I. 371 p. Sales No. E.96.II.A.9;
Vol. II. 577 p. Sales No. E.96.II.A.10; **Vol. III**. 389 p. Sales No. E.96.II.A.11; the 3-volume set,
Sales No. E.96.II.A.12. $125.

Bilateral Investment Treaties 1959-1999 143 p. UNCTAD/ITE/IIA/2, Free-of-charge.
Available only in electronic version from http://www.unctad.org/en/pub/poiteiiad2.en.htm.

Bilateral Investment Treaties in the Mid-1990s, 314 p. Sales No. E.98.II.D.8. $46.

<u>Investment Guides for LDCs Series / UNCTAD - International Chamber of Commerce</u>
http://www.unctad.org/en/pub/investguide.en.htm

An Investment Guide to Mozambique: Opportunities and Conditions.
72.p UNCTAD/ITE/IIA/4. Geneva and New York 2002

An Investment Guide to Uganda: Opportunities and Conditions.
76 p. UNCTAD/ITE/IIT/Misc. 30. New York and Geneva 2001

An Investment Guide to Bangladesh: Opportunities and Conditions.
66 p. UNCTAD/ITE/IIT/Misc.29. New York and Geneva 2001

Guide d'investissement au Mali. 108 p. UNCTAD/ITE/IIT/Misc.24.
http://www.unctad.org/fr/docs/poiteiitm24.fr.pdf. (Joint publication with the International
Chamber of Commerce, in association with PricewaterhouseCoopers.)

An Investment Guide to Ethiopia: Opportunities and Conditions. 69 p.
UNCTAD/ITE/IIT/Misc.19. http://www.unctad.org/en/docs/poiteiitm19.en.pdf. (Joint
publication with the International Chamber of Commerce, in association with Pricewaterhouse
Coopers.)

IIA Issues Paper Series
(http://www.unctad.org/iia.)

Transfer of Technology. p 138 $18. Sales No. E.01.II.D.33

Illicit Payments. p. 108 p. Sales No. E.01.II.D.20 $ 13

Home Country Measures. p.96. Sales No.E.01.II.D.19. $12

Host Country Operational Measures. 109 p. Sales No E.01.II.D.18. $15.

Social Responsibility. 91 p. Sales No. E.01.II.D.4. $15.

Environment. 105 p. Sales No. E.01.II.D.3. $15.

Transfer of Funds. 68 p. Sales No. E.00.II.D.27. $12.

Employment. 69 p. Sales No. E.00.II.D.15. $12.

Taxation. 111 p. Sales No. E.00.II.D.5. $12.

International Investment Agreements: Flexibility for Development. 185 p. Sales No.
E.00.II.D.6. $12.

Taking of Property. 83 p. Sales No. E.00.II.D.4. $12.

Trends in International Investment Agreements: An Overview. 112 p. Sales No.
E.99.II.D.23. $ 12.

Lessons from the MAI. 31 p. Sales No. E.99.II.D.26. $ 12.

National Treatment. 104 p. Sales No. E.99.II.D.16. $12.

Fair and Equitable Treatment. 64 p. Sales No. E.99.II.D.15. $12.

Investment-Related Trade Measures. 64 p. Sales No. E.99.II.D.12. $12.

Most-Favoured-Nation Treatment. 72p. Sales No. E.99.II.D.11. $12.

Admission and Establishment. 72p. Sales No. E.99.II.D.10. $12.

Scope and Definition. 96p. Sales No. E.99.II.D.9. $12.

Transfer Pricing. 72p. Sales No. E.99.II.D.8. $12.

Foreign Direct Investment and Development. 88p. Sales No. E.98.II.D.15. $12.

B. Current Studies

Series A

No. 30. **Incentives and Foreign Direct Investment**. 98 p. Sales No. E.96.II.A.6. $30. [Out of print.]

No. 29. **Foreign Direct Investment, Trade, Aid and Migration**. 100 p. Sales No. E.96.II.A.8. $25. (Joint publication with the International Organization for Migration.)

No. 28. **Foreign Direct Investment in Africa**. 119 p. Sales No. E.95.II.A.6. $20.

No. 27. **Tradability of Banking Services: Impact and Implications**. 195 p. Sales No. E.94.II.A.12. $50.

No. 26. **Explaining and Forecasting Regional Flows of Foreign Direct Investment**. 58 p. Sales No. E.94.II.A.5. $25.

No. 25. **International Tradability in Insurance Services**. 54 p. Sales No. E.93.II.A.11. $20.

No. 24. **Intellectual Property Rights and Foreign Direct Investment**. 108 p. Sales No. .93.II.A.10.$20.

No. 23. **The Transnationalization of Service Industries: An Empirical Analysis of the Determinants of Foreign Direct Investment by Transnational Service Corporations**. 62 p. Sales No. E.93.II.A.3. $15.

No. 22. **Transnational Banks and the External Indebtedness of Developing Countries: Impact of Regulatory Changes**. 48 p. Sales No. E.92.II.A.10. $12.

No. 20. **Foreign Direct Investment, Debt and Home Country Policies**. 50 p. Sales No. E.90.II.A.16. $12.

No. 19. **New Issues in the Uruguay Round of Multilateral Trade Negotiations**. 52 p. Sales No. E.90.II.A.15. $12.50.

No. 18. **Foreign Direct Investment and Industrial Restructuring in Mexico**. 114 p. Sales No. E.92.II.A.9. $12.

No. 17. **Government Policies and Foreign Direct Investment**. 68 p. Sales No. E.91.II.A.20. $12.50.

ASIT Advisory Studies
(Formerly Current Studies, Series B)

No. 17. **The World of Investment Promotion at a Glance: A survey of investment promotion practices.** UNCTAD/ITE/IPC/3. Free of Charge

No. 16. **Tax Incentives and Foreign Direct Investment: A Global Survey.** 180p. Sales No. E.01.II.D.5. $23. Summary available from http://www.unctad.org/asit/resumé.htm

No. 15. **Investment Regimes in the Arab World: Issues and Policies**. 232p. Sales No. E/F.00.II.D.32.

No. 14. **Handbook on Outward Investment Promotion Agencies and Institutions**. 50 p. Sales No. E.99.II.D.22. $ 15.

No. 13. **Survey of Best Practices in Investment Promotion.** 71 p., Sales No. E.97.II.D.11.$ 35.

No. 12. **Comparative Analysis of Petroleum Exploration Contracts.** 80 p. Sales No. E. 96.II.A.7. $35.

No. 11. **Administration of Fiscal Regimes for Petroleum Exploration and Development.** 45 p. Sales No. E. 95.II.A.8.

No. 10. **Formulation and Implementation of Foreign Investment Policies: Selected Key Issues.** 84 p. Sales No. E. 92.II.A.21. $12.

No. 9. **Environmental Accounting: Current Issues, Abstracts and Bibliography.** 86 p. Sales No. E.92.II.A.23.

C. Individual Studies

Compendium of International Arrangements on Transfer of Technology: Selected Instruments. 308 p. Sales No. E.01.II.D.28. $ 45

FDI in Least Developed Countries at a Glance. 150 p. UNCTAD/ITE/IIA/3. Free of charge. Full version available also from http://www.unctad.org/en/pub/poiteiiad3.en.htm.

Foreign Direct Investment in Africa: Performance and Potential. 89 p. UNCTAD/ITE/IIT/Misc. 15. Free of charge. Full version available also from http://www.unctad.org/en/docs/poiteiitm15.pdf.

TNC-SME Linkages for Development: Issues-Experiences-Best Practices. Proceedings of the Special Round Table on TNCs, SMEs and Development, UNCTAD X, 15 February 2000, Bangkok, Thailand. 113 p. UNCTAD/ITE/TEB1. Free-of-charge.

Handbook on Foreign Direct Investment by Small and Medium-sized Enterprises: Lessons from Asia. 200 p. Sales No. E.98.II.D.4. $48.

Handbook on Foreign Direct Investment by Small and Medium-sized Enterprises: Lessons from Asia. Executive Summary and Report of the Kunming Conference. 74 p. Free-of-charge.

Small and Medium-sized Transnational Corporations. Executive Summary and Report of the Osaka Conference. 60 p. Free-of-charge.

Small and Medium-sized Transnational Corporations: Role, Impact and Policy Implications. 242 p. Sales No. E.93.II.A.15. $35.

Measures of the Transnationalization of Economic Activity. 93p. Sales No. E.01.II.D.2. $20.

The Competitiveness Challenge: Transnational Corporations and Industrial Restructuring in Developing Countries. 283p. Sales No. E.00.II.D.35. $42.

Integrating International and Financial Performance at the Enterprise Level. 116 p. Sales No. E.00.II.D.28. $18.

FDI Determinants and TNCs Strategies: The Case of Brazil. 195 p. Sales No. E.00.II.D.2. $35. Summary available from http://www.unctad.org/en/pub/psiteiitd14.en.htm.

The Social Responsibility of Transnational Corporations. 75 p. UNCTAD/ITE/IIT/Misc. 21. Free of charge. Out of stock. Available on http://www.unctad.org/en/docs/poiteiitm21.en.pdf.

Conclusions on Accounting and Reporting by Transnational Corporations. 47 p. Sales No. E.94.II.A.9. $25.

Accounting, Valuation and Privatization. 190 p. Sales No. E.94.II.A.3. $25.

Environmental Management in Transnational Corporations: Report on the Benchmark Corporate Environment Survey. 278 p. Sales No. E.94.II.A.2. $29.95.

Management Consulting: A Survey of the Industry and Its Largest Firms. 100 p. Sales No. E.93.II.A.17. $25.

Transnational Corporations: A Selective Bibliography, 1991-1992. 736 p. Sales No. E.93.II.A.16. $75.

Foreign Investment and Trade Linkages in Developing Countries. 108 p. Sales No. E.93.II.A.12. $18.

Transnational Corporations from Developing Countries: Impact on Their Home Countries. 116 p. Sales No. E.93.II.A.8. $15.

Debt-Equity Swaps and Development. 150 p. Sales No. E.93.II.A.7. $35.

From the Common Market to EC 92: Regional Economic Integration in the European Community and Transnational Corporations. 134 p. Sales No. E.93.II.A.2. $25.

The East-West Business Directory 1991/1992. 570 p. Sales No. E.92.II.A.20. $65.
Climate Change and Transnational Corporations: Analysis and Trends.
110 p. Sales No. E.92.II.A.7. $16.50.

Foreign Direct Investment and Transfer of Technology in India.
150 p. Sales No. E.92.II.A.3. $20.

The Determinants of Foreign Direct Investment: A Survey of the Evidence.
84 p. Sales No. E.92.II.A.2. $12.50.

Transnational Corporations and Industrial Hazards Disclosure.
98 p. Sales No. E.91.II.A.18. $17.50.

Transnational Business Information: A Manual of Needs and Sources.
216 p. Sales No. E.91.II.A.13. $45.

The Financial Crisis in Asia and Foreign Direct Investment: An Assessment.
101 p. Sales No. GV.E.98.0.29. $20.

Sharing Asia's Dynamism: Asian Direct Investment in the European Union.
192 p. Sales No. E.97.II.D.1. $26.

Investing in Asia's Dynamism: European Union Direct Investment in Asia.
124 p. ISBN 92-827-7675-1. ECU 14. (Joint publication with the European Commission.)

International Investment towards the Year 2002. 166 p. Sales No. GV.E.98.0.15. $29. (Joint publication with Invest in France Mission and Arthur Andersen, in collaboration with DATAR.)

International Investment towards the Year 2001. 81 p. Sales No. GV.E.97.0.5. $35. (Joint publication with Invest in France Mission and Arthur Andersen, in collaboration with DATAR.)

Liberalizing International Transactions in Services: A Handbook.
182 p. Sales No. E.94.II.A.11. $45. (Joint publication with the World Bank.)

The Impact of Trade-Related Investment Measures on Trade and Development: Theory, Evidence and Policy Implications. 108 p. Sales No. E.91.II.A.19. $17.50. (Joint publication with the United Nations Centre on Transnational Corporations.)

Transnational Corporations and World Development. 656 p. ISBN 0-415-08560-8 (hardback), 0-415-08561-6 (paperback). £65 (hardback), £20.00 (paperback). (Published by International Thomson Business Press on behalf of UNCTAD.)

Companies without Borders: Transnational Corporations in the 1990s. 224 p. ISBN 0-415-12526-X. £47.50. (Published by International Thomson Business Press on behalf of UNCTAD.)

The New Globalism and Developing Countries.

336 p. ISBN 92-808-0944-X. $25. (Published by United Nations University Press.)

World Economic Situation and Prospects 2002. 51 p. Sales No. E.02.II.C.2. $15. (Joint publication with the United Nations Department of Economic and Social Affairs.)

World Economic Situation and Prospects 2001. 51 p. Sales No. E.01.II.C.2. $15. (Joint publication with the United Nations Department of Economic and Social Affairs.)

D. Journals

Transnational Corporations Journal (formerly **The CTC Reporter**).
Published three times a year. Annual subscription price: $45; individual issues $20.
http://www.unctad.org/en/subsites/dite/1_itncs/1_tncs.htm

United Nations publications may be obtained from bookstores and distributors throughout the world. Please consult your bookstore or write to:

For Africa, Asia and Europe to

Sales Section
United Nations Office at Geneva
Palais des Nations
CH-1211 Geneva 10
Switzerland
Tel: (41-22) 917-1234
Fax: (41-22) 917-0123
E-mail: unpubli@unog.ch

For Latin America and U.S.A to:

Sales Section
Room DC2-0853
United Nations Secretariat
New York, NY 10017
U.S.A.
Tel: (1-212) 963-8302 or (800) 253-9646
Fax: (1-212) 963-3489
E-mail: publications@un.org

All prices are quoted in United States dollars.
For further information on the work of the Division on Investment, Technology and Enterprise Development, UNCTAD, please address inquiries to:

United Nations Conference on Trade and Development
Division on Investment, Technology and Enterprise Development
Palais des Nations, Room E-10054
CH-1211 Geneva 10, Switzerland
Telephone: (41-22) 907-5651
Telefax: (41-22) 907-0498

E-mail: natalia.guerra@unctad.org
http://www.unctad.org

QUESTIONNAIRE

International Investment Instruments: A Compendium

Volume VII

In order to improve the quality and relevance of the work of the UNCTAD Division on Investment, Technology and Enterprise Development, it would be useful to receive the views of readers on this publication. It would therefore be greatly appreciated if you could complete the following questionnaire and return it to:

Readership Survey
UNCTAD Division on Investment, Technology and Enterprise Development
United Nations Office in Geneva
Palais des Nations
Room E-9123
CH-1211 Geneva 10
Switzerland
Fax: 41-22-907-0194

1. Name and address of respondent (optional):

_____

_____

2. Which of the following best describes your area of work?

Government	○	Public enterprise	○
Private enterprise	○	Academic or research institution	○
International organization	○	Media	○
Not-for-profit organization	○	Other (specify) _____	

3. In which country do you work? _____

4. What is your assessment of the contents of this publication?

Excellent	○	Adequate	○
Good	○	Poor	○

5. How useful is this publication to your work?

Very useful ○   Of some use ○   Irrelevant ○

6. Please indicate the three things you liked best about this publication:

_____

_____

_____

7. Please indicate the three things you liked least about this publication:

_____

_____

_____

8. Are you a regular recipient of *Transnational Corporations* (formerly *The CTC Reporter*), UNCTAD-DITE's tri-annual refereed journal?

Yes   ○   No   ○

If not, please check here if you would like to receive
a sample copy sent to the name and address you have
given above   ○

*